THROUGH THE SEASONS
WITH

THROUGH THE SEASONS WITH

Dulcy

The Best of *The Oregonian* Garden Writer
Dulcy Mahar

Compiled and edited by Ted Mahar

Carpe Diem Books®

PORTLAND, OREGON

To Dulcy, Doug and Peggy

Introduction and Dulcy Mahar columns © 2014 Ted Mahar
Photographs and illustrations © as credited below

Carpe Diem Books®
8136 NW Skyline Boulevard
Portland, OR 97229
carpediembooks.com

First Edition

ISBN 978-0-9897104-4-2

Library of Congress Cataloging-in-Publication Data available.

Publisher: Ross Eberman
Project Director: Richard Owsiany
Editor: Peggy McMullen
Designer: Beth Hansen-Winter
Sales: Ken Rowe

Indexer: Cher Paul
Prepress Consulting and Color Management:
  William Campbell, Mars Premedia
Promotional Photography: © 2014 Michael Shay,
  Polara Studio

Manufactured in China: Multicolor Media Production Limited

First Printing 2014

PHOTO CREDITS BY PAGE—Marv Bondarowicz: Cover: Left, ii, iii, v Middle right, xii, xv, 105, 115, 122, 126, 136, 140, 142, 143, 150, 152, 154, 165, 167,170, 175, 177, 179, 182, 224 All, 240; Beth Hansen-Winter: Endpapers, i, vi Top right, vi Bottom left; vi: Bottom right, viii, x, xix, xxiii All but top, xxiv Middle left, xxiv Bottom left, xxiv Middle right, xxv All but bottom, xxvi Both, xxvii All, xxviii All, xxix, xxx All, xxxi All, xxxii All, xxxiii All, 48, 61, 62, 64, 66, 67, 68, 70, 72 Both, 74, 77, 79, 81, 83 All, 84, 86, 88, 90, 91, 93 Both, 95, 98 Both, 100, 102, 106, 109, 111, 113, 117, 119, 120, 121, 124, 129, 133, 135, 137, 141, 145, 148, 149 Both, 160, 163, 168, 173, 184, 185, 189, 192, 204, 206, 221, 233; Ted Mahar: Cover: Right, third from top; Harold Mendelsohn, Universal Pictures: Back cover; Richard Owsiany: Cover: Bottom right; xxiii Top, xxiv Top, xxiv Bottom right, xxv Bottom, 1, 17 All, 20, 32, 36, 42, 46 Both, 50, 60; Sherrie Rieger © 2014 Sherrie Rieger, sherrierieger.com: Cover: Right, second from top; xi, 2, 5, 11, 13, 19, 23, 26, 30, 33 Both, 41, 55, 56, 58, 186, 195, 198, 200, 211, 213, 217, 219, 223, 227, 229, 231,234, 237, 239; Garden plan on page xviii courtesy of *The Oregonian*

Cover: Left: Dulcy enjoying a quiet moment on her back porch. Right, top to bottom: Checkered frittilaries, summer hydrangeas, Halloween flamingos, winter snow. Page i: *Rosa* 'Sally Holmes'. Page ii: A shady bower outside the Pouting Shed. Page vi: Clockwise from top left: The entrance courtyard in winter snow, a rhododendron outside the greenhouse, a fall-flowering *Rudbeckia*, *Daphne* 'Carol Mackie'. Back cover: Paul Newman and Ted Mahar.

Dulcy, Ted and Orville.

Acknowledgments

Heartfelt thanks to the faithful fans who shared their affection for Dulcy in her final days. The throngs who showed up for the sale of *Back in the Garden with Dulcy*, sent letters and emails, paid visits to her garden, attended book signings and shared expressions of devotion continue to provide a heart-felt balm.

Much gratitude for assistance in producing this book of columns and bringing it to Dulcy's readers goes to Mary Volm, Ross Eberman, Dick Owsiany, Beth Hansen-Winter and Peggy McMullen. Many thanks to *The Oregonian* for their sustaining support for this second book of her columns, and for the great working relationship Dulcy enjoyed with her editors over the years.

Contents

New ideas can strike . . .

IN YOUR GARDEN, INSPIRATION IS QUIETLY CALLING

D ULCY.
For more than two decades, you only had to say the one name for Northwest gardeners to know you meant garden writer Dulcy Mahar. Through wildly popular columns in The Oregonian, readers came to know the changing three-quarters of an acre of gardens that surrounded Dulcy's home in Portland's Garthwick neighborhood. Over the years, Dulcy opened her doors for tours, was a top speaker at regional garden events and secured a spot in Northwesterners' hearts. Eavesdrop on a conversation with gardeners and sooner or later someone would say, "Well, Dulcy…"

Her death from cancer in 2011 left readers bereft without her weekly column, so it was no surprise how they dove with relief into *Back in the Garden with Dulcy*, happy to find dozens of her beloved columns and photos of her and her changing landscape. As one of her former editors and faithful fans, I, too, was thrilled to see the compilation.

I had missed my weekly gardening fix from Dulcy. Every week since 1989, season in and out, readers had looked forward to being inspired by what was going on in Dulcy's garden. In winter, they dreamed as she did of what to do in the coming planting season. In spring, they watched along with her for the first emerging tendrils. Summer was about basking in the lushness and worrying about the heat. Autumn was time for harvest and reflection.

Just as with the rest of her readers, Dulcy's influences are everywhere in my garden. There is the pair of flamingos I added the day she died; their black ribbons are gone but they still stand sentry, adding color to the deep shade under a large rhododendron. There are the roses we had the courage to move, the plants we dug out, the shade garden filled with heucheras (a favorite of Dulcy's), pots of colorful annuals interspersed in perennial borders and, most recently, a rabbit planter I added to the vegetable garden for a touch of whimsy.

As I gardener, I still find myself thinking when pondering a seasonal decision: "What would Dulcy do?" So I'm happy to find ongoing inspiration in this second compilation, *Through the Seasons with Dulcy*. Her voice of garden wisdom can once again remind me when to start seeds, give me tips on protecting plants through heat and cold — and nag me not to put winter mulch on too soon (but also telling me not to worry much if I did).

If you are one of her readers who have missed the weekly trips into Dulcy's beautiful gardens, here are 140 more of her best columns. Arranged by months, we Northwest gardeners can once again (or, if you never read Dulcy's newspaper columns, for the first time) let her guide and inspire us through the changing seasons.

Come on. Can't you hear your garden (and Dulcy) calling?

—Peggy McMullen, Editor
The Oregonian's Homes & Gardens of the Northwest
November 2009 through September 2013

. . . from spring . . .

. . . to fall.

Dulcy liked to sit in her garden for hours at a time.

Preface

DULCY STILL GUIDES HER LANDSCAPE

By Douglas Wilson (aka "Doug the Wonder Guy")

MAYBE IT WAS HER CALIFORNIA CHILDHOOD. OR MAYBE SHE HAD SIMPLY BEEN BORN with the innate good sense to stay indoors when it's 35 degrees and raining sideways. Whatever the case, Dulcy's idea of winter gardening was a warm fire, a cup of tea, a bit of chocolate, fuzzy slippers and garden magazines.

In midwinter, if I had a question or idea, I would pull off my boots, roll up the cuffs of my rain pants and head upstairs in stocking feet. Dulcy's office was a sort of comfy battle station, with folding card tables laid out in a U shape, piled high with garden magazines and books, notebooks, and sketch pads. In the center of it all were the twin tomes of *Flora Plant Encyclopedia*. I am proud to own those two twelve-pound books now, the information contained in them — along with Dulcy's highlights and handwritten notes — make them two of my most valued possessions.

In late winter as the *Galanthus* faded and purple and yellow crocus were just opening, Dulcy would be drawn back into the garden. In a purple raincoat, yellow Wellies, and a pink hat printed with kitties carrying umbrellas, she would dash out, offer up chocolates, make a few notes on a Rite in the Rain pad and sprint back in. It was like a sort of multi-colored tiny Sasquatch sighting.

As spring quickened, so did Dulcy. She would often meet me at the gate before she left for work to run through to-do lists and get updated on the progress of various projects. Her excitement was like a second cup of coffee, and spring days slid by like moments until suddenly it was late May and the front gates were swung wide for the first open garden of the year.

Summer was Dulcy's high season. If she wasn't at work, she was in the garden, or out in the plantmobile hunting and gathering. It wasn't uncommon for me to unload her car midday so that she could head out again in search of rare treasures.

In addition to working together, and to-do lists, Dulcy developed a sort of shorthand in the garden. If there were a few spent flowers on the ground in front of a rose just inside the front gate it meant "deadhead the roses." A can of slug bait on the front bench meant "I don't want laceleaf hostas." A garden fork stuck in the ground next to a daylily meant dig and divide this plant. The system broke down a few times. Dulcy, hands full, would set a plant down beside the path and I would come along and plant it there.

Fall was project time. Inevitably another broad swath of sod would need to be removed to make room for new plantings. I remember Dulcy standing on the upper terrace pointing and calling out as I moved a garden hose to outline a perfect kidney shape for the back lawn. John, who has mowed Dulcy's lawn since long before I knew her, has seen his job shrink incrementally. Now I think it takes him longer to unload than to actually mow.

As leaves turned, Dulcy took to wandering the garden in quiet thought, sometimes sitting on a bench for whole afternoons, reading, napping or just watching her garden.

When the Big Rain returned sometime after Halloween, Dulcy would retreat from the garden, and I was left to solitary tasks, cleaning up leaves, gathering up glass and ceramic critters and tucking them into the pouting shed, moving delicate plants into the greenhouse. Without Dulcy, those quiet winter months seem to stretch out a little longer, and the long days of summer are a bit more precious.

For the first couple of years after my friend passed, I simply let the garden grow. I weeded and deadheaded, pressure washed and pruned, but no new projects were started.

Gardens grow and change with or without us. Rambling roses ramble too far, garden thugs spread into their neighbors, flowers that self-seed become weeds, and so industry has returned to Dulcy's garden.

Last fall I started a woodland garden under the big maple on the street; this winter I reoriented and broadened the veggie garden beds to take better advantage of the sun. One week earlier this year, under bright May sun, I kept my promise to Dulcy: I removed the gravel path I had cut through her back lawn so that she could access the garden in a wheelchair, or walker.

She had balked at the idea of cutting the lawn in half, but as soon as work began she became interested, suggesting that we plant succulents in the gravel at the edges of the path. When planting time came, she sat on the terrace and helped me lay out the plants. It was the last project we worked on together. She made me promise that when she was gone I would make the lawn whole again, and now it is once again a pleasing kidney shape.

An upcoming project is to add low voltage lighting throughout the landscape so that we can have open gardens in the evening. Next winter I intend to tackle some long overdue pruning, editing and plant division projects.

Early on my work for Dulcy was pretty straight forward — dig holes, move big things. But Dulcy was very generous and the garden quickly became a collaboration. As Dulcy became ill, I often had to take the lead. The structure and character of Dulcy's garden was established by the thousands of hours we spent working together there. I still feel we have a collaboration and I think Dulcy would be pleased with the progress in her garden.

PASSIONATE TO THE ROOT

Dulcy Mahar wittily chronicles her longtime obsession with gardening

By Kym Pokorny

THIS STORY, WRITTEN BY *THE OREGONIAN*'S GARDEN WRITER, RAN IN THE JUNE 3, 2010, ISSUE OF HOMES AND GARDENS OF THE NORTHWEST.

O N A 24-KARAT DAY, DULCY MAHAR RE-laxed on the veranda of her home, BASKED in the golden day and considered how just one moment 23 years ago could change everything.

Her moment hung on the drip of an ice cream cone and an unplanned drive through Garthwick. Steering slowly through the quiet neighborhood near Waverley Country Club, confection in hand, she and her husband, Ted, noticed a for-sale sign in front of an impressive Georgian Colonial.

Mahar hardly noticed the house. It was the parklike expanse behind the fence she immediately began to covet.

"I remember saying to Ted, 'I don't care what the house looks like. I want this,'" she says with the same absolute clarity she felt that day.

A gardener's desire for more space compelled Mahar to peek over that fence, but it was instinct that persuaded her to move from the smaller house where gardening first got under her skin. In his good-natured way, Ted went along and watched as his wife's fixation intensified.

"Sometimes I can't explain it to my husband," she says helplessly. "But it's a passion you can fulfill without guilt. It's not fattening. It's not bad for your health. It doesn't lead to a life of crime."

Although her garden has achieved local fame through weekly columns that have run in The Oregonian for 21 years, Mahar finds it all a bit overwrought.

"People come here and have great expectations. It's kind of embarrassing," she says, equating it to a quote about Ringo Starr "as one of 1,000 great drummers in Great Britain."

"I'm not being self-effacing. It's an honest assessment."

Many would disagree. With a distinctive dry humor, Mahar writes about her failures, as well as the caprices of nature. Like the time "aphids held an international convention in our *Liriodendron* (tulip tree) and rained down their sticky excrements, reaching their peak performance on the night of a dinner party in our garden."

Helping her out with such unanticipated and other down-to-earth problems is her much-mentioned longtime gardener, Doug the Wonder Boy. Promoted to Doug the Wonder Guy after his 40th birthday, he is coveted by everyone who's ever read a column by Mahar.

Mahar is also well-known for her rapture over chocolate and a public crush on Harrison Ford, whom she dropped for George Clooney when Ford fell in love with Calista Flockhart. "When Harrison Ford attached himself to that skinny broad," she says with disdain, "I lost all respect."

Readers so related to her self-deprecating style that they wrote fan mail and crowded into the appearances she made regularly before being diagnosed with ovarian cancer seven years ago.

"I'm open about my illness, but I don't want to be defined by it," says Mahar, who continues her career as manager of policy writing for Bonneville Power Administration, where she's worked for 17 years.

"When my garden magazines are up for renewal, I ask the doctor, 'Should I renew for one year or three years?' She always says three. That makes me hope."

So do the seasons in her three-quarter-acre garden, which has been strongly influenced by English gardens: first the lushly planted perennial borders characteristic of cottage gardens, then the grand estate gardens with their mixed beds of trees, shrubs and perennials. Annual trips across the pond incited her to new levels.

"Suddenly, it was like going to graduate school," she says.

Gradually, her garden began to show the results of her education. Flowers became incidental as she shifted her affection from perennials to foliage and texture.

"It's a good thing plants are not men," she jokes. "I'd be a true trollop."

But try as she might, roses remain a constant.

"I convinced myself I didn't need roses," she insists. "I tried to give them up, but it's like giving up chocolate. You can only do it for so long. I never made it through Lent; I still have 25 roses."

Mahar spreads the love around. Her passion for gardening may be surpassed by her affection for dogs and cats — vigorously egged on by her husband, who worked at *The Oregonian* as a film critic and reporter for 46 years. When their beloved dog Hector, who appeared in 21 columns, died, he was publicly mourned.

Not unexpectedly, she and Ted soon adopted a new dog. All it took was a letter from the little mutt — ghost-written by a veterinarian and signed with his paw print — to bring Ernie into their lives. Little Ernie, like his predecessors, leaves a mark on the garden. But Mahar takes it in stride. A garden, she says, is meant to bear the signature of the owner.

"Gardening is like spaghetti," she muses. "Everybody loves it, but everyone makes the sauce differently. And it's still good."

GARDENING CHANGES SINCE DULCY MAHAR STARTED 21 YEARS AGO:

- Gardens go organic.
- Lawns shrink.
- Shrubs and perennials mix in beds.
- Old roses and shrub roses make a comeback.
- Gardeners step up interest in autumn plants.
- Challenging the climate zone becomes a sport.
- Gardens go vertical with vines, trellises, arbors.
- Interest turns to foliage, texture and color.
- Glazed pots replace terra cotta.
- Art and ornament find a place in gardens.
- Water becomes integral, from pots to ponds.
- Northwest gardeners pursue cutting-edge plants.

FAVORITE UNDERUSED PLANTS

- *Acanthus mollis* (bear's breeches): perfect foliage perennial
- *Clematis texensis* 'Princess Diana': exquisite rosy-pink bells
- *Fritillaria meleagris* (checkered lily): weirdly beautiful bulb
- *Primula vialii* (a primrose): striking color for the rock garden
- *Kirengeshoma palmata* (yellow waxbells): great foliage, late blooming

- *Lonicera nitida* 'Baggesen's Gold' (box honeysuckle): ideal filler
- *Philadelphus coronarius* 'Aureus' (sweet mock orange): heavenly scent
- *Rosa* 'Mutabilis': very long-flowering shrubby rose
- *Ribes sanguineum* (flowering currant): Imagine, an underused native!
- *Polygonatum odoratum* (Solomon's seal): elegant shade plant

THREE FAVORITE GARDENS

Setting aside Monet's garden in Giverny, France, and Sissinghurst garden in Kent, England (which are everyone's favorites), here are three of Mahar's favorites. All three are private gardens but open to the public.

- Giardini di Ninfa, 40 miles southeast of Rome: Grand in scale but not formal, a garden out of a child's fairy book.
- York Gate, West Yorkshire, England: Just one acre but with exquisitely designed garden spaces.
- Le Vasterival, Normandy, France: The terrifying Princess Sturdza's gorgeous and near-perfect woodland.

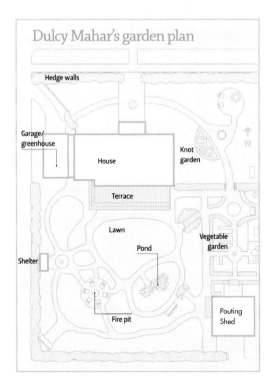

Dulcy Mahar's garden plan

Hedge walls

Garage/greenhouse

Knot garden

N

House

Terrace

Lawn

Vegetable garden

Pond

Shelter

Pouting Shed

Fire pit

Introduction

FACING CHALLENGES WITH CHARM, HUMOR AND COURAGE

By Ted Mahar

DULCY MAHAR WAS THE FINEST WRITER I HAVE EVER KNOWN — BIBLICALLY. Some 30 or so years ago, when Dulcy and I were on the same speaking program, she appeared before me and introduced me with the above observation. I swore that I would do the same to her, but the opportunity never arose — until now.

Now I am introducing a second book of columns from her 1989-2011 career as freelance garden writer for The Oregonian.

Dulcy died at 2:05 a.m. on July 2, 2011, and I was already preparing a book of her columns. I had hoped and expected that it could come out that December. Instead, it came out in November 2013. The delay was my fault. I sadly found that I simply could not continue for several months. Later, when I could finally return to work on that book, I found as I read through her hundreds of columns, I was impressed anew of what a great writer she was.

Dulcy often asked me to read over her shoulder. In the early years, well-meaning friends asked if I really wrote her columns. Dulcy never took offense. It seemed a natural question. I had been an *Oregonian* columnist since 1966. But when Dulcy began her columns in 1989, she had been a professional writer for decades. Aside from peering over her shoulder and suggesting copyediting remarks, I never contributed a syllable to her writing.

From the start we exemplified a line in a long-forgotten 1956 Broadway musical, *Happy Hunting*, that immortal lyric: "We belong to a Mutual Admiration Society." From the very first story Dulcy handed in to me on the University of Oregon newspaper, the *Oregon Daily Emerald*, I saw that she was a real writer. I was simply impressed and always was. Luckily, the feeling was mutual.

I pulled at the oars of *The Oregonian* for 45 years, working with excellent writers. I was proud to be an *Oregonian* writer. But I knew none who surpassed Dulcy. Each of us sincerely thought the other was a better writer.

I can brag my brains out about how great Dulcy's first book was because I had little to do with it, aside from writing a biographical introduction and sorting through her columns. Carpe Diem Books produced a gorgeous volume with great editing, typography and photos. I cherish it.

And now here's Book II.

Dulcy and I were teenagers when we met in January 1960 on the *Oregon Daily Emerald*. Dulcy was decades from developing her gardening obsession. She joined a sorority, Sigma Kappa, a far from ideal site for gardening. Not until her mid-30s did the urge begin, but when it did, it had Mount St. Helens intensity. We never had human children, but gardening was a greedy teenager for Dulcy and she could not get enough of feeding it.

Peering over Dulcy's shoulders for years, I noticed one of the great appeals of her columns — aside from her fabulous sense of whimsy. She methodically indulged in a practice that is, in fact, considered a taboo in some newspaper circles.

Anthropomorphizing.

That is, treating nonhuman — and even nonorganic — subjects as if they were human. Those of us who live with pets know about it, if only subliminally. We even named our automobiles as if they were somehow human. From the beginning Dulcy wrote about plants and gardens as if they were beings with personality, motives, quirks and relationships. She wrote as if they were friends. And so they were. Also her children, in addition to the pets. I have no doubt that this was one of the great appeals of her columns.

I guess Union General William T. Sherman was Dulcy's favorite historical character, for she employed him regularly in similes and metaphors, using the term "marching through Georgia" to characterize morning glory, slugs, raccoons, wisteria, opossums, crabgrass, daisies and various other items that were neither human nor military.

This book takes Dulcy through the seasons, which I believe she might have considered improbable. We have selected columns she wrote in winter, spring, summer and fall — but Dulcy had a formidable challenge her readers may not have noticed. There's far less to write about in November through February. Dulcy considered this her most challenging, creative and imaginative writing.

With gardens languishing in late fall and winter, there was little to say about planting, tilling, trimming and other stuff about which I know conspicuously little. But with the demand to produce a column a week, Dulcy somehow came up with the goods. Sometimes she referred to her December and January columns as "Nothingburgers." That is, they were general essays with no real immediate lessons. I gather that there's little to do in the garden in the dead of winter. But readers loved the columns. I loved them.

I don't know you, but if you've read this far, I like you, and I'll share a secret that's not really a secret. Dulcy's garden was a pricey enterprise. We both LOVED our jobs. Dulcy had a terrific career, worked hard and long and made a great income. I considered myself more than well paid for my career at *The Oregonian*, but my pay was incidental to the family income. I hear that this is a problem in some families; some guys can't deal with a wife who makes more money than they do. If Dulcy had made two or three times what she did, that would have been just swell with me.

The result of her income was that, starting in the late '80s, Dulcy began taking two-week trips with other gals to visit gardens in England, Germany, Italy and France. She came home with ideas and occasionally even a few plants. It was like a post-graduate course. (Dulcy and I vacationed in Europe, Hawaii or Indonesia. Oddly enough, tropical flora was attractive to her but not fascinating. "It's always summer. Of course it's always blooming. So what?")

The great appeal of Dulcy's column was her humor. Some readers seem to have considered her a comic writer — which she often was.

As I was perusing her columns for these books, however, I realized that she was dispensing not just good garden advice but actual wisdom. Good and great garden advice is ubiquitous — practically unavoidable — and Dulcy's popularity derived from her sense of humor. But she really delivered the goods. Gardeners read Dulcy's columns for solid, practical garden knowledge. I actually learned a lot reading her columns for these books. I'll never use it, but it doesn't hurt to know, for example, that Oregon's clay soil is quite the bummer and that you should always add compost.

As you read Dulcy's columns I would like you to realize one thing. Dulcy's cancer came back in summer 2005. Once cancer returns you know that you will die of it, but not when. For Dulcy it was six years. The dates of Dulcy's columns are attached at the bottom of each. From summer 2005 on they were written by a woman knowing that she had a death sentence.

She kept her charm and humor to the very end.

I now indulge a selfish impulse. I am breaking my promise to Dulcy. She strictly forbade the customary obituary boilerplate paragraph about how brave and courageous the deceased had been.

I am willing to believe that the boilerplate cliché is probably true in most cases of lingering death by cancer. I try never to argue with other people's experience.

And it pains me to violate Dulcy's emphatic wish.

But I hope she would not argue with my experience. My mother's father served in the Royal Irish Rifles regiment of the British Army. My uncles Mattie and Eddie were infantrymen in World War II. Eddie was wounded on Anzio Beach in January 1944, and Mattie got through the Battle of the Bulge without a scratch. ("I said three Hail Marys for every dead body I saw, even Germans," Mattie said.)

I was in the National Guard for three years and the Naval Reserve for twenty. I knew genuine heroes.

I lived intimately with the dearest possible, most indispensable friend who woke up every morning for six years knowing that doom was closing in but not knowing when it would strike. I expect to never again be so close to such courage, grace under pressure and philosophical acceptance. I humbly marveled at it but was forbidden to talk about it.

Until now. No, including now.

Dulcy more than once said that, if I blathered on about what a brave little soldier she was, she would come back to haunt me.

Oh, if that could only be true.

THE OTHER SIDE OF DULCY

By Ted Mahar

H ERE IS A LOOK INSIDE OUR HOME, A VIEW THAT FEW OF DULCY'S readers or garden visitors saw. There's also a look at her popular Pouting Shed and some of her collections.

THE FOYER

Dulcy loved this red wallpaper. It was one of the first changes made to the 1915 Georgian Colonial we bought in 1985. The entry area is rife with Dulcy's friendly décor — including a kitten, butterfly, bunny, cherub and several geese. A recent addition is the arrangement on the table; the frame holds an old ad from The Oregonian *of me as movie critic, my face expressing my opinions of various films. The ornate pumpkin is one of her numerous garden-inspired decorations. A coat rack holds quick garden apparel; umbrellas are essential for Oregon. The basket attached to the front door is my invention; it keeps the cats from making their presence known on the mail falling in through the slot.*

THE LIVING ROOM

We added the bookshelves and window seat to store two of our passions. The cabinetry beneath the shelves holds a CD player and speakers; the

storage under the seat is packed with CDs. Dulcy planned the simple décor of this room and the rest of our home so that there is always something to look at, no matter where your eye falls. The fireplace mantel holds Chinese figures and old church candlesticks — some of the few bits of décor I picked out.

THE DINING ROOM

We loved to entertain — and it will be no surprise that most of our guests shared Dulcy's ardor for gardening. The formal dining room had its heaviest use in the

colder months when the veranda was too chilly to use. The lattice feel of the wallpaper and the flower prints put guests in a garden mood no matter the season. The French doors, which are original to the home, lead to a hallway between the kitchen and back garden. While the home's décor is not Asian, the house is filled with vases, statues and other accessories from Japan and China (with a few from India and Korea).

THE KITCHEN AND STUDY

The kitchen was like the galley of a destroyer — dark, tiny and metallic. We took out a wall and expanded the area, updating everything and adding storage. The view of the kitchen table is from the study; the small table at left sits where a kitchen nook had been. The corbels in the wall above had been on an exterior wall. When we expanded the house outward, we kept them in place in the new room.

The brick wall had been buried in stucco; we scraped it clear and regrouted it. The study along the back of the house — which is stuffed with more of our books — is a light-filled work space, thanks to the new skylights and a bay window that looks out onto the garden.

THE POUTING SHED

Dulcy turned the former potting shed and stable into something uniquely hers. In a spirit of whimsy she renamed it the Pouting Shed and filled it with artwork, antiques and garden books, creating a very charming spot for contemplation (or, as the name warns, pouting).

THE COLLECTIONS

Dulcy loved collecting art, and made a point of seeking out the work of Northwest artists such as Carol Grigg (second row center above). Cats and garden life were popular themes. She accrued pieces in a variety of mediums, including oils, acrylics, watercolors, carvings, ceramics and stained glass.

As previously mentioned, we have many Asian pieces sprinkled around the house, such as the cat, dog, teapot and ceramic pieces pictured on the facing page. The small pieces of brass with coral and turquoise inlay are mostly from China, Japan and India (opposite top and bottom right) and were picked up on our travels over a couple of decades. We bought every piece of this form we ever found. The mosaic and brass candelabra for votive candles is sprinkled with little birds in a similar style.

THE CRITTERS

Frogs

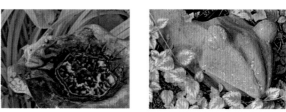

Dulcy's love of frog in sculpture and artwork was rather paradoxical. She loved frogs in that form, but, on the other hand, real frogs jumped into the pond and ate the fish. Now frogs guard the shady area where she is laid to rest in the garden.

Pigs Dulcy grew up on a ranch during World War II. Among the many barnyard animals were pigs, and she loved them. Her favorite friends were a battle-scarred male cat named Mary Anne and a 600-pound porker known as Hoggy Dear. She named both.

Cats and Dogs

It wasn't just our live cats and dogs that Dulcy loved. Her menagerie of household and garden pets just kept growing. These are some of our garden favorites.

CATS OF WWII

Purr Harbor
early 1941

Wormy Pyle — famed
war correspondent

Enemy sub

Flying tiger

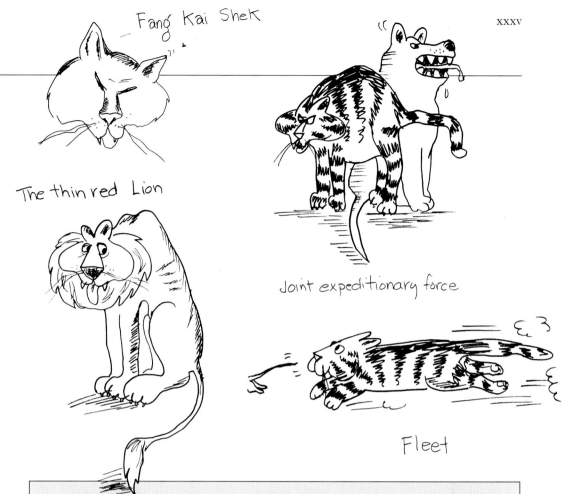

Fang Kai Shek

The thin red Lion

Joint expeditionary force

Fleet

    Dulcy's creative talents extended beyond her writing into visual arts. She took up painting and created many beautiful pieces. She, however, never felt her work was "good enough," and ruthlessly purged her paintings.

    She burned more than a dozen over the years. I practically cried over some of the canvases she incinerated, but her rebuff was unassailable: "They're mine. I can do what I want with them."

    Damn.

    But she considered her cartoons as throwaways. Her memos at work often had cartoons, which she whisked out in seconds.

    These cartoons are from a book she gave me at Christmas, 1979. She bought a book of blank pages, then — playing to my passion for World War II history — quickly sketched in these cartoons and, at the end, included a $100 gift certificate for Powell's Book Store. I have treasured the whimsy for decades and now share some of them with you. In Dulcy's words: "The one volume history — from Pearl Harbor to Tokyo Bay — of the cats who fought in the Pacific."

Famous WWII photograph

Breaking the code

Hellcat

Carrier

Fat Man and
Little Boy

Kamikaze

Dogface

War bride

Peace offering

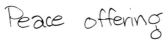

A treasured musician inspired this poem, which Ted read at all three of Dulcy's memorials.

RESURRECTION

The dead girl plays. She plays and plays.
Her elbow weaves her slashing bow.
With savage grace her fingers dance
tarantellas on the strings.
Her gleaming smile and sparkling gaze
illuminate the concert hall.
Her cello sings in her embrace.

Between her knees the dead man lives,
Sebastian Bach. He slipped from life,
he fell from fame. But Mendelssohn
exhumed his art for future ears
and dead girl's hands.

I lounge and hear the dead girl play.
She warms my living room to life.
The drink is cool within my hand.
Her hands are cool within the grave,
Yet on they play and play and play
within my house, within my heart.

Her cello once was living wood.
It died, yet lives beyond its time
As instrument for dead girl's art.
The dead girl played on vinyl disks,
which now are ancient artifacts,
And, even dead, she outlives them.

We never met. We'll never meet,
Yet still she fills my heart with joy,
exhilarates my soul with tears.
My living room's replete with life,
Because the dead girl plays and plays.

In time to come, I'll slip away.
I'm sorry, but we'll all be gone.
But on she'll play
on compact disks or something else.
She'll play and play with savage glee
To charm new ears and stir new hearts.
She'll play and play and play and play.

TED MAHAR

This poem clearly was not inspired by Dulcy but by the brilliant cellist Jacqueline du Pré (Jan. 26, 1945 – Oct. 19, 1987). Multiple sclerosis ended du Pré's career at age 28; she died at age 42. The theme of resurrection and life after death was compelling enough that I read it at three memorials for Dulcy. A few kind friends asked for copies, which I gratefully sent.

Du Pré was most famous for her interpretations of Sir Edward Elgar (June 2, 1857 – Feb. 23, 1934), but I was fascinated by the fact that Felix Mendelssohn (Feb. 3, 1809 – Nov. 4, 1847), created a new knowledge of totally forgotten composer Johann Sebastian Bach (March 21, 1685 – July 28, 1750) whose music still thrives solely because of Mendelssohn. —TM

Part 1

WINTER

Contemplation, Christmas and a Calamity

Evergreens offer structure during bare winter months.

NEVER SAY DORMANT

The terrace project goes full-throttle, while other gardens go to sleep

I THINK MY HUSBAND IS CATCHING ON THAT I've put in a new terrace at the front of the house. The other day, I asked him to go with me to Hughes Water Gardens out on Stafford Road to pick up a giant water bowl. He's still driving around with it, because it's too heavy for us to unload by ourselves.

He's also noticed that I go out in the front and kind of stare into space. What I'm doing is envisioning what it will look like when it's done. In fact, I am having trouble going dormant like a good gardener should.

One should never start a big project late in the year; it just gets your blood stirring. You find yourself lying in bed at night imagining what you will plant or sketching planting schemes when you are supposed to be paying attention in a meeting. Not that I personally would ever do that.

We've gotten as far as removing the front lawn. I don't know why I use the royal we, because Doug the Wonder Boy and his friend did all the work. I have focused on designing the new shape for the flowerbeds.

My vision replaces the old narrow gravel path to the back yard with a wide swath of gravel curving gently like a stream. The previous design simply followed the rut made by the wheelbarrow, when we originally hauled topsoil into the back yard some 16 years ago.

> *One should never start a big project late in the year; it just gets your blood stirring.*

The planting beds will edge the path on both sides (whoopee, no grass). We might even have a few plants that seed themselves in the gravel, a la Provence. This, anyway, is the dream.

I've been using the latest technical advancements to sculpt the shape of the beds. I tried the hose, but it wasn't flexible enough. So I used some old pancake flour to sprinkle a line in the shape of the paths. I figured it's biodegradable and can be hosed away to try new shapes.

Trouble is, I hadn't counted on the fact that dogs like pancake mix. Hector kept following me and licking up the line. I wonder if Capability Brown had to worry about dogs when he designed gardens.

As for the giant water bowl, I envision that it will nestle somewhere on the gravel path. In the planting schemes — the ones I don't do while I'm in meetings — I have it filled with papyrus.

Once the new path is defined, we'll put landscape cloth down to suppress any errant grass seeds that may have been left. This is a sign of maturing. In my early gardening adventures, I made the mistake of putting black plastic beneath a gravel path and ended up with the Okefenokee Swamp. Fortunately, landscape cloth is porous so water drains through it.

We'll put sand over the cloth to level out any bumps and to make a good bed for the gravel, which will probably be quarter-minus size. We tried a finer gravel on some of the paths but found this is not good if you have cats. To put it delicately, it bears an unfortunate resemblance to kitty litter. Don't ask how I know.

I can hardly wait to begin planting, but

that may have to wait until spring. If we make any progress, I'll be sure to report. Meanwhile, if you pull up alongside a dazed-looking man with a giant water bowl in the back seat, it's my husband. As I said, I think he's beginning to realize something's afoot.

NOVEMBER 14, 2002

❧

PLAIN JANE
A little bit of boring goes a long way in the winter garden

L EAVE IT TO ME. WHEN I MAKE GARDENING mistakes, I put them right smack out front. In front of the entry, in fact.

When we moved into our house several years ago, I wanted low-growing, softly mounding shrubs on each side of our entryway. I decided on two viburnums. The *Viburnum opulus* 'Compactum' that went on the east side of the walk is perfectly gorgeous, with beautifully sculpted foliage that glows bronze in autumn. In spring, it has lovely white flowers, and later there are pretty, glossy berries.

On the other side, I planted *V. davidii*, which is not nearly so interesting. Its leaves are leathery and plain, and neither the flowers nor the berries are particularly showy.

Still, the mistake turned out to be the pretty *V. opulus*. The plain Jane *V. davidii* is evergreen, and if you're going to frame your front door, it ought to be with something evergreen, since that's the only part of your garden people see on cold wintry nights as they dash from car to hearth.

When I selected the plants one spring, I thought about a lot of things — shape, flowers, size and fragrance. It didn't occur to me to think of winter appearance. In fact, I had a tendency to associate the term evergreen with stiff limbs and sprouting needles. Conifers are splendid winter plants, but they aren't the only ones that keep their clothes on in winter.

There are, of course, the ubiquitous rhodies, camellias, boxwood, laurel and hollies. But that's where many homeowners stop. Actually, a surprising number of broadleaf evergreen shrubs thrive in Northwest winters.

If your bare winter garden looks like something Hannibal just marched his elephants through, you might consider the following dressed-for-winter shrubs. Mature sizes are approximate, and many are slow-growers or can be kept in check with judicious pruning.

A BUNDLE OF BROADLEAF EVERGREENS

Aucuba japonica 'Crotonifolia': True, the Japanese laurel (6-10 feet) is rather coarse with insignificant flowers, but this highly variegated cultivar makes a bold statement with glossy leaves that look as if they've been spattered with golden paint. Both male and female plants are needed for winter berries. Sun to shade.

Berberis: This versatile genus includes both deciduous and evergreen varieties, so

> *If your bare winter garden looks like something Hannibal just marched his elephants through, you might consider dressed-for-winter shrubs.*

Hardscaping defines the form and function of a garden.

know which you're getting. *B. darwinii* (8 feet) is loved for its graceful fountain shape and hollylike leaves. It is hardy to 10 degrees. The smaller *B. verruculosa* and *B.* 'Chenaultii' (3-4 feet) have glossy dark green foliage, black berries and hardiness to below zero. Sun to light shade.

Cotoneaster: This genus is one of the great berry producers, with several hardy evergreen varieties. *C. salicifolius* (15 feet), *C. lacteus* (8 feet) and *C. congestus* (3 feet) show the variety of sizes that is available. Do your homework to find the evergreen varieties. Full sun.

Daphne: Marginally hardy, but we all know it's irresistible. Improve chances for winter survival by planting it in a sheltered spot and in very well-drained soil. *D.* x *burkwoodii* (3-4 feet) is neatly rounded with fragrant white to pink flowers in late winter. 'Carol Mackie' is a popular cultivar with golden-edged leaves. *D. odora* is the more common but still beloved form. Dappled light or semi-shade.

Elaeagnus pungens: The ordinary form of this large shrub (15 feet) has gray-green foliage, but cultivars are more exciting. 'Maculata' leaves have golden centers; 'Marginata' leaves have silver-white margins; and 'Variegata' creamy yellow margins. Sun to part shade.

Euonymus fortunei: A small (3 feet), shiny-leafed shrub with semi-vining habit, good for mixing in borders. White and gold variegated forms. Golden varieties ('Emerald 'n' Gold') are especially brilliant in winter. *E. japonicus* (8-10 feet) can form a small tree and be pruned into an umbrella shape. Full sun.

Fatsia japonica: Not to everyone's taste, since it resembles a big house plant (5-8 feet) with huge, sculpted leaves. But dramatic in gardens with eclectic or tropical flavors. Unusual fall flowers grow in creamy clusters and are followed by black, berrylike fruits. Shade to deep shade.

Kalmia latifolia: Mountain laurel (10 feet) has all the virtues of a rhododendron, which it resembles, and enjoys the same conditions. A lovely plant for woodland gardens.

Ligustrum japonicum: Japanese privet (10 feet) has dense growth and can be trimmed into formal hedges and topiary. Yellow-green leaves are glossy on top and whitish underneath. Sun to partial shade.

Lonicera nitida 'Baggesen's Gold': A lovely and mysteriously underused shrubby member of the honeysuckle family that can be clipped to shape (5 feet unpruned). Bright golden foliage needs sun to retain its color.

Osmanthus heterophyllus 'Aureomarginatus': Leaves closely resemble variegated holly, but unlike holly this osmanthus (15 feet) also has clusters of fragrant flowers in autumn. Sun or shade.

Skimmia japonica: Two especially choice forms of this neat little (3-4 feet) rounded shrub are 'Fructu Albo', which bears pearly white berries, and 'Rubella', which carries rosy buds through winter before bursting into spring bloom. Plants are aromatic. Part shade to shade.

Viburnum tinus: This dense grower is a good alternative to laurel for a lush, informal hedge (10 feet). Clusters of flower buds dress up the shrub through winter and open in spring. They are followed by dark berries with a metallic sheen.

DECEMBER 3, 1998

~✕~

FANTASIES OF A GARDEN ROOM
On dreary days, indulge your dreams of curling up in a sunny, luxurious chamber

H OW DOES A GARDENER SURVIVE THROUGH the winter?

I, for one, have a fantasy to keep me warm and cheery. It's a garden room, the kind you see as part of houses in magazines such as *Southern Living*. Why do houses in warm places have garden rooms? How indulgent. After all, the residents can go outside nearly all year. It's those of us who live where the days are drippy and dreary who deserve a garden room.

Now let's be clear what we're talking about here. This is not a greenhouse. No, that's another fantasy. A greenhouse is for serious stuff, like propagation or wintering-over fuchsias and geraniums or growing something exotic such as orchids.

But a garden room is pure luxury. Sure, you can use it to start seeds early and force bulbs, but its real purpose is atmosphere. This is where you take tea (it's my fantasy so I can make time for tea) and curl up on a wicker settee with a book.

My fantasy garden room has a brick floor and lots of big windows and skylights. Actually, the ultimate fantasy is one of those Victorian English conservatories, but even fantasies have to be sort of realistic, so I'll settle for an attractive American lean-to.

Of course, the garden room would have a small, round iron table and a couple of those folding chairs you see in French parks. But mostly, it would have big, comfy, wicker chairs with chintz covers. The cats would love it.

On a practical note, the room would have a sink with ample counter room for potting plants and arranging flowers. There'd be a big old armoire for all the vases and pots. Of course, the room would have French doors, and they'd have to open onto the garden, preferably the rose or herb garden.

Lots of plants would be inside. Anyone lucky enough to have such a room really does have a responsibility to force bulbs. This would be the place to house the potted (Italian terra cotta pots, of course) dwarf citrus trees and the dramatic banana plant during winter.

Alas, I don't have a garden room, but I do have the next best thing. We put a huge bay window in a workroom off the kitchen that looks out over the back garden and the fish pond, where Nancy and Tonya have begun to hibernate. The ledge is big enough for lots of potted plants and even for starting some seed trays in late winter.

NOVEMBER 11, 1994

SCENT OF THE SEASON
Memories of holiday traditions waft in the air

ABOUT FIVE YEARS AGO, I DECIDED IT WAS too hard to decorate a fresh Christmas tree each year.

So, in a rare practical mood, we got two faux trees — one for the living room and one for the kitchen. The kitchen tree was the pet tree, and all the ornaments were cats or dogs. Eventually, we collected so many pet ornaments that we had to have a separate cat tree and a dog tree. That's just how silly we are.

A big advantage was that we could wrap the trees, ornaments and all, in netting and haul them down to the basement at the end of the season. The next year

Every tree, whether real or faux, needs a Christmas flamingo.

we'd haul them back up, and they'd already be decorated.

Still, something niggled at me. It was guilt. I just couldn't get past the fact that they weren't real trees. I missed the scent of greens. I missed the tradition. And, I even missed the imperfections. Faux trees are perfect; real trees are not, and some are even little twiggy Charlie Brown trees.

Most of all, I felt that, as a gardener, I had somehow let our side down by not using real greens. I realize this nuance of conscience, coming from a woman who has eight plastic flamingos pecking around in her backyard, is quite laughable.

Nevertheless, this year, the faux trees will stay in the basement. I still don't have the energy for a lot of decorating, but I'm quite content with a small fresh tree sitting in a red bowl on a table in our entryway. I don't even need to decorate it, although I expect

I'll put something on it. I might spruce it up by sticking in some magnolia leaves and berries.

The scent of my little true tree has brought back memories of traditions. Years ago, we always put a dreidel among our ornaments for Jewish friends who spent every Christmas with us. Sol and Lois, both of whom are long gone, would come laden with gifts in pink bags. Lois never used wrapping paper but seemed to have an endless supply of those pink bags. The dreidel is a symbolic top used in celebrating the Jewish feast of Hanukkah.

Another tradition, when I was a child, was stringing popcorn, which the dog always ended up eating. Once we finished the tree, my mother and I would fling silver tinsel all over it. The tinsel was quite tacky and obscured any artistry, but we didn't care. This was our tradition. Besides, the cats loved to bat the tinsel. That tradition ended when I got my own home and realized I didn't love to clean up tinsel-laced fur balls.

I certainly am not implying that there's anything wrong with faux trees. But I am a hopeless traditionalist. I want real mashed potatoes on Thanksgiving. I love it when ladies wear big hats and flowered dresses on garden tours. I would rather have a loose, floppy bouquet picked straight from the garden than a dozen perfect roses smashed together like asparagus in a box, although (ahem) I wouldn't turn them down.

DECEMBER 10, 2009

> *I am a hopeless traditionalist. I want real mashed potatoes on Thanksgiving.*

DRESS HOUSEPLANTS IN A HOLIDAY MOOD

Plant some boughs in the poinsettias, or get merry with berries and colorful twigs

IF YOU'RE LOOKING FOR LAST-MINUTE, FRUGAL ideas to dress up the house for the holidays, you can't go wrong with indoor plants. The trick is to take the plants you already have or inexpensive new ones and do a little dress-up work.

Turn ordinary houseplants into elegant winter decorations by filling in skimpy plants with greens from the garden. Take, for example, three small single poinsettias. Tuck them together into one big brass or elegant Chinese blue-and-white pot and fill them out with branches of greenery from your own garden for a spectacular display.

Similarly, just stick fresh greens into the soil to fill out any spindly houseplant. Poke fresh greens in barren outdoor planters and window boxes as well. Outside, they'll last for at least a couple of months.

Fine-leafed, stiff-stemmed plants such as nandina, juniper, cedar and boxwood are superb fillers. Stems of big, glossy plants, such as laurel or evergreen magnolia, are also elegant additions indoors or out. They combine nicely with needlelike branches to make a contrast in textures.

Use sprigs of berries to add a jolt of color. You can jazz up floral arrangements, too. Instead of investing a small fortune in a full bouquet of flowers, buy just two or three stems of white lilies or a half dozen white chrysanthemums or any flower that will look smashing with greens and berries. With the greens added, you only need a few stems of flowers to have high impact.

Pretty twigs also look charming stuck in among greenery, whether in a potted plant or bouquet. Red and golden dogwood, curly willow, or any moss-covered twig makes an attractive addition. You can hang little ornaments from the twigs for the holidays. I hang some inexpensive, tiny carved birds from Indonesia on a branch or two.

Natural twigs also make pretty stakes for floppy houseplants. Amaryllis in particular gets heavy and tends to emulate the Leaning Tower of Pisa once it blooms. Tie the flower stem loosely to the branches with raffia or ribbon. Tuck smaller branches around drooping foliage of narcissus and other indoor bulbs and encircle them with narrow silk ribbons.

If you don't have a spectacular pot, there are a lot of ways to be creative with containers. Pretty bird cages, wooden drawers, twig baskets, children's sand pails, wooden boxes, cheap terra-cotta pots spray-painted gold, Chinese buckets, bushel baskets, burlap sacks tied with raffia, China bowls and even colorful shopping bags lined with plastic are all creative alternatives.

Or forget trying to find a container. Disguise the ugly plastic pot that plants often come in by wrapping it with moss or twigs and tying it together with a pretty binding such as raffia or a silk or metallic ribbon.

Another way to jazz up houseplants, especially larger ones, is to hide the bare soil at the base of the plant. Green moss is readily available. There's also a silver moss that has a looser, bird-nest texture.

Tuck the moss in under low, leafy plants so it sticks out over the edges. With tall, bare-stemmed plants, such as ficus, heap the moss over the bare soil. The trick is to make a generous fluffy pile.

With large plants, the moss makes a perfect bed to nestle tiny treasures into — a bird's egg, pine cones, ornaments, a charming little carved animal. I confess to copying this and other ideas from a good friend and local decorator, Virginia Burney, who has delicious ways with plants and other ornaments.

As an alternative to moss, drizzle potpourri around the plant up to the rim of the pot. The potpourri and moss have an added benefit. They'll help keep plants from drying out so quickly between waterings.

Another way to make large houseplants look lusher and cover the bare soil is by nesting trailing plants around the edges. Small-leafed variegated ivies and asparagus ferns are ideal. Yet another way to cover soil around a bare-stemmed plant is to mound lemons, tangerines, lady apples or pomegranates around its base.

These little creative projects can be fun as well as inexpensive. I felt like a regular Martha Stewart the other night when I was wrapping moss around old plastic pots. Only, I can assure you, that's where the resemblance between me and Miss Perfect ends. You will never find me looking spotless and coifed in the midst of any gardening project.

DECEMBER 15, 1996

AT THE ROOT OF CHRISTMAS
David Douglas slaked his English countrymen's thirst for greenery with Northwest flora

C ONSIDER YOUR CHRISTMAS TREE. CHANCES are it's a Douglas fir. So is the one at the White House, and that's one holiday tradition that has its roots, literally, in the Northwest.

There's a man behind that tree, and his name isn't Santa. It's David Douglas, a man who left his name liberally around the Pacific Northwest. It's on trees, flowers, a high school, an Oregon county and a few other public places. So who was this guy? He was, according to one English writer, responsible for making England look like the Pacific Northwest (and you thought it was the other way around). "The flowers, shrubs and trees he collected are considered to have had more effect on our gardens than the discoveries of any other plant-hunter," wrote David Hessayon, one of England's best-selling garden writers.

Technically, Douglas didn't "discover" the Douglas fir, just as Columbus wasn't the first to discover America. But, like Columbus, Douglas was the first to bring the discovery to others' attention. (The lesson must be that if you are going to make being a discoverer your career, you had better have a strong minor in public relations.)

The first European to discover the Douglas fir actually was Archibald Menzies, which accounts for the tree's botanical name of *Pseudotsuga menziesii.* Menzies sailed as ship surgeon and naturalist with Capt. George Vancouver on his ship Discovery in search of the Northwest Passage, the illusive link between the Pacific and Atlantic oceans.

Reports of the Pacific Northwest's fabled forests, with trees 300 or more feet high, had fascinated Europeans since the first major coastal explorations in the 1700s. Menzies was aware of these stories when he arrived at what later became known as Vancouver Island, in 1792. It was just after Capt. Robert

Gray had come upon the Columbia River and 33 years before David Douglas visited the Northwest.

It was there that Menzies encountered the huge forests dominated by Douglas fir. The seeds he collected were sent back to England, but little was published about them. In fact, Menzies' contributions are only being recognized fully in the 1990s.

Douglas, on the other hand, had no such PR problems. A Scotsman, he had worked at the Glasgow Botanic Garden before moving to the London-based Royal Horticultural Society. The society, well aware of the growing excitement about New World plants, sent him on botanical explorations for the Hudson Bay Co., based in Fort Vancouver. Though science played its part, the real momentum for Douglas' work was the insatiable appetite in England for new ornamental garden varieties.

Douglas arrived for his first trip to the Northwest in 1825 and stayed two years. During two separate trips to the Pacific Coast, he covered thousands of miles by canoe and on foot. He seems to have been particularly accident-prone, falling out of canoes and losing his botanical notes on at least three occasions. Likewise, his death in Hawaii in 1834 at age 36 seems to have been a ghastly accident. Douglas fell into a bull pit while climbing Mauna Kea on Hawaii and was killed by a trapped wild bull.

His strangest adventure was his quest for the sugar pine. Soon after Douglas arrived at Fort Vancouver, he heard from Indians about a tree with large golden cones. Several months later, while exploring along the Umpqua River, he finally came on the tree. Since the cones were so high up, he tried to shoot them down. The noise brought some unfriendly

Indians, and Douglas barely escaped with his life.

He returned to London in 1827 with hundreds of new specimens. Bored with city life, he was back on the West Coast by 1830, alternating between the Northwest and California.

Although many of the plants that Douglas collected and sent back to Europe had been identified by others earlier, it was Douglas who put them on the botanical map. As a result, many of the plants have been named in his honor.

That is not to say he didn't have his share of discoveries. According to botanical historian James Reveal, Douglas discovered one-third of the West's great conifers and introduced 200 species into modern horticulture. In addition to the Douglas fir and sugar pine, he introduced Europe to the ponderosa pine, Western larch, California laurel, silver fir, grand fir, noble fir, white lodgepole pine, digger pine, Sitka spruce and white dogwood.

Though best remembered for trees, Douglas also discovered a number of shrubs and flowers, including two Western state flowers — the California poppy and Oregon's own state flower, the Oregon grape.

DECEMBER 25, 1992

༄

HAVE A BERRY CHRISTMAS
While flowers are scarce, decorate the table with whatever you find in the garden — rose hips, seed pods, heathers or twigs

CHRISTMAS DAY IS TWO DAYS AWAY, AND all through our house, every creature is stirring except possibly a mouse. There's last-minute list-checking, followed by last-minute panic-buying and last-minute frenzies of wrapping.

And unwrapping too. Sorry, Karma the Cat, you won't get a gift this year. The Perp has unwrapped your catnip pad and is, at this very moment, rolling in ecstasy all over it. We tried to retrieve it, but figured you didn't want something now soaked in drool.

Dried hydrangeas are wonderful in arrangements at Christmas, or any other time of year.

We are observing all the usual holiday traditions, such as finding the hidden tape dispenser, putting coasters under one side of the stand to get the tree straight, and figuring out how to get both strands of lights to blink at approximately the same frequency.

And speaking of traditions, I am reminded of one that Seattle author Ann Lovejoy wrote of in a column several years ago. Each Christmas morning, she makes a point to decorate the table with what her family finds in the garden. It began, she writes in *The Year in Bloom,* as a celebration of the mildness of our maritime Northwest winters.

It's a charming tradition, and one worth copying. It reminds us of what a bountiful and gentle place we live in. Lovejoy's family scurries out and canvasses the yard for treasures such as leftover calendulas and pansies, an early primrose, long-lasting chrysanthemums and the occasional Kaffir lily.

In this first week of winter we still can find a few roses budding. Almost as good are the fat hips of the rugosa roses. The hydrangeas have dried to burnished beauty. There still are glorious grass plumes and a few interesting seed pods. Some brave petunias linger over as well.

But not all is leftovers. The sasanqua camellias are in the first flush of bloom, and the white-green hellebores are unfurling. The winter blooming heaths, cousins to the heathers, are suffused with frosty blooms. The winter jasmine is in bud and promises to erupt into fragrant buttery yellow blossoms at any moment.

Make up for the scarcity of flowers with creative combinations. Sprigs of nandina berries are ideal fillers. Pluck off some of the white quasi-flowers of the tropical-looking fatsia. Gather crimson red twigs from Siberian dogwood or mottled, mossy twigs from almost anything.Add feathery greens of conifers, heathers, boxwood, artemisia, rosemary and nandina again. Its leaves are as fine as its berries. Trail tendrils of small-leafed ivy out of your bouquet for a wild and romantic look.

If you can't find enough to make a full-blown bouquet, carry out the tradition with little tussie-mussies. Tie your sprigs of berries, greens and the odd rose bud with bits of silk ribbon and lace and set them by each plate.

These little nosegays date from Elizabethan England, but despite their fragile prettiness, they have an unsavory history. Aromatic herbs and flowers originally were bundled into the finger-sized bouquets, so strollers could hold them up to their noses to disguise the foul smell of London's streets.

Alas, not all tradition has romantic origins.

DECEMBER 23, 1994

❧

THE GREAT POND CALAMITIES
Slime, mosquitoes and a predator try to sabotage the garden project

WE VERY NEARLY MADE IT THROUGH THE year without yet another disaster. Very nearly, but not quite.

It was the year of The Great Pond Project, which turned out to be a lot like digging the Suez Canal. First, we dug the pond big and deep enough so raccoons wouldn't get the fish. That's when we discovered that a liner large enough to cover a 26-foot-long pond weighs about 400 pounds and takes six teenagers and three cases of Coke to install on a hot day.

Then we put in the gravel and learned lesson No. 2 as the mud roiled up like a mushroom cloud. You're supposed to wash your gravel first. Then mosquitoes arrived from all over the Western Hemisphere to take up residence. Lesson No. 3: Dump in a pail of *Gambusia affinis*, a tiny little fish that regard mosquito larvae the way most of us regard chocolate.

The next event to unfold in the pond saga was a freak windstorm that sent a tree crashing down over the pond, denting an arbor and flattening the water iris. This, of course, conveniently happened four days before a garden group was coming on a tour.

Once the debris was cleaned up, we

thought we were home free. That's about the time summer finally arrived, and the algae turned the pond a slime color resembling the Amazon river in one of those B-moves in which bimbos and piranha figure heavily.

Water plants and a good pump and filter system

> *We keep telling ourselves that a garden without challenges isn't any fun.*

soon took care of that. Finally, the fish went in and so, to our delight, did a couple of frogs, several snails and a turtle. All but the fish were volunteers, and we came to name it Jurassic Pond.

We thought we had arrived at a peaceable kingdom at last. Oh, we couldn't move for three or four days after we raked the fall leaves out. And we had an anxious moment with an early freeze. But although a cascade of water froze over the water iris, the pump kept working, and the fish, though sluggish in their hibernation, were alive and well. Bob and Ray, the two Koi, had fattened up nicely and the 30 or so goldfish had tripled in size. Watching them dart through the water made all the work worth it.

That's when we learned that The Perp ate Ray. Or maybe it was Bob.

The call came last Friday. Vicki, who helps clean our house, called me at work to say there were two dead fish in the den and one fish in the kitchen. In a voice only barely masking disgust, she reported that the kitchen

The pond, forlorn and bare in winter.

fish "is still flopping around and it's a real big one." She put it back, and we haven't seen any fish with X's in their eyes floating belly up. So, thanks to the intrepid Vicki, Ray may have made it. Or perhaps Bob.

Later, she called back to say she had discovered the villain. The Perp was out fishing. The Perp is a very fat — and I might add, very naughty — cat. Her name, short for "perpetrator," should give you an idea of her personality. This archcriminal was foisted off on us by our vet, who assured us she was Grade A feline material and who even threw in a free spaying. We should have suspected something right there.

So much for the theory that if you make your pond with straight sides and a deep spot where the fish can hide, they'll be safe from predators. The problem is that cold weather makes them sluggish and, apparently, stupid. For some reason, Bob and Ray, who perversely hid out under the iris all summer and fall, decided to bask on the surface.

We haven't found any other dead fish around the house. But we had some company, and — I'm not making this up — one person noted that Ralph, our dachshund, had fish breath. You can only imagine the look my husband and I exchanged.

Still, we aren't completely broken. We keep telling ourselves that a garden without challenges isn't any fun. We keep repeating that a garden that's finished is, frankly, boring.

So, we're investing in netting for the pond. We're also looking forward to the days after Christmas when, with new garden books spread out on the dining room table, we can plan the great project of 1994. Will it be a knot garden? An arbor walk? An ornamental vegetable patch? Perhaps a row of espaliered fruit trees? Whatever it is, we're sure it will bring a plague of locusts.

DECEMBER 24, 1993

CHRISTMAS PRESENT
It's time to share the priceless gift of experience

W HAT GIFT CAN I GIVE MY FELLOW GARdeners on such a day as this?

Certainly not routine gardening advice. You have all your new books to peruse for that. I can't suggest something to do in the garden. Who wants to tear themselves from the holiday table to muck around outside?

I decided I could pass on some experience. More to the point, I could tell you all the mistakes (or a lot of them, anyway) I've made through the years so that you don't have to make them.

There is, for example, my first foray into making a flower bed, which I dutifully double dug, just as the books said. First, I dug up a foot of soil and set it aside, then turned over the next foot. I put all the nice crumbly clay soil back in.

Somehow, I missed the part about adding organic matter. Of course, by the following season, the bed again had the consistency of a Los Angeles freeway.

Once I figured out the compost thing, I foolishly thought that adding a couple of truckloads to my clay soil would be enough. I had not counted on this being one's life work. It seems there is no such thing as enough when it comes to compost.

And before we leave this earthy subject, I have to admit that I learned the hard way that new compost takes a long time to "cook," sometimes about a year. The result of adding compost too early was a lot of little weeds and grasses sprouting in a new flower bed.

The good news is that once compost has established itself, the bacterial action that kills viable weed seeds goes much faster.

After the sad experience with double digging, which I never tried again, I got the bright idea of hiring someone to rototill new beds. That's when I discovered that rototilling and old underground sprinkling systems are not good mixers. We didn't have to go to Yellowstone that year to see Old Faithful.

Early on in my gardening career, I found that if one sack of fertilizer is good for the lawn, it does not necessarily follow that two sacks are better. Unfortunately, it was kind of a double whammy, because I learned this lesson the week before my first open garden.

Speaking of open gardens, never again will I underestimate the perseverance of some garden visitors. I've had visitors walk into my back yard at 9 a.m. for an open garden tour scheduled to begin at 1 p.m. They said they wanted to beat the crowds. They found me curling up hoses in my flannel nightgown and fuzzy slippers.

I should get something from Victoria's Secret for the next tour. That would put off the early birds.

Once I joined a garden book club, the kind that sends you a book or two each month on trial. This is not a smart idea if you lack the discipline to wrap and return books you don't want. This, I swear, is the only reason I have Martha Stewart's gardening book. Why else would I buy a gardening book with photographs of a woman digging in the dirt wearing spotless white shoes and white gloves?

Adding a pond opened up a whole new field of errors, but I'll select just one for today. I had a bright idea to bank the far side of the pond with a little hill, all the better to display the plants. The plants showed to a great advantage. But somehow I had overlooked the fact that topsoil runs downhill, right into the pond every time it rains, or you turn on the sprinkler.

I note with interest that 10 years after planting a *Styrax japonica*, the little leaning tree is now a big leaning tree. Somehow I thought it was a plant's nature to grow straight to the sun. It seems little trees, like kids' teeth, need to be straightened early on.

Speaking of little trees, I cleverly pruned some white lilacs into a tree shape. They did make a nice little tree, but it's hard to pick flowers growing 10 feet up.

Then there are vines, which I discovered too late come in different lengths. This was after I planted a 30-footer on an 8-foot arbor. When in bloom, the arbor looked like Dolly Parton's head.

I learned to move swiftly with the pruning shears after my rare variegated-leaf hydrangea sprouted an all-green branch that I failed to snip off. Surprise! The next year, it was a not-so-rare all-green hydrangea.

In the future, if I'm going to try a plant that is marginally hardy in our zone, I will limit the experiment to just one plant. That hedge of hebe I planted flanking the front walk in my old house did not turn out to be a

> *I should get something from Victoria's Secret for the next tour. That would put off the early birds.*

good idea. All 40 plants turned toes up one savage winter.

In our current house, we built garden paths by first putting down black plastic to suppress weeds, then overlaying the plastic with bark chips. The plastic did indeed keep the weeds down. It also helped water pool, turning the paths into a canal system that rivals Venice. The paths will be redone in the new year, with perforated landscape cloth this time.

My husband just chimed in that I must include the bamboo we once accepted as a present. I actually planted some in our very first and very small back yard. I stress this was a really long time ago.

You'd think I would have learned a lesson about invasive plants, but not so long ago I planted some pretty ribbon grass. It is spreading like the Blob in that old Steve McQueen movie of the same name.

There's more. I found that hoses are the one garden accessory you should never look for a bargain on. There is nothing quite so maddening as a kinky hose — unless it is pots that are supposed to hold water but don't.

In the plant world, I thought that growing miniature pumpkins meant that the vines would be miniature, too. And I now know that if you plant 40 seedlings of lettuce on the same day, you will have 40 heads of lettuce ready to eat at the same time, which is OK if you really like salad, three meals a day.

Lovely as it is, I will never plant *Nepeta* x *faassenii* (catmint) again in household ruled by cats.

And here's a mistake I make year after year: (Give me marks for consistency.) Waiting too long to stake floppy plants. The result has been some decidedly odd shapes, once the sprawling stems are corseted up.

So what is the biggest mistake I've ever made? Hands down, it's the time I left my husband unsupervised with some pruning shears. Suffice it to say, we had words over the results.

DECEMBER 25, 1997

ALOHA DAZE
Changeable Northwest weather delights a weary traveler

I JUST SPENT TWO WONDERFUL WEEKS IN MAUI. The weather was generally sunny, the trade winds kept things comfortable, and it seemed to rain only at night. We read books, did crossword puzzles and planned our day around where and what we would eat.

The flowers, to my surprise, were everywhere. We had never been there so late in the year and were amazed to find hibiscus, oleander, plumeria and many other exotic plants all abloom.

Sound idyllic? Well, almost, but I'll take my Eden with Dougie firs. Although we came back to weather 50 degrees cooler, I wouldn't trade home for the tropics. Once again, I'm reminded of how much I enjoy seasons. It was somewhat unsettling to see palm trees decorated with holiday lights and to hear "I'm dreaming of a white Christmas" as we strolled around the streets of Lahaina.

Odder still were some of the decorations, including Santas in hula skirts and painted coconuts. I had to restrain my dear husband from buying an ornament depicting Santa riding a shark. Thanks to him, we already have the Christmas pickle and banana ornaments, which are bad enough.

But what do the islanders have to look

forward to after the holidays? Just more of those same exotic flowers and more of that sunshine. Boring, boring, boring. Just think what we have to look forward to. We get to talk about the weather, which never ceases to fascinate us. In fact, weather now seems to take up a bigger portion of the evening news than either actual news or sports.

We get to wonder if this is the year we will finally have a white Christmas, which has its summer counterpart in speculating whether we will have a ripe tomato before the first frost. We get the delicious anticipation of imagining what will and won't make it through the winter in our gardens. And, we've already begun to cruise garden catalogs in secret hopes that some space will open up.

And before long, we can look forward to our first flowers, which are usually snowdrops in the third week of January. From then on, we can anticipate a steady march of bloom from crocus to daphne before it turns to real spring. These early blooms always bring a delicious joy, almost as if they've never happened before. How I would miss this unfurl-ing of the garden if everything were the same month in and month out.

We gardeners love to walk about our gardens early in the new year and get quite giddy at the sight of a shoot poking up or a little fern uncurling. By the time the hostas are sticking their noses up, we have become besotted anew with our gardens. Talk about falling in love again.I have heard that in the Yukon, the residents celebrate and go a little crazy when the ice begins to break up. I think our equivalent is when new plants arrive in nurseries and the plant sales begin. How can a tropical island compete with this kind of exhilaration?

Excuse my unrepentant prejudice, but I believe we in the Northwest have it just about right. We do have distinct seasons, but not too distinct. We have neither the scorching heat of a Southwest summer nor the bitter cold and dirty slush of a Northeast winter. And, should a season become a little too distinct, we can always escape to a tropical island, just long enough to get bored.

Finally, on a personal note, I would like

Hawaii may be a summer paradise, but see what you miss with only one season?

to end the year with a warm thank-you to readers who sent me such lovely notes and kind wishes. I deeply appreciate your thoughts and prayers. I also loved reading about your gardens, your experiences and your plant triumphs and disasters. I am convinced, once again, that people who garden are especially nice.

The good news is that I am responding well to chemotherapy and look forward to spring, when my hair will be sprouting along with my flowers.

DECEMBER 29, 2005

LIKE FINE WINE
Some resolutions improve with age

THIS YEAR MY NEW YEAR'S RESOLUTION IS, well, to keep some of the resolutions I make every year. It'll be a first if I can manage it.

The garden resolution I unfailingly break is keeping a garden journal. As one of the world's least organized people, I really need a journal. It's amazing, but as long as I've been gardening, I still can't remember what blooms when or even when the garden peaks.

Through the years, I must have started a dozen or so journals, then let them lapse. I started one this year but lost momentum when I found the corners chewed by our new and otherwise adorable dog, Hector. I know, it's like saying the dog ate my homework. But it's true.

The only journal I kept with any success

was my first one, started in the summer of 1982. It's fun to pull it out and see just how much has changed. That first journal was full of conversation about annuals. It also was one of the warmest years on record, and even my dahlias survived without being dug up.

It's also interesting to track how the gardener, not just the garden, grows. In a 1982 entry, I wrote, "The magenta plant is very healthy and blooms continuously." A year later, I scribbled in an entry saying the flower I called magenta plant was really rose campion.

Too bad that journal fizzled out. I wonder how many years it was before I caught on that the botanical name was *Lychnis coronaria*. Still, it bloomed just as well with the name "magenta plant," and to this day, that's how I think of it.

There are other noble resolutions I have a habit of breaking year after year. Near the top are resolutions that deal with being on time.

- I resolve to weed early before those little criminals spread their seeds.
- I resolve to stake early before floppy plants sprawl into forms resembling giant squids.
- I resolve to pull up the zillion little seedlings of lady's mantle, verbena, angelica, tovara and other self-sowers before they spread like measles. This will take all the fortitude I can muster because they look so adorable when they're babies. But I always regret letting them take over the garden, even if it is a friendly takeover.
- I resolve also to bite the slug pellet, or whatever the garden version of a bullet is,

> *As long as I've been gardening, I still can't remember what blooms when or even when the garden peaks.*

and remove plants that (a) are overgrown or (b) don't merit the space they use. This is a particularly tough resolution because ridding myself of a plant goes against my soul. I've had a houseplant for 30 years that is spindly, stunted and generally wimpy. But I can't toss it out.

Snowdrops offer hope for a green future.

- I resolve, too, to label plants whose names I always forget. These, of course, are the ones visitors always ask about. As I recollect, a set of labels has been lying around the garden shed for about two years. Because they're metal, I can't even claim Hector ate them.

I hope my resolve persists into autumn because I also resolve to plant, not just write about, more bulbs. Each spring I regret that I wasn't more ambitious with the fall planting program. Oh, I buy the bulbs all right. It's getting them in the ground that I have trouble with.

One thing I don't have to resolve to do is to build a compost pile. I've got a nice, healthy one going. For those of you who don't, it's one resolution I heartily recommend.

Finally, this is the year I resolve to have a sign made with the name of our property. This is the third home we've owned, and we named the other two.

The first was Toad Hall, for the bilious green color of the house. The second was Monkwell Manor, because the day we bought the house, we saw Agatha Christie's play, *The Mousetrap*. The fictional manor was the setting for the play. In fact, after the play, the cast surprised us with a present of the Monkwell Manor sign.

Although we've lived in this house 12 years, a name has eluded us. This summer, I came up with the perfect one: Blackspot Manor.

JANUARY 1, 1998

༰

WINTER CULL
Storm damage may leave us with a cleaner slate in the garden

THIS IS WHAT WE CALL A "THINNING OF THE herd" winter, the herd in this case being our plants. Not only did subfreezing temperatures lay siege to us for a sustained period, but also the timing was rotten. The first of the December storms hit after a fairly mild autumn, when many plants still hadn't gone into full dormancy. This made them more vulnerable to freeze damage than if the same weather had hit us this month.

If you want to know what you've probably lost, look first to those borderline Zone

Along with being beautiful, snow serves as a protective blanket.

8 plants that we've gotten away with leaving out for the past few winters. This includes New Zealand flax (*Phormium*), cannas and flowering maples (*Abutilon*). I won't even mention true tropicals. I could hear my banana pleading for its life even while in protective custody in the back shed.

We may also lose those marginally hardy plants that survive years of our winters but can't take the occasional extreme event. This will include certain cultivars of hebe, California lilac (*Ceanothus*) and daphne and even a few hybrid tea roses. Plus, anything we planted in late fall, like my crape myrtle (*Lagerstroemia*), may not have produced enough root growth to make it tough enough to survive.

Still, what does survive may surprise you.

The fact that it snowed heavily will have provided some protection for plants since snow acts as insulation (that's why places like Chicago and Denver can grow roses). Snow makes every bit as good a mulch as compost. The most devastating weather for plants is frigid cold with strong desiccating winds and no precipitation.

In that way, snow is our friend. In other ways it isn't. The most difficult losses will be the larger trees and shrubs that could take the freezing temperatures but not the weight of the snow. Some will spring back into shape, while others may be so flattened or have lost so many limbs that they will have to be pruned way back if they are salvageable at all.

I fear our large laurel pruned to look like a tree will have to be cut back sharply. It's not that laurel is an important plant; it's that it was of a size that conveniently hid a telephone pole and lines behind it in the back alley. That asset will be hard to replace.

In general, it's best to wait for at least a few weeks and see what revives. Broken or obviously dead stems can be removed, which will help prevent cell damage from going further. This is especially important for roses. They will fool you and leaf out in spring, then start to die as cell damage from the freeze spreads. Roses seem to have lots of ways of breaking our hearts.

But all is not doom and gloom. There are theories, and I specify theories because I have not witnessed the actual evidence, that a very cold winter will kill off many annual weeds and leaf-chomping critters. Maybe that's why we had Oregon slugs heading to Hawaii nestled in a shipload of Christmas trees. They may be smarter than they look.

But getting back to the subject of thinning the herd, the best way to deal with plant loss is with attitude. I was talking to my friend Denise the other day about the potential losses, and she said she was actually looking forward to having a cleaner slate this spring so she could try some new things. Atta girl. That's the attitude we should start stitching into our samplers for this year.

JANUARY 8, 2009

❧

GENEROUS TIPPER
An experienced hand shares a wealth of advice

RECENTLY I WAS ASKED TO GIVE A LITTLE talk, and the hosts suggested that I speak on garden tips. This is a fairly broad subject, and I can think of numerous tips, such as don't dig up moist earth and put out plants on a hot day because your dog will lie on them. But I think my hosts wanted something a little more generic.

So I jotted a dozen basic tips, and I pass them on for those of you who are starting or refreshing a tired garden in the new year.

1. I'll get the boring one out of the way first, but of course you know this: Good, fluffy soil is the place to start. This is the thing you can't skimp on. Organic compost does the trick. End of lecture.

2. Forget trying to figure out what style your garden should be. Don't copy someone else's idea of the perfect formal or informal garden. Personal style is in, and as you dig in, you will find your own style. Themes (colors, kinds of plants, ornamentation) will emerge as you purchase things that make you happy.

3. Don't worry if you don't have a complete landscape plan. It's good to have a general concept, but the best gardens evolve gradually. If you don't get things exactly right, it's easy in our climate to move plants around. While it's lovely if you do have a plan, don't follow it rigidly. Experimentation is part of the fun of gardening.

4. If, as often happens, you begin to notice that your garden doesn't quite pull together as a whole, there are things you can do. To give a cohesive look, limit the number of colors you use and repeat plantings and shapes. Otherwise, you may get an overly busy polka-dot effect. Also, introducing focal points (an ornament, water feature, gazebo, specimen plant, etc.) can help pull things together by giving the eye a place to rest.

5. Let nature guide you. If you have a wet area, don't fight it. Make it a bog garden or pond. A dry spot would be best for Mediterranean-style plants. The best area for dining may be under a large tree, not necessarily on a shadeless deck off the back door.

6. Introduce elements that appeal to all senses — for example, water and rustling grass for sound, flowers and herbs for scent, soft foliage for touch and, of course, color and shape for sight. A garden should be more than something to look at. Make it an environment.

> *A garden should be more than something to look at.*

7. A flat garden is boring and unnatural. Follow nature and plant in layers, including shrubs and small ornamental trees, as well as flowers and ground covers. A layered garden also is most attractive to birds.

8. Don't be afraid to remove something that's not working — an overgrown shrub, a misshapen tree, a spindly plant or one that casts too much shade. Editing a garden can work wonders to refresh it. And, if a plant continues to be sickly (think a black-spotted rose or mildewy azalea), be tough and put it out of its misery.

9. The best design decision you can make is to ensure healthy plants. Pay attention to plant needs. Plants that love sun will grow spindly and lean toward the light in shade. Similarly, plants that need shade will shrivel or scorch in too much sun. The same is true of plants that need moisture or well-drained soil. They may survive in poor conditions, but they won't thrive.

10. Don't forget garden furnishings and accessories — whether found objects or real works of art. A garden should be a place to have fun and express yourself.

11. Include a little mystery. It's much more fun if you can't see everything at once. That's why so many of the "grand" gardens have "rooms." Even a small garden can have special spaces. It can be as simple as a couple of chairs in a small clearing.

12. Whatever style you choose, do it with gusto. Don't skimp on foliage. A garden that is robust, verdant and luxuriant has innate style.

JANUARY 15, 2004

FEAR OF FREEZING
Winter runs hot and cold, so defend yourself

WE ARE IN THAT NERVOUS PERIOD WHEN we worry that a sudden winter freeze will swoop through our gardens, leaving Antarctica in its wake. The fact is that a freeze at this time of year will not wreak nearly as much devastation as an early or late freeze. Right now, everything in our gardens should be as sound asleep as a snoring grizzly.

It's far more threatening when freezing temperatures hit in November or December before everything has gone quite dormant. In December, some of us have been known to be out there picking off the last rose of the year, rather than letting it go to seed, because it's such fun to tell our friends in Cleveland that, nyaa, nyaa, we've still got roses. But, alas, even that little pluck constitutes a form of untimely pruning.

But the worst weather threat to our gardens lies ahead. It's that combination of early thaw followed by late freeze. It's common to see a few days of false spring in February, when things bud up and a pale sun beats down on our heads, causing us to go a little berserk and forget that it will get cold again. You know that week — there's always some guy in the neighborhood who gets out his Bermuda shorts and starts mowing the lawn.

If you haven't done so, you can protect your plants from that all-too-common event by getting out and adding a couple of inches of good organic mulch on top of your flower and shrub beds right now. Most of us associate mulching with fall, but it's absolutely not too late. A good mulching now will keep the ground cold and help protect plants from breaking out of dormancy when false spring arrives. It's especially helpful for roses.

> *... there's always some guy in the neighborhood who gets out his Bermuda shorts and starts mowing the lawn.*

Don't wait to put the mulch on in early spring (everyone ignores me and does it anyway because it makes flower beds look so neat with that chocolaty cover). The problem is, an early spring mulching will keep the ground

Come summer this winter view will be verdant with foliage and flowers.

cold, just when you want it to be warming up. It's warmer ground temperature combined with longer days that makes things grow.

The other thing you can do in midwinter, if you're just itching to get out in the garden, is some pruning. This is a great time to prune deciduous shrubs and trees because you can see the general shape of the plants. According to *Cass Turnbull's Guide to Pruning*, winter pruning stimulates growth almost as much as spring pruning.

But then things start to get scary. Does your shrub flower on old or new wood? Will pruning it now destroy spring flowers? Well, yes, it will if you cut certain shrubs way back in the manner you would prune a hybrid tea rose (which should wait until late February).

The secret of winter pruning is to prune for shape. Just open up the shrub or tree and remove some branches to give an airy and sculptural effect. That way you'll still have lovely blooms on those branches you left whole. Start by removing water sprouts (those vertical shoots), deadwood and branches that cross or rub against each other. Then approach the plant as a sculpting, not pruning, assignment.

The other winter job is dormant spray. This is light oil applied to fruit trees and other woody plants to kill insect eggs before they have a chance to hatch. Ignore all those books that tell you to do it in March. They are written for parts of the country that don't warm up until then. Here west of the mountains, you need to get dormant spray on by mid-February; otherwise the oil could damage emerging growth. Be sure to follow package directions.

Finally, while you're out there, you may see some of your bulbs coming up and worry that a freeze will do them in. That's not usually going to happen, even if the tips of the leaves get winter burn. The little flower heads should be tucked in deeply enough, like a little duckling with its head under its wing. All except the snowdrops (*Galanthus*), of course. Look for them to bloom about the third week of January.

JANUARY 13, 2005

THE COUNTDOWN BEGINS
Soon it will be time to start your seeds indoors

IT WON'T BE LONG BEFORE CATALOG-PERUSING season edges into seed-starting season. So, like many of you, I'm canvassing window ledges, water heaters and other possible sites where a few seed trays might stay cozy.

The best place in our house is the south-facing bay window off the kitchen. Even that, however, has limitations because there are usually other items on that ledge, including whatever stack of video tapes my husband is viewing, an orchid I'm trying to get to rebloom, books and, of course, a cat sunning her ample belly. One of my winning-the-lottery fantasies involves a working greenhouse, but for now, space is limited. As a result, I tend to be choosy, sticking to seeds of favorite annuals that aren't readily available as potted seedlings in nurseries.

For example, you can always count on nurseries to stock the common tobacco flower (*Nicotiana*). But it's a lot harder to find the magnificent, 5-foot-tall *Nicotiana sylvestris* or *Nicotiana* 'Lime Green', which has flowers of that delicious color. And although common sunflowers are indeed common, starts of a particular creamy white variety, *Helianthus debilis* 'Italian White', aren't easy to find.

The same is true of the castor bean plant (*Ricinus communis*), one of the all-time great foliage plants. It has large blue-green leaves with red veins and stems. The whole plant looks a bit tropical and lends an exotic touch. Some years it's easy to come across, and other years (last year was one) I didn't find any seedlings until late in the season.

Your favorites might be different from mine. The point is, if you don't have the luxury of space, try sowing seeds of hard-to-find plants.

Leave the cosmos, marigolds and petunias to people with greenhouses and acres of room. Better yet, hang around when they're transplanting their plants; some might fall into your basket.

A SEED-SOWING PRIMER

Here's a quick refresher on starting from seed.

- Don't start seeds too early, or plants will get spindly and weak while waiting for the soil to warm up for planting. February through April is seed-sowing season for the Willamette Valley.
- Seed packets give the number of weeks to germination. Count backward from when you estimate is the best time to plant in your garden. That will give you a date for starting seeds.
- Find a site where temperatures will be between 60 and 70 degrees. The best exposure is a south or southeastern window. Take the guesswork out of temperatures by buying heating coils made to go under seed trays.
- Don't plant in garden soil. The planting mix should be light, fluffy and sterilized. Commercial seed-starting mixes are avail-

able, and many garden books have recipes for homemade mixes.

- Sow from six to ten seeds per square inch, depending on the size of the seed. Follow the directions on the seed packet, and don't sow too deeply.
- Some hard-shelled seeds (the packet will tell you) need to be soaked in lukewarm water for 24 hours to soften the shell. Another technique for getting hard-shelled seeds to germinate: Nick the shell with a knife or rub a small section with an emery board.
- Once seeds are planted, water from the bottom by sitting the pots or tray containing seeds in a pan or sink of shallow water. Drain away excess water.
- Keep soil barely moist. If you see a crust forming, spray with a misting bottle.
- Until seeds sprout, keep pots or trays covered with something such as clear plastic that lets in light and holds in moisture. Remove the cover when sprouts appear.
- Rotate seedlings when they sprout so they won't grow sideways toward the light.
- If you use artificial light, use a cool bulb (fluorescent or a special grow light). Place lights about a foot above seed trays and leave on 12 to 16 hours a day.
- Thin and transplant seedlings indoors when they've gotten their second or true pair of leaves. Crowded seedlings will compete, resulting in spindly growth.
- Transplants going into larger pots should be put in a heavier mix such as commercial potting soil, but not heavy garden soil.
- After frost danger is past, put new seedlings outside in a protected area such as on a porch or in a cold frame for a few days to allow them to adjust before planting them in the ground.

• Ideally soil temperatures should be about 60 degrees when you plant outside. In the Willamette Valley, that isn't likely to be until mid-April, and later if it's a cold, wet spring.

JANUARY 13, 2000

THE BATHTUB GARDENER
Wallowing in the season gets ideas flowing for an annual project

L ATE LAST FALL, I WROTE HOW I GET THROUGH the winter doldrums by planning a project. I choose a gardening project for the following spring, and I spend the winter researching (also known as bathtub reading) and dreaming about how I will execute it.

My project for the coming spring is a white garden. This will be a second try. The first was a disaster. I went about it by buying all the white plants I could find and sticking them in willy-nilly.

You might not think it, but a white garden takes planning. I discovered that a bluish-white flower can look washed out next to a creamy white, and the latter can take on a jaundiced look by contrast. It seems that you need to pay even more attention to positioning plants in the same color family and use ample buffers of green and gray foliage.

So, you see, planning a garden project is a swell way to occupy yourself while you're waiting for the ground to get dry enough to plant, which some years can take right up to the Fourth of July.

If you haven't come up with a garden

A knot garden is a focal point year round, but especially so in winter.

project already, here are 10 ideas to jump-start the gardening juices and set green thumbs atwitter. We're not talking large landscaping overhauls, just a teensy project here and there. (As in, "Honey, it will hardly cost anything, and your brother-in-law will help us!")

1. **Got a hot tub that doesn't get much use?** Consider turning it into a pond, replete with fish and water lilies. Cedar-lined tubs make the best ponds, but any tub can be banked up with decking or a berm so it fits into the garden. Think of all the fun you'll have studying up on water plants, fish, pumps and filtration systems.

2. **Have a corner of the yard that lacks interest or a big lawn that needs a focal point?** Plan a knot garden. Spend the winter copying designs and deciding on plants. Boxwood is most the permanent, but germander, hyssop, santolina and lavender are faster growing and can be sheared into little hedges, too. There are more possibilities, but those are for you to look up.

3. **Have you always wanted an herb garden?** Plant a parterre for growing herbs. Parterres are little beds in geometric shapes, very French. A parterre can be as simple as a circle divided into wedges with narrow brick paths between each wedge and a great pot or sundial in the center.

4. **Got a lumpy growth of boxwood?** Lucky you. Take a chance and try a topiary. Birds are easiest, but animals are fun, too. If you don't have boxwood, buy some in a pot. Remember, it's like hair. It will grow back if you mess up.

5. **Does your garden need a structure for accent?** Plan a gazebo, greenhouse or potting shed. Months before we added our gazebo, we circled prospective sites with a hose and plunked down a couple of chairs inside the circle. That way, we tested different spots to see where the gazebo would look best and what the views would be when we were inside it.

6. **Have a small yard but want some fruit trees?** I confess to having always wanted to try my hand at espalier. For this project, you need to check out dwarf fruit trees and pruning techniques. And you need to have a good understanding with your spouse about who wields the pruning utensils.

7. **Got a section of path that is boring?** Plan a pergola. Either design your own structure or line up three or four conventional arbors. Then spend the winter thinking about the climbers you'll try. Will it be flowers such as intertwined roses and clematis, or fruits such as kiwis and grapes?

8. **Already have a pond?** Make it an even more important focal point by planning a bog garden around one end. What fun to make up a list of plants that actually thrive in mucky, wet clay soil! Many bog plants have big leaves and look tropical.

9. **Want to try a different water feature?** Plan a narrow wet or dry stream bed that wiggles or zigzags through a section of the garden. Have it intersect with a path so you can have a little stone or cedar bridge as well. This is a great feature for small front yards and courtyards.

10. **Thinking about a theme garden?** Set aside a space dedicated to a special motif, like my white garden, or dedicated to a plant type, such as alpines. I know eventually I'll try a rock garden because I love those beautiful lewisias, but they really

need a rockery to set them off. Other themes: a cutting garden, a Shakespeare garden, a garden of roses with royal or celebrity names, a Colonial garden, a scented garden, a garden of biblical plants, a variegated garden, an Asian garden or, well, you get the idea.

JANUARY 15, 1998

GREAT PRETENDERS
Tropical look-alikes stand up to winter

B Y LATE 2003, MANY OF US WERE CONVINCED that climate warming was going to mean consistently mild winters, and so we continued our headlong rush into the tropical look. Oh, yes, never holier than thou, I purchased a banana and stuck it in the greenhouse to winter over. Alas, it expired in an unholy mess shortly after last year's January freeze.

Once again winter reminds us that weather is cyclic, and not a steady upward or downward trend. I suspect it's a lesson we will proceed to forget over and over all our gardening lives. I even recall a certain dear neighbor pronouncing before last winter, "Oh, yes, it's getting warmer. We won't have the kinds of freezes we used to."

But although wiser, we remain seduced by that exotic temptress, the tropical look, and it is hard to let go. And maybe it isn't all that necessary. I recall the first time I visited the African savanna at the Oregon Zoo. It really did look like Africa, even to me who has visited the wild game preserves of Kenya

. . . we remain seduced by that exotic temptress, the tropical look, and it is hard to let go.

and Tanzania. The trick, I was told, is that the zoo gardeners used plants that replicated the look of the savanna.

It seems to me that we can apply the same principle of replicating to the tropics if that's a look we still want. I don't have a particularly tropical garden, but I do admit to having a yen for an exotic touch here and there.

The idea is to use hardy plants that have exotic and bold foliage and tend to grow lushly like their jungly fellows. If one uses such hardy plants for "the look," he or she can then insert the tender banana, canna, savanna (couldn't resist that) plant here and there. That way, if a freeze swoops down, the whole scheme isn't lost.

So here are some plants with heroic foliage that are tough enough for any of our winters but could, for all appearances, be at home in warmer climes. All are perennials, except where noted.

Acanthus mollis (bear's breeches): Elegant architectural leaves. Often evergreen, but will die back in a really cold winter. It will reliably return but may take a couple of years to get back to the size it was. Sun, part shade.

Arundo donax (giant reed): Huge (12 feet) grass that is mercifully slow to spread in our climate. Makes a striking and exotic statement for the lion-hearted. Sun, light shade.

Astilboides tabularis (used to be *Rodgersia tabularis*): Leaves can span 3 feet. Sun, light shade, moist soil.

Catalpa bignonioides (Indian bean tree): Exotic, big-leaved tree. Size can be controlled by cutting to the ground in spring, which also will make the leaves bigger. 'Aurea' has gold leaves and grows more slowly. Sun, slightly moist soil.

Darmera peltata (umbrella plant): Big-leaved native; use only if you have the room, because it's a spreader. Colors nicely in fall. Sun, light shade, moist soil.

Fatsia japonica (Japanese aralia): Evergreen shrub to 10 feet with Asian look. Sun or shade.

Ligularia: Lovely, but really must be kept moist or it will droop by midday. Excellent for a bog garden. *L. dentata* 'Desdemona' is particularly beautiful. Sun, shade, moist soil.

Macleaya cordata (plume poppy): Tall (maybe 8 feet) but narrow plant that doesn't need staking (wins my heart). Feathery flowers. Sun, light shade.

Paulownia tomentosa (empress tree): Exotic tree with huge leaves. Like catalpa, can be controlled by cutting to the ground every spring and fertilizing, which will make leaves even bigger. Sun, moist soil.

Petasites japonicus (butterbur): Magnificent round leaves, but also a spreader. Loves a streamside or pond location. Sun, shade, moist soil.

Rodgersia: Lovely underused foliage plant, but will burn if it gets afternoon sun. Upside is that you get big leaves without fear of spreading, also foamy flowers. Shade, moist soil.

JANUARY 20, 2005

❧

DARK PERIOD
Get through gray days by plotting a winter pick-me-up

I KEEP PEERING OUT THE WINDOW HOPING TO catch a glimpse of that much heralded look called the glory of the winter garden. But try as I may, I can't see any resemblance to those photos of frost-rimmed foliage sparkling in a winter sun that you see in books about gardens in winter.

Frankly, my back yard looks more like Beirut. Also, I'm beginning to have very bad thoughts the more I hear that Madame La Niña could mean a late spring. It's obvious this is the dark period for gardeners.

We can either wallow in our misery or we can take remedial action. In the interest of positive thinking, I called a gaggle of gardening pals who came up with a tidy list of 20 picker-uppers they use to get them through the dead of winter.

1. A good place to start is dosing yourself with chocolate. The miracle of chocolate is that it's equally useful to picking oneself up as it is to wallowing in misery.

2. Don't just think about starting something from seed this year. Do it. It doesn't take much room; a windowsill will work for a modest effort. There are all sorts of things on the market from seed trays to warming cables to make germination easier.

3. Turn disaster into opportunity. Start a list of what you will plant in the holes left by plants that didn't make it through winter. I personally expect to have lots of opportunities, since I mulched my cannas rather than digging them up. I'm pretty sure they are now in tropical plant heaven.

4. Widen your repertoire of garden catalogs.

5. Go through photos of your garden in bloom. Each winter I can't believe that this barren plain I see before me could ever again turn into anything verdant. Then I'll come across photos, and they give me faith that it'll be that way once again.

Winter is the time to dream up new designs, initiate new projects, research new plants.

6. Put a bird feeder near a window. People who aren't regular bird watchers forget that winter is the best viewing time. There may be fewer birds, but they concentrate around feeders as other food sources are diminishing.

7. Buy or rent a garden video for wintry nights.

8. Use the bareness of the garden to stimulate design ideas. In winter, you can see things you otherwise would miss — structure and shape, whether things are in pleasant proportion, how paths line up and how focal points are balanced.

9. Read a garden book; I mean really read it. Don't just buy a pretty picture book. Look for the earlier works of established writers before they began putting out coffee-table books. Check out authors such as Christopher Lloyd, Katherine White, Margery Fish, Henry Mitchell, Michael Pollan and Karel Čapek.

10. For inspiration, bundle up and visit a great winter garden or join a botanical garden society.

11. Visit a nursery. Even in winter, you'll find things to delight you, especially if you like garden ornaments and accessories.

12. Grow something indoors that you don't ordinarily grow. Personally, I find that regular houseplants aren't a very good substitute for outdoor gardens, but there are a few plants that do put a little zing in my heart. Having an orchid in bloom is a real picker-upper, despite the fact that I've never gotten one to rebloom.

13. Force an early spring by forcing bulbs and budding branches. Stores still carry com-

mon indoor bulbs such as paperwhites, hyacinths and amaryllis. As soon as you see the nodules of buds on your forsythia, Cornelian cherry, witch hazel, amelanchier, flowering quince, daphne and crabapple, cut off some branches and put them in water for early bloom indoors.

14. Think ahead for next year. Make a list of the plants you really should have in your winter garden. Examples are boxwood and dwarf conifers for greenery and shape. For winter flowers, top picks are hellebores, winter jasmine (*Jasminum nudiflorum*) and two great viburnums, *V. bodnantense* and *V. farreri*.

15. Do something industrious in the garden. Winter is a great time to prune shrubs and trees for shape because you can see the structure and spot dead limbs. Open them up to graceful natural lines but don't overprune. Even spring-blooming shrubs such as lilacs can be pruned if you're just thinning for a little airiness. Don't hard prune unless you're prepared to lose a season's bloom.

16. If you're a wimp like me and don't really want to get out in the cold, do something for the garden than can be done indoors, such as a craft project. Learn how to make a mosaic stepping stone, a trough, a birdhouse, a banner or some other decorative thing that you've spotted with a big price tag and thought, I could do that!

17. Take a class. Community colleges, gardening societies and even some nurseries offer a selection from overall garden design to wreathmaking. Or take a class in watercoloring or pastels so you can try your hand at botanical illustrations.

18. Start your garden notebook for the year. Make your first entry the first time you see a sign that the garden is starting to come alive. It may be the first clump of snowdrops you spot. Then you can compare the dates each year.

19. Take a winter walk around your garden and neighborhood and see how clever you can be in gathering enough pretty things to make a winter bouquet. If you come up short on winter blooms, combine red or moss-covered twigs, evergreen foliage, dried seed heads and berries. At first glance, the winter landscape may look barren, but you'll be surprised at the rich assortment you'll find when you get out and explore.

20. If all else fails to lift your wintry soul, start a savings account for a greenhouse.

JANUARY 21, 1999

COUNTING ON SNOWDROPS
These punctual white flowers brighten winter days

THE THIRD WEEK IN JANUARY IS ALWAYS A milestone moment in my garden. Right on schedule, as if they know they're on the clock, my snowdrops (*Galanthus nivalis*) begin blooming. The oldest clump, right outside the kitchen, is the first to flower. I always go out and give them a little round of applause to welcome them.

The Victorians, who admittedly were a bit silly in their romantic symbolism, designated the common snowdrop as the symbol of hope. I think they got it right with this flower. These bulbs, which produce clumps of nodding white flowers, are the earliest bulb to bloom, and they do indeed signal the awakening garden.

Don't worry if yours don't bloom this week. I'm in Portland's so-called banana belt, down by the river and away from gorge winds, so bloom time may be later in other places, but it will be dependable. The small flowers look delicate, but I have seen pictures of them blooming in snow, so they must be tough.

It won't be long now until we begin to see other harbingers of spring, but don't worry overly much if some of the usual signposts are missing. After our snowy winter, spring won't bring devastation, but it will bring mixed messages. Plants that set buds in late fall, such as forsythia, may not flower this year but will still be healthy. It just means their buds froze.

Do not be overly anxious to replace what you've lost. Some plants that are normally evergreen in our winters (acanthus being one) do die back to the ground in colder climates. That's how they protect themselves. I've had plants die back and show no signs of life until June. Then, just as I was about to put something new in, I'd see little green sprouts poking up.

But beware of wolves in sheep's clothing. I recall one winter when my 'Cecile Brunner'

Chances are, trees and shrubs shrouded in ice during deep freezes will survive undamaged.

rose died completely back. I was overjoyed when late new growth came up from the ground. But it wasn't poor Cecile; it was some wild, rangy rose that Cecile had been grafted onto. It was a good lesson as to why it's important to choose roses grown on their own rootstock.

Alas, some plants will start to sprout leaves in spring, but will slowly die as the interior cell damage becomes apparent. Roses have a way of breaking your heart this way. I've also heard that yellow roses tend to be less cold hardy than roses of other colors. However, I'm still betting that the snow helped insulate roots and likely saved plants that would otherwise have died when temperatures dipped.

Meanwhile, I'm going to enjoy my snowdrops and hope for the best, although thinking of snowdrops reminds me of a failed experiment. In autumn 2007, Doug the Wonder Boy planted clumps of small bulbs in our back lawn. He chose very-early-blooming varieties so that they would be over and done with by the time the lawn needed mowing.

The bulbs did come up last spring, but, although we thought DTWB had planted a sufficient number, the little flowers were too sparse to produce the effect we were after, which was one of those flower-filled lawns you see in English gardening magazines. Ours looked rather anemic by comparison, but if we had waited a few years, the bulbs might have multiplied.As it turned out, we took up the lawn and put a new one in, not because of the bulbs, but because the old lawn was looking like a threadbare rug.

Finally, dear readers, this is the last time I will refer to my garden helper as Doug the Wonder Boy. He has turned 40, and I have promised to upgrade him to Doug the Wonder Guy.

JANUARY 22, 2009

❧

ROAD TRIP

Winter excursions to a nursery reveal true nature

I F YOU'RE LOOKING FOR A GARDEN FIX IN THE dead of winter, here's a suggestion: Visit a nursery. You may be surprised at how much life there is in the so-called dead season. So put on your slickers, because here are 10 good reasons to visit a nursery in winter.

1. **Enjoy the quiet.** You can wander around without any crowds. It's peaceful. You'll see things you wouldn't notice in any other season.

2. **Notice the shape of plants.** Stripped of foliage, you can appreciate the lacelike tracery of branches, the winding corkscrews of certain twigs and the elegant vase shapes of shrubs such as witch hazels.

3. **Discover the colors of winter.** Far from being a drab period, winter glows with burnished colors — the crimson and gold of willow and dogwood twigs; the warm browns and dove grays of other shrubs and trees. You may even fall in love with bark. Look for the cherry *Prunus serrula*, which appears to have been wrapped in mahogany-red satin ribbons.

4. **Find out what really is evergreen, even in the deadest of seasons.** You'll notice that not all evergreens are conifers and not all conifers are Christmas-tree green. They also come in blue, silver, gold, chartreuse and dark green.

Winter gardens glow with color through bark, foliage, winter bloomers, and well-placed garden art.

5. Stumble upon a jewel of a plant that you wouldn't have given a second thought to in any other season. For me, it was the lowly bergenia. Lowly, that is, until I

came upon it in winter to find its foliage utterly transformed into glowing crimson fans. Check out *Bergenia* 'Sunningdale' or 'Bressingham Ruby'. You might also develop a fondness for heaths and heathers, which come into their own in winter. Heaths (*Erica*) are winter bloomers, while heathers (*Calluna*) have colorful winter foliage.

6. **Select winter-flowering plants when they are in bloom so you can get the finest color.** Look for hellebores in that exquisite violet with a speckled throat or a *Camellia sasanqua* in virginal white or palest pink.

7. **Discover that there's more to bare-root plants than roses.** I didn't give much credence to bare-root planting until three years ago when I got a bare-root weeping crabapple and a flowering cherry. The pair looked like mere sticks, but cost just $5 each, so I took a chance. They flowered the first season and are growing like Jack's beanstalk.

8. **Take advantage of the fact that nursery folks have more time to help you.** They can answer questions, give you ideas or just chat amiably about our favorite subject. I have some friends who just bought a new house and wanted to start their new garden with a peony. They went to a nursery and asked what the chances were of finding one at this time of year. "Slim to none," was the answer. Still, the nursery employee went out and looked, and, lo and behold, found a beautiful peony.

9. **Check out what looks good if you've been flirting with the idea of year-round interest in your garden.** If you wait until spring or summer, you won't see the beauty of winter plants. Some, such as winter jasmine, look insignificant at any other time of year. You need to see the winter bloom, color and structure of the season's choice plants. Many nurseries group seasonal plants so you can see good companions. I call it seduction alley and admit to being a fallen woman (plantwise, you understand).

10. **And the best reason of all to visit a nursery in the quiet season?** Go to wallow in the experience, the feel and scent. For those of us who are dedicated — or possibly decadent — gardeners, there is nothing quite like the springy feel of a nursery path or the heady scent of rich, humusy earth. It clears the head, stimulates the senses and reminds us . . . there will be a spring.

JANUARY 22, 2004

EYE CANDY
Some pretty plants have a nasty bite

RECENTLY, TWO ALERT READERS WROTE OUT of concern because I had recommended planting seeds of the castor bean plant, *Ricinus communis*.

Both pointed out, correctly, that the plant is poisonous, and that I should have mentioned it.

Therein lies the dilemma. So many common plants are poisonous. Does pointing one or two out imply that others aren't?

On the other hand, one can argue that some plants are deadly, while others will merely give you a small tummy ache. And some plants are more dangerous because of certain attractions. A child is more likely to sample pretty berries and interesting pods than to actually eat a stem or leaves.

This makes the castor bean particularly dangerous on two counts. It bears large shiny seeds that attract attention, and they are highly toxic. One source said that as few as two beans can cause death. So thank you, dear readers, for the alert.

The whole area of plant toxicity is confusing at best and something of an issue at present, given people's fondness for creative salad making and experimental tea brewing. The same plant can be both beneficial and deadly, with the difference being a matter of dosage.

Agatha Christie proved this point when she handed one of her villains a near perfect murder weapon: the common foxglove. Digitalis, derived from foxglove, is a heart medicine, but brewed in a cuppa tea, it's a different matter.

Even edible plants aren't entirely edible. The stalks of rhubarb are edible, but the leaves are toxic. The seeds and leaves of apples, apricots and peaches can make you ill. So can the seeds of asparagus.

And three popular edibles belong to a pretty toxic plant family (Solanaceae). In addition to the deadly nightshades, this family embraces tomatoes, potatoes and eggplants, and the leaves of all are indeed poisonous.

Tomatoes were shunned by Europeans when the plants were first brought from the New World because people thought all parts were poisonous. We have the Italians to thank for debunking that myth. Potatoes also were shunned, but that was a simple case of snobbery.

Some of the most common houseplants, such as philodendron and *Dieffenbachia*, are toxic. The latter is commonly called dumb cane because, if you chew the stem, it can cause the tongue to swell painfully, making speech impossible for a time. Maybe it should be placed near another houseplant, *Sansevieria*, called mother-in-law's tongue.

Some plant families run to the toxic. The buttercup (Ranunculaceae) family is one. And some plants are known fairly widely for being dangerous; for example, monkshood (*Aconitum*). But who would have thought the sweet little lily-of-the-valley (*Convallaria majalis*) is one of the nastiest plants. It has been said that people have been poisoned by drinking water that the flowers sat in.

For several more common plants that can be toxic, refer to the following lists. As for the castor bean that prompted this discussion, I will still grow it, but I would not if I had young children or grandchildren. And I promise that if you are visiting my garden and start looking hungry, I will throw my body between you and the plant. Or at least hold up my cat, The Perp, between the two of you.

COMMON PLANTS THAT ARE TOXIC IF INGESTED:

Aconitum (monkshood), whole plant; *Anemone*, whole plant; *Aucuba japonica*, berries; *Clematis*, whole plant; *Daphne* spp., whole plant; *Hedera* (ivy), leaves, berries; *Caladium*, whole plant; *Convallaria majalis* (lily-of-the-valley), whole plant; *Datura* (trumpet flower), whole plant; *Delphinium* spp., whole plant; *Digitalis* (foxglove), whole plant; *Euphorbia pulcherrima* (poinsettia), whole plant; *Helleborus*, whole plant; *Hydrangea macrophylla*, whole plant; *Ilex* (holly), berries; *Ipomoea tricolor* (morning glory), seeds; *Iris* spp., leaves, rhizomes; *Laburnum*, whole plant; *Lantana*, whole plant; *Lathyrus* spp. (sweet pea), whole plant; *Lobelia cardinalis*, whole plant; *Lupinus* spp. (lupine), whole plant; *Nicotiana* spp. (tobacco flower), whole plant; *Physalis alkekengi* (Chinese lantern), berries; *Pieris* spp., leaves, nectar; *Podophyllum peltatum* (May apple), everything except fruit; *Ranunculus* (buttercup), whole plant; *Rhododendron, azalea* spp., whole plant; *Ricinus* (castor bean), seeds, pods; *Taxus* (yew), whole plant; *Wisteria*, pods.

Even frozen euphorbia can cause a rash.

COMMON PLANTS THAT CAN CAUSE SKIN IRRITATION:

Achillea (yarrow), *Anemone* spp., *Artemisia* (mugwort), *Aster, Chrysanthemum* spp., *Daucus carota* (Queen Anne's lace), *Dicentra spectabilis* (bleeding heart), *Dictamnus albus* (gas plant), *Euphorbia, Pelargonium* (annual geranium), *Primula* spp. (primrose), *Rudbeckia* (black-eyed Susan), *Ruta graveolens* (rue), *Tagetes* (marigold).

SOURCES: *BOTANY FOR GARDENERS* BY BRIAN CAPON AND *THE GARDENER'S COMPANION* BY ROBERTA COUGHLIN

JANUARY 23, 2003

DIRTY WORK
The reward for labors now is smoother sailing in spring

TOWARD LATE JANUARY, SOME OF US START feeling as though we should be doing something besides downing chocolates and grazing through plant catalogs. I think it's the snowdrops that pop up now. They must emit a hormonal substance that prompts those first stirrings of "itchy trowel finger."

We sense we should do something. But we don't know what it is we're supposed to do. Winter isn't like the other seasons when plants are screaming at you — plant me, fertilize me, cut me back. No, the voices whisper now.

Maybe it's because we don't really want to hear what our garden is saying, since it seems to be muttering those "chore" words. I'm hearing chants about pruning and spraying, not fun stuff like planting and designing.

Still, some jobs done now will save on later chores, and some, such as dormant spraying, can't be put off if you're going to do it at all. Such insecticide and fungicide sprays, which must be applied before buds or leaves appear, combine horticultural oil and copper or lime sulfur. If you wait too long to apply them, the oil will coat and destroy new growth.

Dormant sprays kill tough bugs and diseases that winter over, such as scale, mildew and leaf curl. They are commonly used on roses and fruit trees but also are effective for any other shrubs and trees that suffer from leaf problems. A great advantage is that a single dose in winter can prevent having to spray several times later on.

Before you spray, clean any leaves left on your roses or on the ground that could be harboring disease. Bag the leaves and put them in the garbage, not in your compost. Then spray the branches, trunk and ground within the drip line. Make sure to spray into the crotches of branches, since bad things like to hide out there.

Don't get ahead of yourself in your bug-deterrent program. Hold off on injection-type insecticides until spring. Systemics work because they travel with the rising sap into the branches and emerging leaves. Any systemic treatment now would be wasted.

The other big winter chore is pruning to rejuvenate overgrown or lopsided shrubs or those that no longer flower as they should. Because branches are bare, you can see the shape of things and attempt some artistry. Another advantage of winter pruning is that diseases and insects aren't active and won't slither into open cuts.

Other than getting out deadwood, you don't want to prune anything that blooms in spring unless it's really in bad shape. If you do, you won't kill the shrub, but you will kill this season's bloom. (Leave rose pruning for mid- to late February.) Stick to shrubs that flower on new growth, such as hydrangeas. This means most late bloomers, because new growth needs time to get established, which is why the flowers are late.

This also is a great time for pruning fruit trees and many other trees, but I'm of the leave-that-to-the-professionals school.

If you've still got some energy, throw some compost over flower and vegetable beds and under shrubs. This may surprise a lot of people who think mulching is a spring or autumn job.

> *This also is a great time for pruning fruit trees and many other trees, but I'm of the leave-that-to-the-professionals school.*

But we're about to enter the trickiest period of the gardening year. Those seductive false springs in February get plants all giddy and they start budding out too early. Then, whoosh, along comes a cold snap that kills the tender new growth and maybe even the awakening plant. A layer of insulation will keep your plants firmly footed in cold ground so they won't be fooled.

Five golden rules of winter chores:
1. Don't prune or spray if plants don't need it.
2. Leave heavy or high pruning to professionals.
3. Don't spray on windy or freezing days.
4. Read labels on sprays carefully.
5. To recover, apply cups of hot chocolate and another good catalog.

JANUARY 25, 2001

SWEET SUNSHINE
Witch hazel and other yellow-flowering shrubs lend enchantment to winter's darkest days

I SOMETIMES THINK YELLOW IS MY LEAST FAvorite flower color. In spring, it is too strident among the tender violets, pinks, blues and chartreuse greens. In late summer and autumn, it looks downright anemic among the tawny oranges, golds, brick reds and purples of the late garden.

But in winter I am of a different mind.

Next to chocolate, of course, there is nothing like a buttery yellow flower to cheer you up on a gloomy wintry day. That must be why some of the choicest winter plants bloom in bursts of sunshine.

Among winter plants, there is simply no equal to the witch hazel (*Hamamelis*). It should be called bewitch hazel, for it deserves all the hyperbole you can throw at it. It blooms almost boisterously throughout winter, giving us flashes of sunshine in the darkest of days, and it smells sweetly divine.

You don't want to plunk witch hazel down in the midst of perennials or crowd it with other shrubs. It is a shrub that should be given room to show off its graceful vase shape. Underplant it with bulbs in sunshine or partial sun and leave it alone. It requires little or no pruning.

Although it may eventually grow to 10 or 12 feet, it has an elegant open structure that never looks like a black hole in summer as do some of the larger flowering shrubs.

Throughout most of the winter, its bare branches will be covered with tassels of brilliant yellow flowers that scent the area around it. I have mine by the driveway where I can catch a whiff as I get in and out of the car, and this cheers me enormously. There are a number of cultivars, and some, such as 'Diane', have brick-red flowers. I planted 'Diane' next to my *H.* 'Pallida' in hopes it eventually will be tall enough to stand as bridesmaid to my golden bride.

Witch hazel picked up its common name when English settlers in Virginia came upon *H. virginiana* and thought it resembled the hazel back home. The "witch" appellation was attached because the early settlers also used it as a divining rod to find water, which was a bit witchy.

Most garden-variety witch hazels are not the shaggy American variety the settlers found, but the far more elegant varieties from China (*H. mollis*) and Japan (*H. japonica*) or a hybrid of the two, *H.* x *intermedia*.

Despite the common name, the hazelnuts (*Corylus*) and winter hazel (*Corylopsis*) are not the same as witch hazel. The latter is another delicious winter shrub, blooming a bit later than witch hazel. Like witch hazel, winter hazel has glorious sweet-scented golden blossoms. But these hang in tiers of bell-shaped flowers. Winter hazel, which is oddly underused, also likes sun or part shade and is a great companion to rhododendrons.

Winter jasmine (*Jasminum nudiflorum*) is another shrub that produces sunshine in the midst of winter. That, I'm afraid, is the only thing to recommend it. Otherwise, it is a floppy plant that can't quite decide if it's a shrub or a vine. It needs to lean against something like a fence or be tied up around a doorway. Its leaves are uninspiring, but mercifully its thin arching branches are easy to hide among other plants in spring and summer.

But come winter, the ugly duckling becomes a princess, bursting with buttercup-yellow stars all up and down its naked branches. The flowers aren't fragrant, but they bloom early and long, beginning in late November and often lasting into February. So winter jasmine definitely earns its place. And, make no mistake, this is one jasmine that is hardy.

So ask me in winter, and I'll tell you my favorite flower color is yellow. Sunshine yellow.

JANUARY 27, 2005

YOU'RE ABOUT TO MUTATE

Beware: Your garden is about to exert its seductive pull, changing your appearance, your speech, your very being

S O YOU'RE HEADED DOWN THE GARDEN PATH. You thought you'd start a garden this year — a real garden, not just a patch of grass, a clump of rhodies and a wedge of deck.

The garden path may seem benign, but beware, dear reader, it is fraught with peril. And, it is the duty of a responsible garden writer to alert you to the pitfalls ahead.

Appearance will be first to go. The uniform is baggy pants, baggy T-shirt, baggy (also faded) flannel outer shirt, rubber boots and aged straw hat. Oh, the gardener rampant is a lovely sight to behold.

> *The garden path may seem benign, but beware, dear reader, it is fraught with peril.*

Say good-bye to long fingernails. In fact, say good-bye to clean fingernails. Save money on Chanel. No amount of perfume will overcome the scent of Humus No. 5. Dogs will love you.

Conversation goes next.

Watch yourself become boring, boring, boring as you bring up powdery mildew, drip irrigation and potassium at dinner parties.

Fight it all you want, but words and phrases such as deadheading, damping off, heeling in, hardening off, leaching, layering, rootstock and runners will come tripping off your tongue.

It won't be long before that dreaded, snobbish, insufferable Latin starts to creep in. Before you know it, you'll forget there ever was such a thing as a dogwood. It'll be a *Cornus kousa*, if you please.

Eventually there will be personality changes.

Watch as a heretofore unimagined streak of viciousness surfaces. It happens to the gentlest of us when we see our first crop of seedlings decimated by the evil slug empire. You will become a stomper, smasher, salter, zapper and/or sprayer overnight.

You will plumb depths of hypocrisy you did not know you possessed as you dump killer chemical on your weeds, all the while looking furtively over your shoulder at your environmentalist neighbors.

Expect compulsive behavior. By night, you will lie awake thinking of how to restyle your yard. By day, you will go through strange rites of draping your hoses around in odd patterns.

Watch your discipline crumble. You'll read books and make careful plant lists. Then at the first spring visit to a nursery, you'll pile up three wagonloads of plants with names you'd never heard of.

You will become abusive, forcing your spouse or children to hold the flashlight so you can get those last plants in the ground after the sun has gone down. As for dinner, your motto will be "let them eat cake."

You will become a fickle lover, waxing lyrical over the fragile fritillaries and delicate dogtooth violets of spring. By late summer, you will have succumbed to the floozy charms of outrageously orange and red mophead dahlias.

While Congress debates tax cuts, you will fret endlessly over such things as how to pronounce clematis (Klem-atis or klem-Mah-tis);

whether to stick with 'Early Girl' tomatoes or try a new variety; whether to prune roses in November or February.

Sooner or later, you will become obsessed with compost, perhaps going so far as to trade recipes or sources. Ultimately, you will hit bottom, or at least the bottom of the garden path. That's when you start looking in the want ads for manure.

FEBRUARY 3, 1995

CURB THAT URGE TO PRUNE

Warm weather, sunny days and a pair of pruning shears can have dire consequences

FALSE SPRING COMES EVERY YEAR, FIRST SEducing us, then throwing us over. And we're suckers every time. We see it coming. We know it won't last. And still we get out and plant something too early in soggy ground or prune something just in time for the next big freeze. My downfall is pruning.

When the weather soared into the tropical 50s last weekend, I was out there with clippers in hand, trigger finger itching. Oh, I had good intentions. Just a bit of clean-up work, a snip here and there.

Alas, once you make that first snip, it's hard to stop. The first insight I had into this phenomenon was when Jack Catalano helped my father prune my mother's oleanders back in the 1950s. My parents came close to di-

vorce over the incident. As for our neighbor Jack, it took several gift bottles of his remarkable homemade wine vinegar before my mother decided to forgive him.

Mom and I had been to church. When we left, we had a fine flowering hedge of oleanders all across the back fence. When we returned, we had a row of neat, leafless stumps and a fine view of the backs of the neighbors' houses.

It was many years later when I finally understood what had come over my father. In short, there is a primal urge that takes hold when one's fingers close over a pair of good clippers. I felt the first stirrings of this compulsion last weekend with false spring full upon us.

I remember standing out by the driveway eyeing some rose bushes, when around the corner came the neighbors, Walt and Rosemary, walking their dog, Lucky Louie. Walt smiled. Lucky Louie wagged his tail. But Rosemary eyed me suspiciously. You see, she knows a thing or two about gardening. I tried to hide the clippers and make up something about checking out the new shoots. But I knew she knew.

There is a primal urge that takes hold when one's fingers close over a pair of good clippers.

Thank goodness that brought me to my senses, and I didn't prune the roses. Otherwise, I would have guaranteed Portland would have had a record-breaking freeze. It was a close call.

Now that I'm inside, away from those dangerous rays of sunshine, I can admit it's just too early. Give it another two or three weeks. Advice from the Oregon State University Extension Service is that the time to

I mean, really, look at the bare stems of that shrub; how can any self-respecting, pruning-shear-wielding gardener resist that obvious plea for help?

prune is when the forsythia blooms. My personal signal is National Rose Pruning Day, which some people insist on calling Presidents Day. The trick is to prune late enough to avoid a prolonged freezing spell, but early enough to promote new growth so you have roses by late spring.

With pruning duties creeping up on us, it is time to brush up on techniques. Hybrid teas will need the most attention. The first things to cut out are all obviously dead or broken branches and, except on very young bushes, anything smaller than the thickness of a pencil. Then remove branches that cross or touch each other.

The idea is to work toward a bowl shape so that you open up a shrub. That will give you good air circulation and help prevent the dreaded fungus and bacterial diseases that thrive in damp summers. To encourage the bowl shape, prune branches just above an outward pointing "eye" — a swelling bud — to encourage branches to grow away from the center. The cut should be at a 45-degree angle slanting down toward the interior of the shrub, presuming the eye is facing outward.

Some people swear by radical pruning for hybrid teas, taking the bush down to three or four branches and pruning them about 18 inches from the ground. That kind of pruning will divert more of the plant's energy into flower-making and produce bigger blooms. That's what you should do if you're planning to enter your blooms in a Rose Festival contest.

Others prefer to prune lightly to encourage a more natural shrub shape even if the blooms are smaller.

For roses that are healthy, the style of pruning is simply a matter of personal taste. Hard pruning is the best remedy to rejuvenate roses that are less than healthy. You can give aged roses new life by cutting out some of the old woody canes to allow the new green canes to take off.

The same pruning principles, though on a gentler basis, apply to standard and miniature roses. Old-fashioned roses are supposed to be full and rambling, so they don't really need much pruning other than light grooming to keep them mannerly. Cut them back only when they've gotten truly sloppy or are skimpy bloomers.

Whatever your pruning style, be sure to have a good set of pruning shears. If you are cutting away diseased growth, clean your shears before cutting healthy stems. If you succumbed and pruned too early or if you pruned at the right time and there is a late freeze, you may get some dieback. The best remedy is to do a second pruning, cutting at least an inch below the dead wood.

FEBRUARY 4, 1994

✎

IT'S ALL LATIN TO ME
What's in a name? My self-esteem.

I HAVE THIS TENDENCY TO FORGET LATIN NAMES over the winter. This can be embarrassing because, right about now, the lecture circuit starts. Someone is bound to ask me to identify a plant on the screen when I'm showing slides. Fortunately, people in the audience helpfully shout out the Latin name, and very few of them mutter "you idiot" under their breath.

I was building up confidence that I had this Latin thing conquered when I came across a magazine article that listed some common Latin mispronunciations. Out of 15 flower names, I had been pronouncing only three correctly. It took a whole bag of M&Ms to recover my confidence.

I mean, would you believe that it's pen-STEE-mun and not PEN-stih-mun and it's la-VATT-er-a and not lav-a-TEER-a. The killer was that my favorite shrub, the smokebush, is really pronounced KOTT-ih-nus, not koh-TINE-nus, as I have been broadcasting far and wide.

This is particularly embarrassing because I was a National Merit Latin Scholar in Sister Mary Reginalda's ninth-grade Latin class.

At least garden art doesn't require complex furr-eign names (or purr-fect pronunciation).

The thing is, I was really good at memorizing. I could remember things just long enough to pass a test. It's not that I ever actually understood the stuff.

The best advice I've ever heard about Latin pronunciation came from Sara Mauritz, who wrote on the subject for the Portland Garden Club's newsletter a few years back. Her advice was to pronounce every single vowel. Hence, words such as davidii that end in double "i" are pronounced "ee i" at their end.

This would have helped in my early gardening years when I was still referring to my cotoneaster as my cotton-aster. Using the pronounce-every-vowel system, I proceeded for several years to speak of my co-TONE-ee-as-ter with confidence. Then I find that it's really "co-tone-ee-ASS-ter." Darn.

With my ignorance unraveling before my very eyes, I decided to learn more about pronunciation. I plowed through penults, diphthongs and stressed vowels. I ran into competing schools of pronunciation: classical Latin, liturgical Latin and reformed Latin. Then came the exceptions — "a" is never pronounced "ah" unless the word contains "r" plus another consonant. Arrrrrgh! (That would be pronounced ahrrrrrgh.)

By now, I had followed the M&Ms with a bag of Cheetos and a Classic Coke chaser. At this point I decided to apply the "prudent-man principle" to botanical names. It is recognized in law — at least as practiced by television lawyers — as a benchmark for what a reasonable person would do.

Applying the prudent-man principle, it makes sense that gardeners learn botanical Latin names because there's a good reason for them. Many different plants share the same common name (bluebell, bellflower and tulip tree, for example). Latin names also provide information about plants, such as origins (*alpinus*), color (*purpurea*) and growth habit (*prostrata*).

But really, does pronouncing a botanical name correctly serve any purpose? Well, it might keep people from muttering "you idiot" if you're giving a garden talk. But other than that, I'd say let's agree to apply the prudent-man principle and not get too exercised over the fact that I say "CLEM-ah-tis" and you say "clem-AT-is," or vice versa.

FEBRUARY 22, 2001

TRAVEL BUG
Cabin fever sends gardeners packing

ABOUT NOW, WITH WINTER STILL NIPPING AT our little green toes, we start to mull (or at least daydream about) a spring or early summer garden trip. It's obvious from the number of questions I've been getting that some of you have a serious case of wanderlust. I know the symptoms well.

The question I get most often is whether it's best to go on a garden tour or customize your own trip. That's like asking which is best, white chocolate or dark chocolate? Both are lip-smackingly delicious.

If, however, you are a first-timer, an organized tour has advantages. It's the best way to get directly to exceptional gardens when you aren't familiar with the terrain. Also, if you detest logistics as much as I do, it's comforting to have someone else take care of details.

It's also fun to be around people who share your interests. They can be quite amusing. On one memorable tour, my husband and

I were the only non-senior citizens, and the rest of the group called us "the kids." (We were in our 40s at the time.)

One of the senior ladies had, to put it delicately, a dalliance with the bus driver. Another couple argued continuously and, midway through the trip, began sitting at opposite ends of the bus, asking the rest of us to communicate messages between them. It was great; we had a live soap opera as well as terrific scenery.

One reader recently asked where she could find a trip for novice gardeners; she worried she'd feel intimidated because she didn't know all the horticultural terms. I have heard others worry about this. Truthfully, on any trip there are likely to be some people who pong esoteric Latin plant names back and forth and generally display a superior knowledge of just about everything. Usually, they turn out to be very nice people if you get to know them, and the decent ones are great mentors.

Mostly, it is our own lack of confidence that gets in the way of a good time, not the people we perceive to be snobs. On my first garden trip to England several years back, there were five of us from Portland, and the rest were from Seattle. The Seattle crowd was mostly professional nursery owners, landscape designers or very sophisticated gardeners.

Our little Portland group was simply a collection of amateur but ardent gardeners. We spent much of the time feeling ignored and intimidated by the Seattle contingent. After all, they went off to dinner on their own, sat at separate tables in the pub at lunch and largely ignored their poor cousins from Port-

land. Of course, we were offended, and it's even possible a nasty comment or two may have escaped our lips.

Last summer, I went on a garden tour of Tuscany, and, what do you know, three of the Seattle folks happened to be on the same trip. I got to know them, and they were absolutely lovely people. One night at dinner toward the end of the trip, one of them said, "You know, we used to think you Portlanders were such snobs because you always went off to dinner by yourself and sat at separate tables."

HITTING THE ROAD: The garden tour is no longer the province of wealthy lords and ladies with great manor houses and sweeping gardens. More and more of us polyester-clad ordinary folk are strapping on cameras, hoisting guidebooks and jetting off to grand gardens all over the world. Here are tips to help you plan.

WHERE TO GO: Most Northwesterners head for the British Isles (including Ireland, Scotland and Wales) because the climate is similar to ours and we can grow most of the same plants and adapt many of the ideas. Also, because the British are so crazy about gardening, there are more public gardens and resources available to travelers. France, Italy, Belgium and the Netherlands, in particular, also have a wealth of gardens with western-style plants, and New Zealand is turning out to be the place to head in winter. Plus, there are a growing number of garden tours in the Eastern and Southern United States.

THE PERFECT TRIP: Many Northwest travel agencies offer garden tours and are

> *It was great; we had a live soap opera as well as terrific scenery.*

gaining expertise in such customized trips. Also look for trips advertised in newspaper travel sections, garden magazines and horticultural society newsletters.

THE BEST TIME: June and July are peak months in England, but the gardens are beautiful all summer. I prefer July for northern England and Scotland. Mediterranean gardens are fresher in April through mid-June before the summer heat. Spring is the time to go to Holland if you want to see bulbs.

CHECK THE ITINERARY: Many general tours include visits to gardens in addition to stops at manor houses and historic and literary sites. Some garden tours include side trips to nearby sights or time for antiquing. But dedicated garden tours seldom allow for much else besides visiting gardens, and they won't look kindly on you if you want to deviate from the schedule. Examine the itinerary carefully before choosing, or opt for a customized trip if flexibility is important.

LIMIT YOUR SCOPE: If you try to take in too broad an area, you will spend a lot of time on the highway, not traveling scenic back roads through charming villages.

DON'T MAKE THE CITY YOUR BASE: It may look like it's an easy drive from London, Paris or Rome to garden sites, but it can take two hours just getting out of the city in the morning rush hour and the same coming back in the evening. Make smaller towns your base, and tag the city on at the beginning or end of your trip.

INVESTIGATE: Visit the travel section of your favorite bookstore for research. Whichever guide book you use, make sure it includes garden addresses, highlights, history, directions, hours, fees, facilities (restaurant, restrooms, wheelchair access). Also, if you're going to England, pick up the unique Yellow Book, officially called "Gardens of England and Wales: The National Gardens Scheme." It lists private gardens that are open throughout the two countries. The Web site is www.ngs.org.uk.

CHECK RESERVATIONS: Some very famous gardens, such as Sissinghurst in England and Monet's garden in France, may require advance booking for crowd control. If you are going on your own, check this out before you arrive.

BRINGING PLANTS BACK: My advice is, don't. It's complicated, and there are restrictions. Each plant brought to the United States must be labeled by Latin botanical name and go through agricultural customs. The plants have to be bare root, which makes their survival iffy if they haven't been packed professionally. Finally, the Northwest's horticultural professionals are so leading-edge, you'll be hard put to find a plant elsewhere that won't soon be available here.

FEBRUARY 8, 2001

✧

CHRONICLES OF A CIRCLE SKIRT

Record your green successes in a garden journal

A FEW YEARS BACK, RUMMAGING IN AN OLD desk at my mother's house, I found the diary I kept when I was 15. I opened it truly expecting an enchanting read of quaint girlish observations on life in general, insights into the 1950s, or, at the very least, the story of the sensitive transition of a young girl into womanhood. I could hear the publishers panting already.

Silly me. Talk about banal — the diary

Don't forget shrubs for winter berries and buds. You'll be surprised by how red berries in the dark days of winter can lift your spirits.

Fortunately, my next attempts at keeping a journal three decades later proved more successful. I have kept a garden journal off and on for about 10 years now. I've found that by observing and noting what's happening in a garden, you'll begin to see patterns that you might not otherwise spot. Again, still humbled by my earlier experience, I offer these tips on what to look for and record in a garden journal.

WEATHER: If you live in the Northwest, you've got to be obsessed with the weather. After all, we have lots of it. Note yearly weather variations and how they affect your garden. You may be surprised. For one thing, you'll probably find August and September, not May and June, are premier months for Northwest gardens.

FROST DATES: Sure, you can get average dates for last and first frosts for the city out of books, but elevation, exposure to winds, nearby trees and slope can mean different frost dates for your property. Understanding your own site will help you know when to place plants in and out of protection and when to start seeds.

THE TENDER: This will tell you what plants are chancy in our climate zone and should be planted sparingly and given special mulching attention come late fall.

was replete with descriptions of things like the "darling circle skirt with the poodle applique" I had just gotten and how I was swooning for a stitched-down pleated Pendleton skirt. Clothes in general were a big theme. So was gossip about which guys my girlfriends and I thought were "neat" and which girls had suddenly turned into snobs (generally a title accorded all girls who had boyfriends before we did).

LEAF-OUT TIMES: This is useful to know so you can underplant with bulbs and early flowers that bloom before shrubs and trees leaf out and cast dense shade.

SEQUENCE OF BLOOM: Knowing what blooms when will help you with plant selection and placement. By paying attention to length of bloom, you may find some plants aren't worth the trouble if they take up space and flower for what seems like mere seconds.

GENERAL PERFORMANCE: As the season progresses, record which plants rate a perfect 10 so you can try more of them. Note which ones are wimps that need to be mercifully dispatched.

THINGS TO DO AND WHEN: Inconveniently, plants have different timing needs. Note when particular plants need to be pruned, moved, divided, sprayed, fertilized, mulched or otherwise chucked under their little chins so that when the time is ripe, you're on top of the job.

LIGHT CHANGES: Observe which areas get morning sun, afternoon sun or both and how this changes as the year moves on. This can give you insights into how to site everything from flower and vegetable beds to a greenhouse.

SPONGY AREAS, STANDING WATER: Watch in the rainy season or after watering to know where the problem areas are. This can lead to several choices, including improving drainage or (my vote) selecting plants that thrive in wet conditions.

PEAKS AND VALLEYS: With our long growing season, Northwest gardens go up and down like the stock market. A common pattern is profuse spring bloom when roses burst open, followed by a let-down, then a pickup. Knowing your garden's patterns can dictate what plants to buy to fill in the down periods, or even when to plan garden events.

FLOWERS THAT FLOP: Wait too long, and you'll find trussing up plants that have already swooned makes for some very unnatural shapes. The trick is to have scaffolding in place for the plant to grow into.

IDEAS FROM OTHERS: A good gardener is original. A great gardener is both original and unashamed about stealing ideas from others like mad. Jot down plants

I've found that by observing and noting what's happening in a garden, you'll begin to see patterns.

and features you see elsewhere. Clip out pictures from magazines and slip them into your journal.

RESOURCES: Write down interesting new books, seminars, nurseries, open gardens, shops and events as you hear or read about them so you'll have a reminder.

LOCATION, LOCATION: It's easy to forget where bulbs are after the foliage dies. Make note of other plants that lose their foliage after bloom or you'll end up inadvertently digging them up.

ADDITIVES: Note results of fertilizers, soil amendments, insecticides and fungicides. The summer we heavily fertilized the tomatoes, they grew Jack-in-the-beanstalk foliage but dinky little fruit. We learned a good lesson about overfertilizing.

PLANT WISH LIST: Save lots of room for this section.

FEBRUARY 18, 1999

COLLECT CALLING

What is it about certain plants that triggers a passion to possess?

IN THE PAST COUPLE OF YEARS, DOUG THE Wonder Boy and I have developed a joint passion for hellebores. I'm not sure whether we originally put our heads together over this or independently fell for them and just came together.

It doesn't matter, because together we have become like indulgent parents adopting new offspring — me buying hellebores whenever I spot some, him bringing over seedlings from his own garden or some that another gardener gave him. Good neighbor Rosemary also has contributed some of her seedlings.

We have spread them along the woodland path (our fancy-schmancy name for the side of the lot shaded by big trees). I had never realized the enormous variety. We have them in shades of cream, chartreuse, pink, violet and a yummy yellow. There are flowers with freckles, colored throats and ruffled edges. In one leap into extravagance last year, I bought a double-flowered variety offered at a plant sale, even though it cost as much as a pedigreed dog.

What is it about certain plants that makes you want to collect them? This is not the first passionate craze I have had by any means. When the first of the fancy-leafed varieties of *Heuchera* (coral bells) came on the market, it started a craze. 'Palace Purple' may not have been the very first, but it seems to have triggered that hunter-gatherer gene.

Soon came 'Silver Veil', 'Chocolate Ruffles'

Hellebores are the queens of winter. Imagine. Flowers in January!

(I had to have that), 'Persian Carpet' and, more recently, 'Amber Waves' and 'Obsidian'. I had a similar experience with the first blue corydalis, 'Blue Panda'. It was exquisite, but difficult. Soon I discovered 'China Blue' and 'Pére David', both easier to grow for me. Before I knew it, there were purple, pink and cream-flowered cultivars, and now there's 'Golden Panda', which is supposed to start with a flush of golden leaves.

Oh, lordy, I want them all. It's hard to recall that not long ago, all we made do with was the perfectly acceptable yellow *Corydalis lutea*.

Rose lovers, of course, have always known about the passion to amass as many plants as

> *I bought a double-flowered variety offered at a plant sale, even though it cost as much as a pedigreed dog.*

you can. Clematis is another one that's hard to resist once you get started. I guess some plants are like a box of chocolates. You can't stop at one.

Regarding perennials, it may be different plants for different people, but there are some plants, such as coral bells and hellebore, that seem to be particularly tempting to a lot of gardeners. Hosta too. In fact, what is it about plants beginning with H? I suspect I'm beginning to want every hydrangea known to man.

Down the street from me, Rosemary is starting her own collection, although, ever self-effacing, she would probably pooh-pooh the label "collector." In her case, it is lilies. It started small, with a few catalog orders. Now she adds new ones each year and even goes to seminars on lilies, which is a sure sign of someone in the grip of a consuming passion.

Another sign is when you start buying books devoted to a single plant. Looking at my bookshelves, I'm thinking it may be time to call in some friends for an "intervention." I fear that, at the very least, I'm in need of Hydrangeas Anonymous.

FEBRUARY 10, 2005

✿

IS YOUR BELOVED A WALLFLOWER?
You may dig gardening too much

IN JUST TWO DAYS WE CELEBRATE ST. VALentine's Day, a day to revel in romance, passion and even obsession. Yes, yes, I am talking about feelings for one's garden. It strikes me, in fact, that gardening is one of the few actually benign obsessions. It certainly seems to be rampant in the Northwest. Maybe you are wondering if you've advanced to that stage.

In the interest of public-spiritedness, I've devised a little test to help you determine if indeed you are in the throes of a gardening obsession. If the majority of the following items describe you, take two chocolates and call a nursery in the morning.

- Come spring, you feel strange stirrings, and they have nothing to do with Harrison Ford (or the appropriate gender or generation counterpart).
- You no longer regard dirt under your fingernails as tantamount to a lowering of social standards.
- Latin is not a dead language to you.
- You prefer the scent of compost to that of Chanel No. 5.
- You can stump your friends in a game of Scrabble by using words such as "pergola," "friable" and "corm."
- You worry about whether it's pronounced CLEM-mah-tis or clem-MAT-tis (not that it matters, but it's the first).
- Your car automatically turns in to nurseries.
- You buy flowers at the supermarket because you don't want to disturb your garden.
- You have more garden books than cookbooks.
- You'd prefer a gift of ZooDoo over anything in a box from Victoria's Secret.
- You sit in business or committee meetings furtively drawing sketches of garden plans (to all the people I work with, I need to say that I have never, ever done this).
- If you were to throw seeds in the back of your car, there is sufficient dirt that they might sprout.
- You knew better than to buy a tropical plant, and you did it anyway and will probably do it again, even after this win-

Whimsey in the garden can take many forms.

ter (which reminds me, I have to replace my banana).

- You think instructions that say plant 36 inches apart were written for someone else.
- You have been in the cashier's line at a nursery, spotted something in someone else's wagon and gone back to get it.
- You go early to plant sales even if it means standing in line.
- When someone refers to Sexy Rexy, you know they are talking about a rose, not their boyfriend.
- You even enjoy plant catalogs without pictures.
- You have actually gardened so late that you have had to use a flashlight.

- The questions "where will it go" and "how much does it cost" have lost all meaning to you.

FEBRUARY 12, 2004

CULTIVATE A MENTOR
The experienced dig deep to share knowledge with young sprouts

ST. VALENTINE'S DAY GOT ME TO THINKING about sweethearts I've known. No, not the romantic ones, but some special friends. My gardening mentors. In fact, if I could give but one piece of advice to a new gardener, it would be to adopt a mentor. A gardening mentor will give you a wealth of information, education, inspiration and, if you're lucky, some plants thrown in, too.

Long before I began writing about gardening, and certainly long before I knew very much about it, I adopted some mentors. Most of them are probably unaware that I adopted them.

The first mentor, besides my parents, of course, came along close to 20 years ago. I'd take walks around the neighborhood and came one day upon the most delightful cottage garden surrounding a gray-shingled Nantucket-style house.

In place of a front lawn, the house had a charming, not quite neat, garden of old-fashioned favorites — santolina, love-in-a-mist, cranesbill geraniums, lady's mantle, lamb's ears, thyme, lavender, peonies, rosemary, bee balm, iris, Madonna lilies, foxgloves, campanula and alliums.

Even the curbside had been dug up to make room for vegetables. But of all the plants, it was the roses, spilling over everywhere, roses such as I had never seen, that transfixed me. Immediately I fell in love and imagined that surely Miss Marple's twin lived here.

Finally one day I found the owner, Alice Frazer, in her garden. I introduced myself and confessed my infatuation. Alice took me through her garden and told me wonderful tales about how the roses got their names. This was long before old-fashioned roses were all the rage. Smoky violet 'Tour de Malakoff' was named for a Crimean war battle at that site where the rosy smoke lingered in the air for days. There were roses named for kings'

Naturally, by the time I got home, I'd lost or mixed up the tags and didn't have a clue what was what.

mistresses, roses of the warring houses of England's royalty, roses for famous beauties and heroes.

Alice even had the very same rose, 'Maiden's Blush', whose petals fall in one of my favorite paintings, Sandro Botticelli's *Primavera*. Alice sent me home with cuttings and a new vision that there was more to roses than hybrid teas. Years later, when I moved, she brought over two little twiggy sticks with teeny roots. I planted them, and now they've grown into white lilacs more than 12 feet tall.

Next came a mentor who certainly has no idea she performed this service. A few years ago, Cynthia Woodyard, now a garden photographer, and two friends held their annual Three Ladies Plant Sale in Cynthia's back yard.

I had barely graduated from beds of petunias and marigolds, and knew next to nothing about perennials. Cynthia intuitively sensed I was ready for more but was definitely uneducated. Instead of scaring me away with a flow of Latin names that would have set my head spinning, she simply took me in hand and said, you need this and this and this, as she loaded up my little wagon.

Naturally, by the time I got home, I'd lost or mixed up the tags and didn't have a clue what was what. But everything I planted turned out splendidly. Those plants remain some of my favorites and the backbone of my present perennial borders.

Next came Margaret Willoughby, who introduced me to the perennial garden as a whole. Again, on my walks I'd noticed her garden, and, fickle me, fell head over heels for it. I wasn't alone, for Margaret's garden has now appeared in a number of magazines as well as in a book and video.

I suspect that Margaret, with her great generosity, is mentor to half of the gardening population in Portland. Strangers who stopped by her garden often left with not only a number of seedlings but also a "cuppa" tea and cookies to boot. I left with a lifelong friendship.

Then there is Virginia Burney, who taught me more than anyone about the artful garden. Virginia, a decorator, has an exquisite flair for putting things together both inside and outside the house. She has inspired me with her color combinations, textures and ways to display treasures — whether whimsical finds or true art — throughout the garden.

I don't have — and never will — her discipline, but I admire it. For example, her garden is all primary colors, so pink just plain has no place. Occasionally, the errant seed drops or the naughty cultivar reverts back to its pink parents. Lucky me, I get these discards.

I have another new mentor now, and like the others, she probably isn't even aware that I snoop and study her garden and draw inspiration from it whenever I'm lucky enough to be there. Since Rosemary Ellis lives only four houses down, I manage to get there with some regularity.

Her yard is about a half the size of my own. But she and her husband, Walt, have managed to create little garden rooms of great charm, ranging from an herb and vegetable garden with an old-fashioned umbrella-type clothesline on a pole to a fairly sophisticated Japanese garden. The latter was created around a lovely granite stone lantern that Walt bid for at an Oregon Symphony auction.

If there is one common denominator among these mentors, it is that they take genuine joy in gardening and are delighted to share it. Despite all my garden books and magazines and trips to English and French gardens, I have learned more from these people than I have anywhere else.

So, my advice to all new gardeners is to look around and adopt a mentor. Most of these people will be too busy filling your head with wonderful information and your hands with wonderful plants to even notice you've adopted them.

FEBRUARY 16, 1997

TERM LIMITS
Plant descriptions don't tell the whole story

NO DOUBT YOU'VE HEARD THAT CHARMING definition of a weed — that it's any plant growing where it's not wanted. Even *Taylor's Dictionary for Gardeners* falls back on a quote by Ralph Waldo Emerson, who called a weed "a plant whose virtues have not yet been discovered."

This is just one example of the many charming ambiguities in describing plants. But to many, these ambiguous meanings may be more confusing than captivating. Take perennials. All too often, gardeners wring their hands thinking they've done something wrong when certain plants don't come back.

But the words "perennial" and "forever" are not synonymous. Some, such as peonies and daylilies, really do seem to go on forever. But others, delphiniums and columbines come to mind, are quite short-lived.

So here's a primer to help you sort through the tangle of terms.

Perennial: Technically plants that come back three or more years. The longevity range is quite wide. Colloquially, most people use the term to mean herbaceous perennials.

Herbaceous perennial: Soft-stemmed plants such as flowers. They usually die back to the ground in winter. But some, such as acanthus, don't always die back.

Woody perennial: Trees and shrubs.

Hardy plant: A term sometimes equated with perennial, but it's more about a plant's ability to survive in a given location. For example, a perennial that's hardy in Oregon may not be hardy in Minnesota. Loosely, a hardy plant is one that survives winter. In England, which does not have a wide variation of climates, the terms perennial and hardy are interchangeable.

Marginal: Botanically speaking, marginals are plants that grow along the water's edge. Sometimes it's used, less correctly, to identify plants whose survival is "iffy" in our winters, such as cannas. In this context, we really mean plants that are marginally hardy rather than marginals.

Annual: True annuals complete their life cycle in a year or less. Often these are plants that flower so profusely they exhaust themselves after one season. But others that are commonly called annuals in our climate are really perennials in their native frost-free habitats.

Tender plant: A tender plant is one that dies or is damaged by frosts and freezing.

A perennial that's hardy in Oregon may not be hardy in Minnesota.

Tender or hardy annuals: Ah, the exception. When the terms "tender" and "hardy" are used to describe annuals, they refer to how the plant is sown. A tender annual is sown under protection, such as in a greenhouse, and later transplanted into the garden as a seedling. A hardy annual, on the other hand, can be sown directly into the ground in early spring.

Biennials: A unique little group of plants, biennials develop roots and top growth in one year, then bloom, set seed and die in the second year. Sometimes it's difficult to recognize biennials because they seem to keep coming back. That's because many set seed and produce new plants. Common foxglove is an example.

Herbs: Not a separate botanical classification but a common name applied to plants grown for special uses, such as medicine, cooking, dyes or scent. They include perennials and annuals.

Subshrub: Not a small shrub, but rather a plant that looks like a perennial but has woody stems at its base and soft growth at the end of branches, such as caryopteris.

Alpine: Often used interchangeably with the term rock-garden plants. Both are small, low-growing plants that grow in rocky, well-drained soil. But true alpines are native to mountains, where they've adapted to wind-swept rocky scree.

Native: It depends on context. Usually, people mean plants indigenous to the Northwest. But the term also covers plants of the West and the United States. For example, when garden books refer to native dogwoods, they almost always mean dogwoods indigenous to the United States, as opposed to Japanese dogwoods.

Specimen: A plant that is so striking it looks best set off by itself, rather than mixed in with other plants. Obviously, the definition of a specimen plant is in the eye of the beholder.

FEBRUARY 21, 2002

SMALL GARDENS, GRAND IDEAS
Make a lasting impression with a limited space

THE SMALL GARDEN IS AN INCREASINGLY popular subject for gardening books.

It's an apt subject, as land-use planners allow smaller and smaller lots so that more greenspace can be preserved. Then there are the baby boomers who, with more sense than I have, are opting for simpler living spaces, including condos and town houses.

Unfortunately, many books about small gardens are written in England and show designs for long, narrow gardens. Our small gardens tend to be shallow spaces across the back of the house. Other books on so-called small gardens are written by estate landscapers who have not yet landed in the "get real" zone. I wince when I see them talking about a "small garden of less than an acre."

So does that mean that people gardening in tight spaces, including those with only a balcony or small patio, can't enjoy a lovely garden area? Nope. The key is to think in terms of an oasis, a jewel of a space that can be something that my rather unwieldy three-quarters of an acre can never be. It can be perfect.

Here are some tips to get there:

- Container planting is the answer for a really tiny space. Cluster pots or tubs of different shapes and sizes on a terrace, balcony or even an unused driveway. Even where there is yard space, containers make nice accents and can be used to add seasonal interest.

- Since small gardens are often shady, think beyond bright annuals and include lots of leafy plants, including shrubs and grasses. Most do well in containers. Just as with a large garden, lushness is the look you want.

- Don't try to scrunch in a deck across the back of the house if your yard is very small. It will divide an already small area rather than integrating it. Instead, make a little central paved or graveled clearing that is big enough for a table and chairs, and let lush greenery wrap around you.

- Scrap the grass. A puny patch of lawn doesn't enhance a small space, and it is still labor intensive. Pave your open space. Stone or brickwork will be more affordable and possibly more dramatic in a small space.

- If the view from your small garden is a garage wall, turn it into an asset. Cover it with a trellis and plant vines, paint a mural or, at the very least, paint it a striking color that will give your garden some zip. Just don't invite the neighbors over to see what you did with the back of their garage.

- Fences in small gardens tend to be up close and in-your-face. So either make the fence disappear with plants or make it an object of art with colorful paint. Or use it as an easel for hanging everything from pots to art (carved wood panels, lanterns, ceramic plaques, metal sculptures).

A single colorful pot can make an enormous impact on a small garden.

- A small space cries out for a focal point, but don't be cowardly and go small-scale. Look for a grand urn, pot, tiered fountain, birdbath, sculpture or even a dramatic architectural plant.
- It's easier and more affordable to install lighting in a small space, so seize this advantage to add drama.
- Select plants for multi-season interest. This doesn't mean you are limited to evergreens. A small deciduous tree that has a lovely branch structure will look sculptural in winter.
- Keep a small garden scrupulously clean. Large gardens can look "natural" if the grass gets a bit long, leaves aren't raked up and plants get overgrown and shaggy.

But what looks natural in a larger garden just looks messy in a small space.

- Use vertical space. Trellises, arbors and obelisks come in all shapes and sizes and will allow you to create a layered effect.
- Make use of built-ins. A rock wall surrounding a terrace or built-in benches around a deck will provide seating for entertaining without taking up as much space as chairs.
- Small gardens can be noisy. Incorporate the sound of water, either a fountain or bubbler, to mask street noise or the neighbors' snide comments about what you did to their garage.

Finally, trying to make your space look bigger isn't always best. Play to what's good about a small space — the feel of an oasis, coziness, the evocation of the walled courtyards of New Orleans. In other words, a lush wall of green hemming you in may work better than putting up mirrors or other gambits to make the space seem larger.

FEBRUARY 26, 2004

PONDERING ANOTHER POND

A glaze of scum is all that remains from the last attempt at a water garden

LAST WEEKEND'S SNOW DID HAVE ONE GREAT garden advantage. It was deep and soft enough to design with. What, you say, is this madwoman talking about?

It's true, there's nothing like a good snow-

Unseen hazards lurk in the murky waters of a pond.

fall to redesign your yard. When it's heavy enough, it erases all the existing features. What you're left with is the rare clean slate.

Since you can't see where the existing lawn ends, or flower beds and paths begin, you can start all over. You can try out new shapes by just walking through the snow to create patterns. I walked out the new pond.

That's our big project for the coming season. To kick it off, we held a meeting of the Pond Committee. This is a meeting where you get a group of friends together, and you spread out a bunch of garden books on the dining room table. Then you eat cinnamon toast and drink tea and everyone says, "Oh, look at this one."

Of course, "this one" usually is a picture-perfect pond lined with 600-year-old Cotswold stone and stocked with $1,000-apiece prized koi.

Ours will certainly be more humble, but it should definitely be an improvement on the Great Failed Experiment. The experiment began with high hopes. We dug a small but satisfying hole, draped it with a pool liner, bordered it with rocks, stuck in a small pump and stocked it with fish. The pet store unromantically labeled the fish "feeder fish," in other words, the fish nerds of the aquatic world, not cool ones like koi.

Nevertheless, we showered them with affection and gave them proper names, usually the names of battleships, which is what comes of living with a World War II nut. Eventually, we got six fish: Hiryu, Soryu, Kaga, Akagi, Shokaku and Zuikaku — all aircraft carriers in Japan's Pearl Harbor strike force.

All was well for a while. The fish flour-

> *All was well for a while.*
> *The fish flourished. . . .*
> *The algae flourished even more.*

ished. If you squinted your eyes real hard and looked in a certain light, you could sometimes see them. The algae flourished even more. The pond looked very pretty tucked in a shady nook. This strategic siting of course meant that none of the water plants bloomed because no sun reached it. It also meant that falling leaves would clog up the pool in fall.

But disaster struck well before fall. It was August. No raccoon has been sighted in our neighborhood in 30 years. But somehow, the animal tom-toms began to beat, and the little critters came. And they came back every night.

They had very good taste. The Japanese carriers were the first to go. Soon, a fleet of 40 was reduced to a mere seven, and those seven were carried in a bucket on a mercy mission to a friend's pond.

The fish debacle was only half of it. Raccoons are playful, which can be very cute when it's not your yard. They tipped over the plants, took exactly one bite out of each leaf, and when they left, the pond area looked like a mobile home court after a hurricane.

The dogs, of course, were useless. The oil man won't deliver oil and the meter man won't read our meter unless we are home because the canine corps is too scary. But apparently, wild forest creatures can enter our yard at will without disturbing the beauty sleep of our dogs.

The whole pond episode was so depressing that we abandoned it for two years. It has filled with leaves and, when it isn't frozen, will sport a nice glaze of scum.

Perhaps it was last year's drought, perhaps the optimism that renews itself every spring, but we are going to try again.

As we plan for a new pond, we strive to avoid some, not all of the old mistakes. We will make the pond much deeper, with places for fish to hide. It will have steeper sides to deter any furry waders. This time, we're going to try for a small water drop to add the sound of water. A member of the Pond Committee has volunteered her husband, who is handy with wiring and plumbing.

On the other hand, we have thought it out carefully and have decided to make some mistakes over again. The pond will stay on the shady side of the yard, where it looks most natural, despite the fact that the leaves will drop into it and the water lilies won't bloom. When it comes to a choice between the prac-

tical and the aesthetic, gardeners are notorious for throwing good sense out the window.

As soon as the weather softens, we'll be out there with the hose, trying out shapes and sizes. Our resident garden designer on the Pond Committee advises staying with simple natural shapes, rather than going for the dramatic. The waterfall won't really be one, just a small drop over a flat shelf of rock to give some music. The Pond Committee vetoed the cascade-type fall on the grounds that there are only two types — too expensive and too tacky.

There will be one other change: We are retiring the fleet; the fish will be postwar in name.

FEBRUARY 26, 1993

Ponds are not their most attractive in winter. But then again, what is?

ROOM WITH A VIEW

Plant a garden corner for a rainy day

IT WON'T BE LONG BEFORE THE DORMANT SEAson slips away. In the Northwest, that happens long before the end of calendar winter. By February, there are sufficient bulbs popping up, bare-root roses wrapped for planting and primroses parading on supermarket shelves to bring us padding out of our caves.

So, in these last days of garden downtime, let us recall the lessons of winter.

One lesson is the importance of a room with a view. A soul-satisfying view from my favorite window does almost as much for my spirits in winter as my entire garden does in midsummer.

In particular, there is a small plot in a corner of the front yard that I can see directly from my kitchen window. A large fir once dominated the corner but was removed several years ago after a storm damaged the tree.

It was amazing how things lightened up when the tree came out. I was about to sod the bare spot when it occurred to me to make a little winter garden in that corner, nestled between a picket fence and a holly hedge. Because it was near the driveway, I would see it even on drippy, cold days when I was getting in and out of the car. I hadn't counted on the view from the kitchen window.

I moved a witch hazel there and added wintersweet, winter jasmine, hellebores and euphorbia, which stays evergreen most years. Lots of early bulbs also went in. For a touch of whimsy, the garden includes a boxwood topiary in an ornamental pot.

Now I have a splendid view as I stand at the kitchen sink and execute complicated culinary concoctions, such as ripping the wrapping off ramen.

If you have just a tiny spot for a view, plant it to be at its best when the weather is too cold to spend much time outside. That's especially important if you, like me, are not a hardy, foul-weather gardener. I lose my will to live below 40 degrees, which is probably due to the shameful fact that I grew up in California.

An alternative to winter-flowering shrubs is an evergreen garden. Here's a perfect place to put conifers or, if you're really in an experimental mood, a knot garden. After all, the original idea behind medieval knot gardens was to put them where they could be seen to best advantage from an upstairs window. If you have room, add plants for autumn color. Worry last about impact in summer because that's when you're outside and least need a view from the house.

My other favorite view is from our home office. When I'm sitting at my computer doing intellectual things, such as playing solitaire and pushing The Perp off the keyboard, I love looking out at the pond. It was specifically sited to be viewed from the house because we entertained the fantasy the pond would be filled with koi. That was before we learned that blue herons the size of 747s would be stopping by for breakfast.

Still, the view is delightful, which more than makes up for the fact that in all other respects, the pond could not be more ill-sited. It is under a tulip tree that rains blossoms and leaves like ticker tape at a parade. Also, the

> *That was before we learned that blue herons the size of 747s would be stopping by for breakfast.*

Hardscape and structure make even winter views interesting.

tree casts so much shade in summer that only one water lily has ever managed to bloom.

I've had some accidental successes with views, as well as these planned ones. Most fortuitous was planting a *Viburnum* x *bodnantense* shrub outside our living-room window.

The sweetly scented pink flowers bloom from late October to early spring, but they're so tiny they would be lost were they not right up against the glass. Because this viburnum is 10 feet tall, it easily reaches window height.

Sometimes it takes judicious pruning to open up a view that already exists. Many old houses are banked by overgrown foundation plants that block light and views. And if the shrubs are extremely large and dense, pruning them down might produce a collection of big stumps.

A better option with camellias and rhododendrons, two common foundation plants, is to remove lower branches and thin them to create graceful, multi-stemmed trees. The tracery of boughs can frame a vista in a most attractive manner.

The vista you see should not be banked against the house or distanced so far that you can't see the flowers of winter shrubs. If you don't have a convenient corner, consider creating an island bed designed to be seen from your favorite window.

You can anchor it with anything from a pond to a birdbath. And remember, the piece of garden meant to be viewed from the house also is the perfect spot for a bird feeder to increase your viewing pleasure.

FEBRUARY 26, 1998

Part 2

SPRING

Fixes, Foliage and a Flock of Follies

❧

The fragrant flowers of Magnolia stellata *perfume the air in late March.*

MARCH MADNESS

This is the month that separates the die-hards from the dabblers

I'D LIKE TO MAKE A CASE FOR MARCH. WHEN it comes to gardens, it's highly underrated. Poets don't write about March the way they do April, May and June. No one writes a classic calling it The Cruelest Month. No one dances around Marchpoles or brags about being a March bride.

Nevertheless, in some ways March is the best month in the garden. It separates those of us who have got "it" (gardening) really bad from the dilettantes who just want some pretty flowers around. Those of us in the first category experience an enchanting silliness this month.

How else can you describe eager gardeners who wander around and whimper in joy at everything that's poking up or leafing out, as though it has never happened before? Who else but the ardent gardener gets such a rush at seeing those teeny nodules on branches, confirming that the twiggy, dead-looking thing really has some life in it? I say, who needs romance novels when you can get these kinds of cheap thrills out of your garden?

For those of us thus besotted, discovering one's garden anew is more fun than seeing a glorious border in bloom. Of course, the surprise factor in my garden is always enhanced by the fact that, for the life of me, I can't really remember what I planted in certain spots. I'm always wondering about some strange green thing that's popping up.

We can uncross our little green fingers in March. At last, we can look at this budding growth and feel fairly confident that an arctic front won't roar down and nip the life out of it. We can be pretty sure that our marginally hardy babies will make it, although I wouldn't take tender plants out of protection just yet.

Some perennials even bloom as early as March for us to swoon over — perky primroses (*Primula*), Lenten roses (*Helleborus orientalis*), freckled lungworts (*Pulmonaria*) and bergenias. The latter are much, and I believe unfairly, maligned as being peasant plants.

But the best of the March plants aren't necessarily the ones in flower. Part of the charm of the month is watching plants that emerge in interesting ways. My favorites are the ferns and Solomon's seal (*Polygonatum*) that come up in tight coils and gradually unwind, and the hostas that start out as tight furls before they fan out into their glorious leafiness. As you can see, I am easily amused, and poor Fabio doesn't have a chance.

THINGS TO DO IN MARCH

- If you left ornamental grasses uncut for their winter beauty, cut them back now so new shoots have room to poke through.
- Prune roses if you haven't already done so. Waiting won't hurt them, but the longer you wait, the longer you put off flowering.
- March brings weeds. Get ahead of them before they take over.
- Slug babies are on the march, and they especially love hosta shoots. Run a drip line of your favorite slug deterrent around crowning plants that are susceptible.
- Pollard (cut back severely) shrubs grown for winter color, such as red-twig dogwoods. Also, cut back smoke bushes (*Cotinus*) to promote redder leaves and to keep this favorite shrub in scale with flower borders.
- Don't jump the gun and start planting if soil is still soggy. You can do more harm

than good by working our notorious clay soil too early.

MARCH 1, 2001

DESIRE AND DORMANCY

On a winter day, a friend's contagious enthusiasm revives the passion for gardening

I HAVE TO ADMIT TO OCCASIONAL LAPSES WHEN I wonder if I am losing the passion to garden. At times, I think what it would be like to travel more, to take up painting again, to be free of the tyranny of weeding. But usually, sometime after the first of the year, the juices of my gardening passion begin stirring again. I remember the exact day it happened this year.

It was in January, right after we'd had a run of record-breaking warmth. My neighbor Rosemary dropped by, catalog in hand. It is our custom to order a few things together. She had clippings of some new plant introductions and had zeroed in on a new orange-gold echinacea called 'Mango Meadowbrite'.

"I'm just sooo excited," she squealed. I looked over at her, this lovely middle-age friend who was in the throes of a pure child-like thrill, and then I remembered why I garden. Her enthusiasm was contagious. Once again I was caught in the cyclic passion of the season.

Like me, she always has a project for the new year. On that January day, she told me how she wants to redo the borders along her front walk and maybe put in some hebes. Her face lit up and she said, "Do you think it's too early to go out to Cistus?"

"Rosemary," I said, "it's still January.

They're not even open yet." I felt like a heel as I watched her face fall. But she was great therapy for me. She reinvigorated me, and all thoughts that the passion for gardening was gone had evaporated.

Next day I went out with Doug the Wonder Boy, and we talked about possible projects. Perhaps, I suggested, we could do a dry streambed back here where nothing grows. He liked that idea because he likes to work with rocks. Then I said I'm thinking of removing the central part of the boxwoods in the vegetable garden to make room for parterres. With that, he took on the look of one resigned to saintly patience.

By the shed, in a space we call the Zen garden, we talked of putting a laceleaf Japanese maple where we'd lost a maple to disease. It will have to go in a pot since the disease may still be in the soil. He said it should be an earthy-looking pot. I'd been thinking of a sophisticated high glaze, but maybe he's right. We'll work it out.

In the front, I said I didn't like the way the shrubs were crowded, and we needed to widen the beds. With that he immediately sketched out a new line in the soil with his

A concrete gunnera-leaf fountain provides the lovely sound of burbling water that no garden should be without.

foot that looked good. It's good to have the passion back. I've been particularly inspired by two books. One I've written about before is *The Jewel Box Garden* by Thomas Hobbs; the other is *A Garden Gallery* by George Little and David Lewis.

Little and Lewis are the artistic team that has produced the gorgeous concrete leaves and pillars featured in a number of garden magazines. Last summer, at a garden seminar, I visited their garden on Washington's Bainbridge Island. It was truly a magical place.

Both books have pushed me to think about being more daring in my garden, to be braver with color, texture and even ornament. Most of all, they taught me that I should never buy a plant because I need something to fill a space. I must absolutely love the plant.

Anyway, since that January day with Rosemary, I have gone to sleep practically every night dreaming of the garden and planning what to do. So, March, thank goodness you're here. I'm ready at the starting gate.

MARCH 3, 2005

❧

PLANT PRENUPTIALS

Protect yourself when you enter a dalliance with dazzling new varieties

IT IS THAT TIME OF YEAR WHEN NEW PLANTS are trotted out like new puppies for us to examine their teeth and their pedigree. Magazines, catalogs and newspapers all dazzle us with new versions of familiar plants.

There are new cultivars with spotted leaves, petals as ruffled as a can-can dancer's petticoats, and more colors than a jumbo box of crayons. New introductions from faraway places have arrived with exotic foliage, tropical leanings and fantastical new names.

It's as if a voracious appetite has been unleashed, and we can't get enough new things to try. I would like to say that I am immune to all this razzle-dazzle and will stick with my reliable boy-next-door plants, but I know that by season's end I, too, will be in the thrall of some new infatuation.

Unfortunately, infatuations can lead to disaster. Expensive disaster, because often new plants are pricey. So, here are some guidelines that will help those of us who can't navigate a nursery aisle without being spellbound by new plants pleading, "Take me home, please take me home. I promise to be good."

1. If you are new to gardening or feel you have a brown thumb, you can still enjoy new varieties. Just stick to new cultivars of plants that have proved to be nearly indestructible, such as daylilies, hostas, iris and heuchera. It seems there's always a new cultivar of heuchera.

2. Forget the old rule about buying three of everything when it comes to an expensive new cultivar. Yes, you do want to have drifts of flowers for a lush look, and the best way to get that is with tried and true plants. Use expensive specimen plants like spice, offering an accent here and there.

3. Set single specimens out in a way so they won't be lost. Place them where companion plants won't swamp them by midsummer, or lift them up in pots set right in the border. It's particularly a good idea to keep a tender plant in a pot so you can move it to protection next fall.

4. Recognize that some spring-blooming perennials die completely back when it gets

hot. For example, many of the new cory-dalis cultivars disappear in midsummer. You haven't lost them, and they'll be back. But if you don't use plant labels, keep a map of where you put certain plants so you don't inadvertently dig them up.

5. If you have a particularly pricey new plant, be vigilant about slugs. I lost a $35 plant to the little beasts, and I am afraid it has quite changed my attitude about loving all living creatures.

6. If you've purchased a new variety for its unusual foliage color, cut back any branches that sprout in the old color. If not, they will eventually take over and your once golden or variegated plant may revert to plain green.

7. Be temperate with tropicals, which will be available in a far wider selection than ever before. By all means indulge in those newly available semi-hardy plants, but don't buy more than you can afford to lose.

8. ... Or change your attitude about semi-hardy plants. Most don't cost much more than annuals, and if you get a couple of years or more out of them, then you've

The fairly new bleeding heart cultivar 'Gold Heart' is a bit dear but worth it for its gorgeous bright leaves in the spring.

had a good run. Just don't think of them like diamonds. They are not forever.

9. ... Or face the fact that you have no resistance, and invest in a modest or not-so-modest greenhouse to winter plants over. You are probably at this point if you find yourself buying a lot of tender plants such as those elegant succulents (aloes, agaves and echeverias) that are suddenly flooding the market.

MARCH 6, 2003

❧

BLACK MAGIC
The path to a great garden is lined with compost

THERE IS A MYTH ABROAD THAT THE WORLD is divided into those with green thumbs and those whose thumbs shed nary an emerald glint. As one friend who considers herself in the latter group said recently, "My plants come with sympathy notes." A lot of people like her think the greenies were simply born with a magic touch.

Not true. I am here to tell you that, at least in the maritime Northwest, there is nothing wrong with anyone's thumbs. We are living in one of the most verdant spots in the world, where it's almost impossible not to grow things.

But like every paradise, there's always a serpent. Ours is called clay soil. If you're having trouble, the problem isn't your thumb. Clay soil, which so many of us have, is rich and fertile, but it is also made up of minute particles that cling together so tightly that it stays soggy and gets little air circulation. Not good for roots. The cure, you've probably heard, is to add organic material to condi-

The key to a lush garden is great (read: "amended") soil.

tion clay. The organic material has to be well composted, which means broken down through bacterial action so that it has a crumbly brown texture and a sweet earthy smell.

At this point, some of you more experienced gardeners are going to think you've heard all this before, but I am going to depart from the gardening books. They tell you what to do, but I am going to tell you what you don't need to do.

Forget fancy formulas for compost ingredients. Forget about driving around the countryside trying to find a mushroom farm. It's nice to start your own compost pile, but forget about using it right off the bat because it will take several months to "cook" up a good batch. If you have a small garden, your local nursery will likely have sacks of compost. If you need to buy in bulk, you can find plenty of sources under "Compost" in the Yellow Pages of your telephone directory. Many deliver. Sure, if you've got the dedication, you can do some research and find out how much organic material, nutrients, lime and other stuff will produce the perfect mix.

But folks, this is taxing, and you've got to save your energy for digging. Any well-composted organic material will be good for your soil. It's kind of like making spaghetti sauce. There's no one "right" recipe, and almost any is pretty good. Don't try to figure out how many cubic feet you need. Unless you are a math whiz, this also is too taxing and likely to send you back to the lounger and a bag of potato chips. Just shovel the stuff in — the compost I mean, not the chips. And then shovel some more.

The formula is easy. Do what you can until

either your back or your pocketbook gives out. You probably won't have done enough, but a little is better than none, and you can add more compost a bit at a time as you dig holes for new plants.

If you've heard about double digging (conditioning the soil two spade lengths down), forget it unless you are into pain and mind-numbing boredom. If your clay is severely compacted, till down one spade length, then buy some good friable topsoil and pile it on top. Then, each year in late fall, top off your soil with an inch or two of compost to protect your plants in winter. Repeat in late spring for weed control and water conservation. You don't have to dig it in. This is called mulching. Gradually your horrid wet clingy clay will build up into the most deliciously crumbly mound, so light that your spade slips right in.

I get kind of giddy just thinking about such soil.

If you still have places that look like a Los Angeles freeway despite all your hard work, don't despair. Until you get your soil in prime condition, opt for plants that have a reputation for doing well in clay. They're great confidence builders. Over time, as your soil improves, you'll not only be able to grow a wider array of plants, but also those plants that grow well will be all the lusher. Plus, all your friends will go about marveling at your shiny green thumb. No sympathy notes for you.

CLAY BUSTERS

The following plants are pretty reliable in clay soil. But while they will survive, they will look far lusher in improved soil.

GROUND COVERS: *Ajuga, Hypericum* (St. John's wort), *Lamium*

FLOWERS: *Acanthus* (bear's breeches),

Peonies hate wet feet but are worth the trouble.

Aconitum (monkshood), *Alchemilla* (lady's mantle), *Anemone* (Japanese hybrids), *Aruncus* (goat's beard), *Aster, Astilbe, Astrantia, Bergenia, Camassia* (camas), *Crocosmia, Digitalis* (foxglove), *Eupatorium* (Joe-Pye weed), *Helenium, Helleborus* (hellebore), *Hemerocallis* (daylily), *Hosta, Inula, Iris, Ligularia, Lysimachia* (can be invasive), *Paeonia* (peony), *Persicaria* (can be invasive), *Rodgersia, Rudbeckia* (black-eyed Susan), *Solidago* (goldenrod)

SHRUBS/VINES: *Aucuba, Berberis* (barberry), *Buxus* (boxwood), *Chaenomeles* (flowering quince), *Cornus* (dogwood), *Cotoneaster, Euonymus* (spindle), *Forsythia, Ilex* (holly), *Kerria, Mahonia* (Oregon grape), *Rhododendron, Ribes* (flowering currant), *Salix* (willow), *Sambucus* (elderberry), *Spiraea, Viburnum, Weigela, Wisteria*

MARCH 13, 2003

GARDEN FRILLS
Fashion a new garden look with accessories

FROM THE SPATE OF RECENT HOME AND GARDEN shows, it would appear that accessories are in. That doesn't mean plants are less important, only that we're expressing more individuality in our gardens. Think of it as trimming the tree year-round.

While we've had lots of good advice through the years about what plants to select, we're all relatively new at this ornament business. Since Martha hasn't stepped up to offer guidance in selecting garden decorations and accessories, here I go. My guidelines start with basic questions.

"But where will you put it?" This is the elemental question that spouses have asked for centuries. I'm sure Eve was ready to tell Adam where he could put that apple. You can always tell a wise and long-married spouse by the bite marks on his or her lip. Ignore this question. If you love something, you will find a place.

"If one is nice, will more be better?" Some accessories obviously stand on their own, such as a gorgeous glazed pot. But little items can make a bigger impact if clustered. I've even thought pink flamingos had a certain charm when flocked in a sprinkling of birdseed. Last summer, I cornered the market on some lovely glass dragonflies because they looked spectacular buzzing en masse around my new pond.

"Do I have a friend who would like one?" Of course you do. This is a great way to get more toys. You tell yourself that you are buying extras as presents for your gardening friends. Occasionally, these items actually get to your friends, but often not. It's called creative rationalization, and it's an art you mas-

ter with practice. (I had intended to give away some of those dragonflies.)

"Does it fit my style?" You may adore an elegant Japanese stone lantern or one of those bamboo stems that channel water into a hollowed-out stone. But if you have a cottage garden or a formal rose garden, it may not be the proper accessory. But what if you adore it? Exercise some discipline and restrain yourself. Or, throw caution to the wind and read the next question for a helpful solution.

"Can I create a whole new area to justify it?" My neighbor Walt Ellis successfully bid on a magnificent stone lantern at a symphony auction. But where to put it, since he and Rosemary had a cottage-style garden? The answer was to carve out a new garden area to accommodate the lantern. The pocket-size Japanese garden is surrounded by shrubs and reached through a wooden arch. It includes a small pond and a stone bench and is marvelously restful. This is called creative justification.

"Is it a one of a kind?" Ever get the idea you've seen the same bunny statue a thousand times? Handcrafted ornaments are especially choice because you know that there will be no two alike. It's even more fun to make your own. But how many times have you seen a clever item and passed it by because you think, "Gee, I could make that"? Ignore that voice. Buy the ornament you like, because the truth of the matter is, you probably won't ever get around to making it.

"If it's one of a thousand, should I avoid it?" If you like something, buy it and find ways

> *We had to remove a silver reflecting ball from our pond because Hector would look at his reflection in it and bark maniacally.*

Whimsical or elegant, found-art or artisan-made, art adds personality to a garden.

to make it individual. Place the bunny on a wonderful pedestal. Personalize a plain birdbath by planting succulents in it or filling it with colored stones and shells you've collected. My neighbor Rosemary took some common pottery fish that the rest of us had staked by our ponds and instead staked them in a sea of waving grass. The effect is spectacular.

"Does it serve a practical purpose?" It's always easier to justify something if you can claim it's functional. Make those pretty copper wands with glass balls on top work as hose guards. Use those lovely tiles as edging. Use wrought-iron scrollwork as a tiny fence to support floppy flowers. It always helps when you can say, "Well, honey, it wasn't that expensive when you consider that we can use the urn as an ice bucket for our anniversary party."

"Will it survive the assaults of squirrels, birds, cats, dogs, raccoons and other critters?" We had to remove a silver reflecting ball from our pond because Hector would look at his reflection in it and bark maniacally. If you're a cat person, you may want to collect something other than birdhouses. If you have raccoons, make sure your pond ornaments can withstand their roughhousing.

"Would I want it myself?" Some items seem to be designed exclusively for someone to give as a gift. Generally, the earmark of such items is extreme cutesyness. But if it's something you wouldn't consider having in your garden, don't get it for a friend. It may, however, be the perfect gift for a relative who always gave you clothes when you were a kid.

MARCH 29, 2001

GOING FOR THAT EARLY SPRING GLOW

Those fleeting moments of stunning color are worth planting for

THERE IS A CERTAIN MOMENT IN VERY EARLY spring when color takes on a quality that is unlike any other time of the year. It usually comes on a brightly overcast day when the sky has a brooding quality, backlit with a hint of sun behind a cloud.

It is at these times that colors seem to pop out. The green of the lawn becomes luminous. The violets, roses, yellows, lime and apple greens of very early spring seem lighted from within. Colors take on a neon but somehow not gaudy brightness.

This peculiar vibrant light always reminds me of the sky just before the tornado hit Dorothy and Toto. Fortunately, we don't have that in store here in the Northwest. But unfortunately, these moments of shimmering color are heartbreakingly fleeting.

Still, they are moments so sublime, they are worth planting for. Part of it is the newness of the season. Emerging leaves have an apple green freshness that will dull to darker, dustier green later on. New roses and peonies have a radiant rosiness that also will disappear.

Of all early spring's colors, the one that seems most closely identified with this season is chartreuse. Golden, yellow, limy green pulsates with light, giving color excitement to a still barren landscape. This is its hour. Chartreuse in all its green-gold variations is brilliant in early spring, but later, it will wash out and lose some of its electric quality as the sun grows stronger.

For now, though, it is the perfect foil to purple-black tulips, early species iris, blush-

Euonymus fortunei *'Emerald 'n' Gold'* with its bright but delicate new spring growth.

ing Japanese primroses and the dawn-tinted flowers of currant (*Ribes sanguineum*) and quince (*Chaenomeles*).The sublime limes of spring can in their turn be set off by under-

Nothing says spring like pink tulips.

carpets of blue-flowered lungwort (*Pulmonaria*), purple pasque flower (*Pulsatilla*), old-fashioned violets and the rose-glazed leaves of *Epimedium* x *rubrum*, one of the loveliest ground covers there is.

No plants capture the glow of chartreuse quite so well as some of the euphorbias, also known as spurge. *Euphorbia polychroma* is a small mounded perennial, not much more than 18 inches high, that starts lighting up as soon as it pushes up from the earth. This sweet, no-care plant does a little self-sowing, but it's not pushy about it.

Euphorbia characias and its subspecies *E. wulfenii* are as dramatic as any plant you'll find. They prefer to be magnificent, rather than conventionally pretty, with their glowing yellow-tinged green mounds of flowers topping nonbranching stems.

Some gardeners avoid these two euphorbias because they are evergreen, and during cold winters they lose their lower leaves and look ungainly by spring. You can avoid that by cutting the stalks that have flowered down in early fall, so that new stems can take their place in spring.

> *There is, after all, nothing quite so charming as the limy froth of lady's mantle that washes a garden with its glow.*

Both *E. polychroma* and *E. characias* prefer a sunny spot and will prove drought-resistant. But *E. villosa* is a brilliant euphorbia as well that begs for moist shade.

You'll also find lime green or green-tinged white flowers among the spring-blooming hellebores (*H. orientalis*, *H. corsicus* and *H. foetidus*). Of course, they'll be even more smashing paired with rose- and wine-colored hellebores and white flowers with speckles of rose. Look for hellebores with names such as 'Cosmos', 'Lilac Picotee', 'Aquarias' and 'Capricornus' for the freckled blossoms.

Iris pallida is another must-grow plant for anyone who wants that early spring glow. While it has purple flowers later on, this is one iris you don't grow for the bloom. You grow it for the stunning greenish yellow stripe up and down the leaves.

For sheer jolt power, nothing can beat a golden *Euonymus fortunei* shrub, particularly the cultivar known as 'Emerald 'n' Gold'. It can be pruned like boxwood to present an imposing mound shape or left on its own. Whichever, it will shine like a beacon on the grayest of days.

For a daintier glow of green-gold, try the smaller shrub honeysuckle called *Lonicera nitida* 'Baggesen's Gold'. This is one honeysuckle that isn't a vine. In fact, it most resembles boxwood and can be pruned into neat mounds or topiary shapes.

For a looser chartreuse-leafed shrub, there's *Spiraea bumalda* 'Goldflame' and 'Limemound'. These small, dainty shrubs mix nicely in a flower border as well as among other shrubs. Of late, they seem out of fashion, possibly because some garden designers feel they've been overused, but that shouldn't stop you.

And, if you're lucky, and the spring has been warm, maybe one of the prettiest of all plants will begin its bloom earlier. There is, after all, nothing quite so charming as the limy froth of lady's mantle (*Alchemilla mollis*) that washes a garden with its glow. One can almost forgive it for seeding itself everywhere, and one is almost tempted to let it do so with abandon.

MARCH 16, 1997

FOR WANT OF A CUCUMBER
Ambitious plans for the vegetable garden germinate

FORGET WHAT I SAID ABOUT BEING DISCIplined. Forget what I said about limiting your palette and not trying every new fad. Forget about not coveting thy neighbor's wagonload of plants. It's spring, and it's time to experiment.

The fact that my garden has "no room"

left has not deterred me from a "must have" list of 30 or so plants. And Doug the Wonder Boy and I have come up with a doozy of an idea for The Annual Project.

This is an especially joyous spring because I have just ended another series of chemo treatments and once again have beaten back what John Wayne called The Big C. There's nothing like a second lease on life to give you the courage and the zeal to try something new, or even silly.

So this year, Doug and I are digging out some of the boxwoods that frame the vegetable garden. Never fear, they will be replanted. Originally, they lined narrow beds

of hybrid tea roses, which were all but dead when we moved into the house 18 years ago. I wasn't up on the virtues of crop rotation then, so I replanted new roses, and all turned out sickly.

They were replaced with a white garden. This grew to be messy and also a target for birds, which expelled seeds of yellow calendula, blue morning glory and red tomatoes in my so-called white garden. In fact, the only really healthy vibrant-blue delphinium ever to grace my garden came by way of birds and landed, you guessed it, in the white garden.

Since then, the area has been our veg-

Vegetable gardens don't have to be plain and utilitarian.

etable garden. But alas, the narrowness of the beds is confining. We have little room for twining and vining plants such as cucumbers, and everyone knows that sun-warmed cucumbers right off the vine are the very best.

Last year, we had "The Incident." I had watched a cucumber ripen gradually until finally I declared it perfect, mixed some vinaigrette and went out to pick. Alas, it was gone. Later Doug, who does have picking rights, and I had a little conversation. Suffice it to say, I put dibs on the next cucumber.

It would be wonderful, though, to have room for more than one vining plant. To this end, we are moving some of the hedging and will open up the area to make parterres (geometrically shaped beds) around a central feature, such as an ornamental pot or sundial.

I realize this is a step back into traditionalism, not at all what the modern cutting-edge gardener should be about. Rather than growing vegetables, I should be nurturing spiny things that make a "statement," such as aloes and echeverias. Instead of parterres, I should be turning loosely shaped gravel beds into Mediterranean gardens.

But, again, what can you expect from a woman who has a gnome? Beneath this not-so-sophisticated exterior is a country girl who really did grow up on a ranch and was once the Radish Queen. So a veggie garden it will be. Our derring-do should give us a larger space to grow healthy food to counterbalance my routine diet of Cadbury's chocolate. It will give us space to mix in annuals, such as calendulas and nasturtiums and sunflowers, very much in the French manner.

Or so I envision. It might turn into a mess. The transplanted boxwoods might die. The years of compacted soil in the current paths may prove impermeable. Some ghastly worm may beat Doug to the last cucumber.

MARCH 17, 2005

THE MIGRATING SPIRIT
Seeds, bulbs and cuttings brought West by pioneers 150 years ago commingled with the native plants and flowers

WITH THE 150TH ANNIVERSARY OF THE great migration over the Oregon Trail, renewed speculation will focus on how much the remarkable spirit of the pioneers shaped Northwest life.

It may not be a stretch to say the roots of the region's great gardening tradition lie in the migration as well.

After all, the trail came to a significant crossroads. One fork led to California and gold, the other to Oregon and verdant farmland. Those who elected to take the northern trail were people who had made a distinct choice. Land, not gold, was their goal.

Oral histories and diaries tell of unimaginable stresses — birth and death on the trail, encounters with friendly and hostile Indians, exhaustion, hunger, dangerous rivers and mountain traverses.

During the endless days as slow-moving wagons lumbered across grassy plains and deserts, small joys — such as finding a clump of new flowers — must have relieved the monotony and fortified their spirits.

It would have been early spring when the settlers rolled out of Independence, Mo. As they headed out across the plains, the settlers would be sailing through a sea of grasses just awakening with wildflowers. If they were early enough coming to the Rocky Mountains, the settlers may have discovered some of the jewel-bright alpines still blooming. Among the sky-blue dwarf columbines, Rocky Mountain iris and creamy windflowers, the pioneers may have glimpsed the pink lewisias, seen by European-descended people only decades earlier in the Lewis and Clark expedition.

After the Rockies, the land was dry and barren until they hit the mountains and came into the greatest conifer forests in the world. Here were towering fragrant trees such as pine, fir, spruce, hemlock, larch, cedar and cypress.

Coming out of the mountains along the Columbia the settlers would have had their first view of the Promised Land. Winter would be descending and settling in would be their first priority. Still, everywhere they turned would have been evergreen shrubs — salal, kinnikinnick, huckleberries and Oregon grape. They may have traded goods with the Indians for the wild camas bulbs that could be ground and pounded into flour.

The following spring must have seemed like a miracle. Now they could explore one of the greatest cradles of plant life in the world.

The Pacific dogwoods, vine maples, Garry oaks, water birch and Oregon ash would be leafing out. Native deciduous shrubs, that later would become world garden favorites, would be exploding into bloom — serviceberry, wild lilac, mock orange, red-flowering currant and red huckleberry.

The woodlands would be carpeted with an array of ferns, wild ginger, and delicate-hued flowers such as dogtooth violet, trilliums, foam flower, false Solomon's seal, fairy bells, adder's tongue, checkered lilies and several native iris species.

The meadows were embroidered with white-flowered bear grass, also known as Indian basket grass, purple-flowered wild onions, blue dicks, mariposa lilies, harebell and violet-blue camas or Indian hyacinth.

Along streambeds and in bogs, they'd find the sedges horsetails, skunk cabbage, deer cabbage and umbrella plant.

It wasn't long before many of these native plants made their way into cultivated gardens. Here, they joined non-native species, for the settlers had brought their most precious possessions with them — seeds, bulbs and cuttings. Some of the rose bushes and lilacs carted along in the wagons still survive in the Century Farms dotted throughout the state.

MARCH 19, 1993

NO TIME?
Mix these ingredients for an instant great garden

IT IS SAID THAT A GREAT GARDEN REQUIRES discipline, planning and patience. Unfortunately, about this time of year, I'm pretty short on those virtues. My soul craves instant gratification. I want my garden to look great. Right now.

The nice thing about gardening is that you can have it both ways. To a degree, you can fake a mature garden while taking the time, perhaps years, to perfect your garden. And, if you're lucky, you'll never get it perfect because, for many of us, gardening is about the thrill of the hunt.

Here are some tried-and-true tricks to make a garden look more mature, finished, done, cooked to perfection while you're wait-

A well placed garden ornament can fill the gap as a young plant matures.

ing for the stately yew hedge to grow and the statue of Aphrodite to arrive from Greece.

- Make a virtue of your favorite vice. Go ahead and overplant. With few exceptions, plants are eminently movable. When things get crowded, you'll find homes for the newly dispossessed, if not in your garden, in appreciative friends' gardens.
- Cover that bare ground between plants not with — gasp — bark dust, but with rich, chocolate-y compost. It makes bare spaces look as though they're supposed to be that way.
- Conventional wisdom calls for planting annuals while waiting for perennials to mature. Tall, full annuals — not short bedding plants — are what you want, and cosmos is the perfect annual filler.
- Height adds character to a garden. Think vines while waiting for slow-growing trees to mature. Train them up trellises, arbors and tuteurs. Try annual vines while waiting for that romantic clematis and rose combination to take hold.
- Until you can afford the paving of your choice, create paths and terraces with gravel. It's relatively cheap, quick and easy to install, and it makes a satisfying crunch when you walk on it.
- Pots are the impatient gardener's salvation. Cluster potted plants and found objects in bare spots. Nestle pots filled with shade plants under a tree. Clump flower-filled pots around the base of a sundial or birdbath to make either look more important.
- Add focal points: a piece of art, a sundial, an ornament. But think of ornaments as spice; too many, and you'll have a circus. A few select focal points give a garden a polished look.
- Don't forget the magic bench. Pull up a bench almost anywhere, and you've designed a sitting area. Benches are like the cherry on top of a sundae.
- Then there's the pot trick. Not the little terra-cotta flower holders, but a big, fat, glazed pot that is so magnificent it doesn't even need a plant. See that bare spot where something died during the winter? Put the pot there. I guarantee, everyone will think it was on purpose and that you're a swell designer.

QUICK GROWERS

Ground-hugging spreaders: creeping Jenny (*Lysimachia nummularia*), blue star creeper (*Laurentia*), thyme (*Thymus*), oregano (*Origanum*).

Shrubs that perform in one season: tree mallow (*Lavatera*), hydrangea (*H. macrophylla*), willow (*Salix*), shrub roses (*Rosa moyesii, R. rugosa*).

Perennials that fill out quickly: euphorbia, bear's breeches (*Acanthus spinosus*), masterwort (*Astrantia*), red valerian (*Centranthus ruber*), daylily (*Hemerocallis*), ligularia, plume poppy (*Macleaya*).

Annuals that mix well with perennials: pot marigold (*Calendula officinalis*), spider flower (*Cleome*), larkspur (*Consolida ambigua*), candelabra tobacco flower (*Nicotiana sylvestris*), cosmos.

Quick edgers: annual nasturtium (*Tropaeolum*), perennial lady's mantle (*Alchemilla mollis*), dead nettle (*Lamium*).

Leafy plants that fill out in a season: rhubarb, castor bean plant (*Ricinis communis*), wormwood (*Artemisia*).

Quick-growing perennial vines: clematis (*C. paniculata*, *C. montana*, *C. tanguta*), Hall's honeysuckle (*Lonicera japonica* 'Halliana').

MARCH 30, 2000

JUMP-START THE SEASON
Woodland flowers quietly signal spring

Many of spring's earliest flowers are woodland plants. Perhaps they bloom early — many when the calendar says it's still winter — because they know they have to get their flowering over before the trees leaf out. If I didn't already have shade, I would plant a small ornamental tree or shrubs, such as rhododendrons, just to create a shady corner so I wouldn't miss out on these flowers. They help jump-start spring.

Woodland flowers aren't showy but have rather an elegant and delicate beauty. Somehow, in early spring, a tiny, twinkling blue pulmonaria delights as much as the over-the-top blue delphiniums do later.

My all-time favorite woodland plant is *Polygonatum*, commonly called Solomon's seal. One of the joys of early spring is watching the little coils of Solomon's seal unfurl into arching stems that drip with faintly scented white flowers. Over time, Solomon's seal will plump up into a solid colony, but it's never invasive. It is especially dramatic edging a woodland path or pond because of its arching habit. There's a variegated variety, *P. odoratum* 'Variegatum'. All Solomon's seals can take reasonably deep shade and need little water once established.

I am also a sucker for one of the most enduring of cottage garden flowers, *Dicentra spectabilis*, or the common bleeding heart. Bleeding heart is best grown as a specimen, not in a clump, so its graceful plumes of dripping hearts can be shown to best advantage. There is a white variety, 'Alba', and now a golden-leafed variety, 'Gold Heart'. Bleeding heart will die back by summer but will return next spring. Other lovely dicentras, such as 'Bacchanal', don't die back. They are shorter and their flowers aren't as showy, but they are long-lasting. Dicentras do best in filtered, not deep, shade. You might notice that the fernlike leaves of dicentra are similar to corydalis, a small mounding plant. The two are indeed related. Most of us are besotted with the newer blue varieties of *Corydalis flexuosa*. I found 'Blue Panda', which requires superb drainage, a little hard to grow, but I have had excellent luck with other blue cultivars, such as 'China Blue' and 'Pére David'.

By the way, one shouldn't shun the more common yellow-flowered *Corydalis lutea*, which is one of the longest-blooming flowers in the garden. It self-sows, but discreetly. Corydalis likes moderate or filtered shade and should be put in your best soil, since the plant will not tolerate heavy clay. Corydalis also tends to die back in summer's heat, but it'll be back, often in the fall.

Pulmonaria (lungwort) is another one of

my early spring favorites. This is one of the few plants my neighbor Rosemary and I disagree about. She doesn't like them. They are a bit plebeian, but I like them for both the speckled leaves and the very early flowers. Bloom starts in January at my house, or at least it did this past warm January. Pulmonaria is low-growing like a ground cover but is not by any means a takeover plant. It just forms a nice, polite clump with a modest spread. While there are many excellent varieties, some favorites are blue-flowered 'Lewis Palmer', white-flowered *P. officinalis* 'Sissinghurst White' and rosy-flowered *P. rubra* 'David Ward'. Pulmonaria can take fairly deep shade and is often evergreen.

Tiarella (foamflower) is a modest small plant with frothy pink or white flowers that usually arrive in late spring. With interesting new introductions of foliage variations, it is beginning to go the way of *Heuchera* (coral bells). That is, it's beginning to be grown more for foliage than flowers. *T. cordifolia* has leaves that look somewhat like a green-leafed *Heuchera*, while *T. wherryi* has leaves that are more sculpted and often infused with a bronze blush. There are, of

The exquisite Corydalis flexuosa *'China Blue' with lady's mantle.*

course, other lovely woodland plants, such as trilliums, ferns, bulbs, epimediums, brunnera and primulas.

MARCH 20, 2003

RUTHLESS RELOCATION
Listless plants can thrive with a change of scenery

THIS TIME OF YEAR COMES WITH A GOOD deal of yearning, blood-rushing, pulse-quickening, heart-throbbing and assorted stirrings. If you are having the above-mentioned symptoms, you are either reading a cheap romance novel or you are a gardener.

It's spring, it's spring, it's spring. Oh, joy. And in this case our fancy turns to . . . yes, yes, yes . . . plants. But before we get too far into the delirium of buying and siting new plants, preliminary work awaits.

The furniture might benefit from rearranging, so to speak. One great thing about gardening in the Northwest is that you can correct mistakes and fine-tune, and nothing can rejuvenate a garden quicker than some thoughtful plant moves. The garden is still spare enough so that we can see the trees for the forest, and young plants are easier to move.

Doug the Wonder Boy and I have been moving plants right and left. I don't know why I always say "Doug and I." It's more like I'm Cecil B. De Mille with the megaphone shouting "Action!" and he is the cast of thousands doing all the work.

Here's what we look for.

Things that get too crowded. There are always some plants that look great for a while, then get lost by midsummer when the garden achieves its fullness. We just moved a lovely aralia. It's always splendid until about mid-July, when suddenly it disappears under the spread of a neighboring *Hydrangea aspera*. Both plants need a little space so their elegant lines stand out.

Proportion gone awry. Who hasn't fallen in love with an adorable little mound only to have it grow into Godzilla? Remember all those little pots of red-leafed ninebark (*Physocarpus* 'Diabolo') that suddenly appeared at nurseries about five years ago? Well, by now they're 8 feet or more. I know I can't be the only one who bought one.

Places that are too spare. This becomes a place to move things to. I have one bed in the front that never quite fills in because we never really dug enough compost into the soil. Flowers don't thrive. But we've found it's an excellent place to move shrubs that have gotten too large. The not-so-perfect soil keeps the Godzillas in check.

Plants that have gone all wimpy. When a plant doesn't respond to fertilizer or proper watering, it may just be unhappy with its site. I have moved a number of anemic-looking plants to different spots, where they've suddenly perked up. So, before tossing a plant, try a change of venue.

Places where the light has changed. As trees and shrubs mature, some formerly sunny places become shady, and the sun-loving plants under them no longer thrive. Similarly, other places have opened up to the sun. We lost a tree, so the hostas beneath it are making like little wildebeests in a mass migration to a shadier spot.

Plants that have lost their luster. Yesterday's infatuation may now seem just blah. Such plants that are too healthy to dispatch with a clear conscience need to be moved to a more obscure site to make room for new guys. For example, we have a perfectly healthy euonymus, but lately the golden leaves that made it such a nice accent plant have turned plain green. It is being moved to background duty in another part of the garden.

Plants that need to be sent to their reward. I hesitate to say this, because in the past when I have mentioned dispatching plants I have horrified some gentle readers who feel that no plant should be discarded. But this year, with great sadness, I have dug up my beloved Graham Thomas rose (may it rest in peace) because it had become a hotel for black spot. Someone once told me I was crazy because I dug up some rare Exbury azaleas, but what's the point in growing a crop of powdery mildew each year? If you have a plant that needs heavy chemicals to look halfway decent, I say, "Off with its head."

MARCH 27, 2003

> *The not-so-perfect soil keeps the Godzillas in check.*

GARDENERS COME IN TWO VARIETIES

On one hand, we have Latin-spouters; on the other, lovers of pretty landscapes

I HAVE THIS THEORY THAT THERE ARE TWO paths to gardening and that eventually they merge. Like most of my theories, it has

*Mexican mock orange (*Choisya ternata*) fills the garden with sweet scent.*

absolutely no scientific basis. But that's not going to stop me from telling you about it.

According to my theory, people approach gardening from two schools of thought, the Pretty Landscape School and the Serious Horticulture School. There's a test to tell which school you started in. Did you pay attention to the second Latin word in a plant name? If so, you're from the serious side.

The pretty-landscape people often start out knowing zilch about plants. They began dabbling in the yard simply because they have an artistic urge. They approach their garden the way they approach their house: as decorators. Their thrill is creating an attractive landscape.

The serious plant people, on the other hand, adore individual plants for their own sake, may even collect certain kinds, and savor the hunt for new ones. Their thrill is a new discovery to try out.

Eventually, according to my theory, the twain meet, so to speak. The design people start to get interested in individual plants. And the plant people, as they acquire collections, start to mull over the idea of creating a more attractive setting for their plants.

I emerged from the first group. My interest in gardening grew pretty much from a vestigial artistic urge. It's not, heaven forbid, that I had actual talent, but nevertheless the urge was there.

My theory about the two approaches to gardening was further strengthened on a trip to England last summer. It was fascinating to watch how each of us approached the same garden in entirely different ways. Some of us stood back and looked around, noting the design or ornamentation and mentally racking up the ideas for a new layout or combination of plants.

But there were two people in our party who were always hunkered down, nose to petal, intensely focused on the plants. Occasionally, these two would stop by a new specimen, squeal out a string of Latin names and go into paroxysms of pleasure at a new discovery. At first I was amused by all this, but then I began to find their excitement infectious.

I started to look at actual plants, not just color combinations or attractive pairings. I'm beginning to think I may be nearing the merging point between the two schools. I don't expect to become the serious collector, and I certainly will never get my Latin right, but I do feel the first stirrings of the thrill of the hunt for individual plants.

MARCH 17, 1996

THE GAME MATE
What's a gardener without a willing accomplice?

DOWN THE BLOCK AT THE ELLIS HOUSEhold, Rosemary has been busy with seedlings she started in the greenhouse Walt built for her last fall. I should tell you that Walt is the ideal gardening spouse. Not only does he like to garden with her, but he also is handy.

Truly I don't covet her spouse, but at times I covet his handiness. My own husband is the second-best kind of gardening spouse. He has zero interest in gardening and is about as handy as our dog, Hector, but he does meet certain other requirements admirably.

If you are going to garden seriously, you should have the good sense or good luck to pick the right partner. In case you are looking, I have compiled a list of what makes a good gardening mate. These are the kinds of things they do not tell you about on Internet dating services.

A good gardening partner:
• Never asks how much those plants in the back of the car cost.
• At the end of the year, when doing taxes, does not add up all the credit-card charges for nurseries. (My own near-perfect spouse did mutter, "Does add them up but discreetly does not mention them.")
• Faithfully drives you to nurseries on the weekend and sits in the car listening to "Prairie Home Companion" while you shop. Then unloads plants from the car for you.
• Patiently and largely without comment holds the flashlight when you are trying to get the last plant in after dark.
• Does not get apoplectic because there is dirt in the back of the car, and something mysterious seems to be growing back there.
• Does not regard grass as a sacred object and won't feign a heart attack when you start digging up more lawn.
• Agrees with you about such things as whether the roses should be pruned in fall or late winter and whether they should be in their own bed alone or mixed in with other plants. (All gardeners know that roses are the No. 2 cause of marital disharmony, after lawns, of course).

Ernie, the gardening friend, loyally keeps an eye out for nasty invaders.

- Is capable of an occasional grand gesture such as digging a hole.
- Shops for presents at Smith & Hawken rather than Victoria's Secret. Or in the case of the female partner, shops for you at the hardware store rather than someplace that sells ties.
- Is silly about pets and does not rant on about what they do to that precious lawn.
- Does not visibly shrink away when you come in smelling like Compost No. 5.
- When you are away, reads and follows instructions, to wit: "Water my plants, and if any die, you die!"
- Limits theatrics to a barely perceptible roll of the eyes rather than clutching chest and swooning when you announce a new project.
- Comes out and compliments what you've been up to in the garden before returning to a) the football game, b) the John Wayne movie or c) doing the taxes and pretending not to add up how much you spent on plants last year.
- Surprises you with that to-die-for birdbath that you adored but said was way too expensive. Really.
- Never says something like, "Those flowers are nice, but you should have seen my mom's dahlias."

MARCH 16, 2000

PLANTS WITH AN ATTITUDE
The furry, the spiky and the chartreuse may not be pretty, but they're intriguing

WHEN I WAS A YOUNG GIRL, IF YOUR friends told you that you looked "interesting," it clearly meant they thought you weren't pretty. And if they went so far as to say you had "personality," that was a sure sign they thought you were ugly as a warthog.

The same can be said in the plant world. There are a number of plants that simply aren't pretty, and a few that are downright ugly.

And every garden should have a few of these oddities. For the fact is, they really are interesting, and they do indeed give an otherwise conventionally pretty flower bed some personality.

Take mullein (*Verbascum*), for example. It is a staple of those romantic English flower

Carex grayi *distinguishes itself with its fabulous spiky seedheads.*

gardens. The best that any garden book can say about mulleins is that they are stately. That's because *Verbascum bombyciferum* reaches a splendid 6 feet. It has yellow flower spikes above largish gray-green leaves that tend to be on the furry side. Purple mullein (*V. phoeniceum*) is about 18 inches shorter and has purple flowers.

Speaking of plants with furry leaves, there's mealy-cup sage (*Salvia farinacea*). It has large feltlike silver leaves and sends up a profusion of purple flower spikes on hairy stems. It blooms for a long time, and its flowers are a favorite with people who want them for drying.

Eryngium is certainly a different flower with spiny leaves and spiky flower petals that have an unusual amethyst cast. The flower petals, which look as if they'd prick your finger if you touched them, radiate out from a greenish, cone-shaped center.

I've seen wonderful specimens in local gardens, but if you had one that didn't make it, try again. They really must have well-drained soil (and where have you heard that before?).

For those with shade gardens, Jack-in-the-pulpit (*Arisaema*) is an interesting little plant that earns its nickname from its spadix, which looks as if it is popping up out of the flower. It is ideal for people with woodland gardens, and although it's an East Coast native, it does very well in natural gardens that rely on native plants.

Yellow hardhead (*Centaurea macrocephala*) and its close relative, *Centaurea* 'Pulchra Major', are nearly, but not quite, pretty. The leaves are coarse, and the flowers on the thistle side. But they are magnificent in borders with their unusual and good-sized yellow and purple flowers, respectively.

Sometimes it's hard to tell if a thing is gorgeous or ghastly. Take our Rex cat. She's practically hairless and looks decidedly odd, and less-than-tactful visitors have pronounced her homely. But the more discriminating note she has the sleek beauty of an Egyptian sculpture.

That's what some euphorbias are like, not that they're sleek. But, depending on your mood, they can either be strangely beautiful or just plain strange. The *Euphorbia characias wulfenii* has large clusters of chartreuse flowers that don't exactly look like flowers. But at all times they are a magnificent presence in any garden.

Even if you only have a terrace, you can have an offbeat plant. The pineapple flower (*Eucomis*) is as odd as they come but is charming and does very well in a pot. Its greenish flower looks very much like a pineapple. It blooms from mid- to late summer, and doesn't need to be taken in for protection during the winter.

A couple of summers ago I pulled up a stand of Jerusalem sage (*Phlomis*) after I decided it was homely. Now I regret it. It had character, and I miss it. The plant bears whorls of lemon yellow flowers wrapped at intervals around square, hollow stems.

If you have lots of room and especially if you have a creek or large pond, you'll want to try a plant with the wonderful common name of dinosaur food (*Gunnera*). Once you see the huge leaves, you'll know where the plant got its nickname. The curious flowers are large, brownish and under no circumstances, I am sorry to say, can be called pretty. Fortunately, they are unobtrusive.

Gunnera will make it here but is a bit tender. It needs to be in a protected semi-shady exposure and mulched heavily over its crown for the winter.

Speaking of mulching for the winter, I've learned that my cardoons (*Cynara cardunculus*) would have made it through the winter if I had cut them back in the fall and mulched them. So here's another peculiar plant to try. If you've seen an artichoke, then think of a cardoon as a slightly more silver, slightly taller, slightly more dramatic version. The purple thistle-type flowers are profuse.

Often in English gardens, you'll spot a real thistle, but not just any old thistle. The favorite is *Cirsium rhinoceros*, and I'm not sure where it got the reference to a rhino. This plant is said to be sculptural and have character, which is a sure sign that it has lots and lots of personality, and we all know what that's a code word for.

APRIL 28, 1996

◦✗◦

A DIRTY LITTLE SECRET
It's okay to break a few rules

MODERATION IN ALL THINGS IS DARN GOOD advice. And that includes moderation in following garden rules.

Now, I'm not against rules per se. They're pretty good guidelines, and you really should know them before you break them. After all, it's not much fun breaking a rule if you don't know you're doing it.

So, here are some rules to think about — and to ignore every now and then.

Rule No. 1: Place tallest plants in the back of the border, medium plants in the middle and shortest in front. This makes fairly good sense, but followed rigidly it could lead to an unappealing stair-step effect. There's nothing like pulling a tall bloomer toward the front to give an exciting dynamic to your border.

Rule No. 2: Always buy plants in threes. That's excellent advice, especially for a beginner, because plants look better in drifts, the way they grow in nature. But once you get the drift, or drifts, have a little fun with punctuation marks. A single, character plant, such as a verbascum, or a tall spray of grass, can do wonders to pep up a border.

Rule No. 3: Space plants loosely to accommodate future growth. Oh, go ahead and break this rule if the plant's a perennial, rather than a shrub. Frankly, we all do. Who wants to wait three years for a garden to fill in? A dose of instant gratification is good for the soul. Besides, most plants transplant wonderfully.

Rule No. 4: Prune regularly and judiciously. People tend to follow this to the point where they don't stop to look at a shrub or tree to decide if it really needs pruning. Clipped is nice. But fluffy can be nice, too.

Rule No. 5: Set aside roses in their own space. This is probably worth following if you're growing roses for show. But otherwise, mix things up. The English (also known as David Austin) roses, old-fashioned roses, flo-

Roses mixed with perennials, grasses and bulbs make for an elegant border.

ribundas and grandifloras are better mixers than hybrid teas. That doesn't mean you have to set your hybrid teas in bare earth. It's okay to undercarpet them with a dainty ground cover (sweet woodruff is a nice companion), as long as you choose something that doesn't have deep roots to compete for water and nutrients. On the plus side, an undercarpeting can help keep weeds out.

Rule No. 6: Shade plants need shade, sun plants need sun. It's not that simple. For one thing, a number of shade plants will do fine in sun if the soil isn't allowed to dry out completely. And what is shade? It can be anything from lightly dappled to deep forest gloom. Experiment a little. You might find you can get more color in shade than you thought, or grow a big, fat, healthy hosta in full sun (I've seen it happen).

Rule No. 7: Choose plants according to climate zone. Don't pass up a wonderful plant just because it isn't hardy in our zone. Simply think of it as an annual. Mild-weather-loving New Zealand flax (*Phormium tenax*), variegated in the colors of the rainbow, makes a great garden accent. You may get lucky and have it live over a winter, as phormiums did this year. Or, it may be a winter such as the previous year's where the phormiums died. You'll have to decide if the price is worth just one season.

Rule No. 8: Pick a garden style and stick with it. Cottage, formal, Asian or woodsy — the choices are too much like the dessert tray. I want to say, "One of each please." Sure, things might get chaotic, but why not experiment to find your own personal style? Now, there's a gardening rule to live by.

APRIL 17, 1997

3Bs OR NOT 3Bs — MULTILEVEL PLANNING IS THE ANSWER

Making a home for birds, bees, butterflies means creating shelter as well as food source

WHEN IT COMES TO NATURAL HABITAT, each creature has its specific needs. My cat The Perp, for example, believes her natural habitat includes an extremely soft mattress, a fluffy quilt and a cupboard well stocked with small and pricey tins of food.

But then, the needs of a very large and very spoiled cat are easily met with or without a garden. Not so with the three B's — birds, bees and butterflies.

The needs of these most welcome garden guests are not so precisely met, especially in an urban environment. Still, with a little artful attention to habitat, any garden, even a tiny one, can be made hospitable to a surprisingly diverse array of fluttery friends.

In today's conservation-minded society, there is no end to articles on how to attract wildlife to a garden. So why am I bothering to bring up the subject? Many articles are limited to one element — food. They helpfully describe berries, thistles and nectar-producing flowers and occasionally, in an expansive mood, also remind us to include water features.

From such articles, one gets the impression that a bright cottage flower garden surrounded by a picket fence is the ideal habitat. The picture is charming, but it's not accurate. If you want your garden visitors to do more than eat and run, you've got to think about shelter and space arrangement as well as food and water.

To convince the three B's to hang around,

A layered garden provides shelter, resting spots, nesting spaces and places for rearing new generations of birds, bees and butterflies.

you've got to provide cover for escape from predators (not every cat is so well-fed and sluggish as The Perp), shelter from weather extremes, perching and resting spots, and breeding and rearing spaces.

When it comes to shelter, a garden built in layers is the five-star hotel of habitats. A layered garden — different levels of plants, from trees to ground covers — is the most efficient way to build a diverse habitat in a small space.

Where space permits, include at least one large tree for an overall canopy, as well as smaller understory trees. On the other hand, in a small space, a canopy tree actually may be inhospitable to wildlife if it casts so much shade that nothing else will grow.

Whatever size trees and shrubs you can accommodate, be sure to include both evergreen and deciduous varieties. Conifers, such as cedar, fir, pine and juniper, are particularly important as shelter during winter months. Picket fences may be picturesque, but hedges provide precious habitat. In addition, they act as windbreaks, which is vital if you want to welcome butterflies.

Large twiggy hedges, such as laurel, are especially useful to birds year-round. On the other hand, dense hedges, such as trimmed boxwood, do not offer easy access and therefore afford little protection from predators. If you want to build a bird's street of dreams, plant hedges made up of a variety of shrubs, not pruned into formal shapes. And if some of those shrubs include thorns (e.g., *Rosa rugosa*), better still, because this adds even more protection.

Trees and shrubs aren't the only forms of cover. Butterflies, and many small birds, are happiest nesting and resting in piles of twigs and brush, so save some of that debris from last winter's storms. Nuthatches, flickers and woodpeckers are especially happy with dead tree limbs.

The arrangement of space is as important as the variety of plants when it comes to welcoming a diverse array of visitors. In nature, the greatest animal diversity often occurs in spaces known as "edges," that is, where two habitats come together, such as woods and a clearing or meadow and marsh.

There are a number of ways to replicate an edge in a garden. A stand of shrubs or small trees can simulate a thicket. A bog garden along the edge of a pond essentially becomes a marsh. And while many wildlife enthusiasts eschew manicured lawns in favor of wilder habitat, actually a small space of lawn can be the equivalent of a forest clearing. But big sweeping lawns tend to deter all but the ubiquitous robins. They're simply too open for timid visitors. Islands of flowers and shrubs will make them more wildlife friendly, and, if there's space, let some of the perimeter lawn go wild. Letting grass go to seed will be a bonus.

Unlike us, birds aren't put off by seedy housing.

APRIL 24, 1997

❧

SPRUCE UP THE GARDEN
Ornamentals and patio trees enhance an urban lot with grace and beauty

THERE IS MORE TO OWNING A HOUSE THAN paying a mortgage. We live in an old neighborhood where the ghosts of residents past hang on tenaciously. People would say to us, when we moved in, "Oh, you live in the Dahl house." It seemed as if we'd have to

A favorite crabapple accessorizes a pretty structure.

live here for about 100 years before people would stop referring to our house by the previous owners' name.

I found a way to speed up the process. In the eyes of the neighborhood, planting a garden was like a merit badge. You were awarded expedited ownership of your home. Of all the things you could do to make a home your own, planting a tree was the best.

The first tree I planted happened by accident. One morning I walked out and found an old plum tree in a disturbingly lateral position. We'd had no wind storm, no ice; the beast had simply keeled over.

Like many people, I have an urban lot, so the replacement had to be dainty. Also, I hadn't been smart enough to start gardening or to buy this home when I was 14, so I wanted something that wouldn't take a lifetime to fill out. That directed me to a group of trees that garden books fondly classify as "small ornamentals" or "patio trees."

I found the perfect tree for the spot among the crabapples. Now, about seven years later, I continue to adore this delicate little tree with its pleasing umbrella shape. It is a true multiple-season plant. In spring, it has delicate rosy buds that glow for weeks before bursting into pink popcorn. In autumn, it drips with reddish fruits about the size of large berries. In between, it requires no care, no special treatment.

Alas, I do not remember the cultivar name, and some varieties are susceptible to disease. But I saved an article from *Fine Gardening* that recommends the following disease-resistant selections: 'Adams', 'David', 'Donald Wyman', 'Indian Summer', 'Malus floribunda', 'Molten Lava', 'Prairie Fire' (outstanding fall color), 'Professor Sprenger', 'Red Jewel', 'Sugar Tyme', 'White Angel' and 'Zumi Calocarpa'.

Now, after this winter of our discontent, I am once again in the market for a small ornamental. I lost a ceanothus that, while technically a shrub, had gotten to be the size of a tree. So, I'm searching for the perfect little tree to fill an unexpected hole.

Among the small ornamental class, the hall of famers for Northwest gardens are Japanese maples, magnolias and dogwoods. You can't go wrong with these trees, with one exception. The American dogwood (*Cornus florida*) is prone to fungal diseases, so look for the Asian varieties (*Cornus kousa*).

If you already have these favorites, it may be time to expand your plant horizons. In selecting an ornamental tree, the first question to ask is what do you want out of it. If your garden peaks in spring, you may want a flowering tree. If you want to shore up your autumn garden, you'll want good foliage color.

It's also important to remember that both flowers and leaf color are fleeting, so above all, select a tree that has a pleasing shape and nice foliage when it isn't spring or fall. All of the following selections fill the bill and peak at 15 to 30 feet or grow so slowly beyond that they fit neatly into small gardens.

Small trees that have it both ways (spring flowers and good autumn color) include serviceberry (*Amelanchier*), hawthorne (*Crataegus*), Japanese snowbell (*Styrax japonica*), *Stewartia monadelpha*, *Stewartia pseudocamellia* and Persian parrotia (*Parrotia persica*). The latter three trees are truly four-season plants because they also have handsome bark that stands out in winter. If you live east of the Cascades, add redbud (*Cercis*) to your list. It will do fine in your area, but it doesn't really like the coastal maritime climate.

For showy spring flowers, it would be hard to beat the Chinese fringe tree (*Chionanthus virginicus*). This graceful, multistemmed tree smothers itself with white stars in spring. The silverbell, also called snowdrop (*Halesia tetraptera*), is another tree that flowers in spring and is multistemmed. It blends beautifully with rhododendrons.

If you're looking primarily for fall color, don't forget small maples other than Japanese maples (*Acer palmatum*). Three that glow in fall are the shrubby vine maple (*Acer circinatum*), Amur maple (*Acer ginnala*) and paperback maple (*Acer griseum*).

Another under-used fall beauty outside the maple family is the Franklin tree (*Franklinia alatamaha*). It turns a brilliant

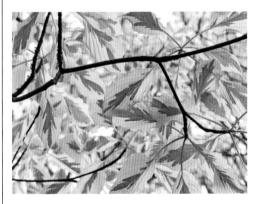

Cornus controversa *'Variegata'*.

orange-red in the fall after bearing camellia-like blossoms in late summer.

If you want to try something even more offbeat, here are two choices. The yellow wood (*Cladrastis lutea*) has a pleasing round shape with bright green leaves that turn buttery yellow in autumn. It will flower brilliantly, but may take several years.

Or to really be the envy of your neighborhood, plant a dove tree (*Davidia involucrata*). It is one of the most exquisite trees you can grow — if you are patient. The white blossoms, which may not appear for 10 years, are like the wings of doves.

APRIL 7, 1996

PETTICOATS FOR YOUR BORDERS

Underplant shrubs with low-growing perennials for a pretty effect. It's also a great way to keep weeds down.

I, FOR ONE, THINK SUCH THINGS AS SOULS, FAN-nies and earth should not be bared in public. Because I have minor credentials in only one of these areas, I will limit my opinions to earth, as in dirt.

Cottage gardeners long ago learned that the best way to keep weeds at bay and reduce watering is to pack plants in tightly. The rule is: no bare earth. Not only does this make maintenance easier, but the look is lush and dramatic.

But many gardeners do not have flower borders, or, if they do, only part of their garden is used for flowers. Drive down any city street and what you will see are shrubbery borders: lots of rhodies and azaleas, camellias, pieris and witch hazels.

More often than not, these lovely shrubs sit on bare ground with no underplanting, resembling nothing so much as elegant gowns with bare feet sticking out. It's time we tucked some petticoats underfoot. The tried and true ground covers — such as ajuga and vinca — are perfectly serviceable but a bit boring all by themselves.

By introducing some of the low-carpeting perennials in shrub borders, you can create something much more exciting, a veritable Persian carpet of color and texture.

Here are suggestions for both shade and sun. Most have a tendency to spread, which is desirable in a ground cover, but none is rampant in the extreme like the thug-like ribbon grass (*Phalaris*) or bishop's weed (*Aegopodium*).

Let's start with plants that thrive in shady, somewhat moist places, since many of our shrubs, especially rhodies, enjoy these conditions.

Alchemilla mollis: Lady's mantle is the perfect petticoat plant, soft and billowy, with froths of chartreuse flowers and pretty dew-catching leaves. It can go in sun, too, but prefers a little shade.

Bergenia: I've never understood why people consider begonias elite plants and turn up their noses at the peasanty bergenia, which resembles some varieties of begonia. The splendid broad-paddled leaves with ruby blushes are terrific for fluttering out beneath shrubs.

Brunnera macrophylla: Brunnera resembles forget-me-nots, but, while it does seed some, it won't drive you quite so mad by seeding all over the garden the way forget-me-nots do.

Convallaria majalis: Lily-of-the-valley is another spreader, but it's a sweet and sweetly

Huge hostas planted in front of a weeping red Japanese maple.

scented plant if you've got the room. The upright structure, rather like small iris, is a nice foil for mounding shrubs.

Corydalis: Corydalis forms a soft lacy mound, and both the yellow-flowered and blue-flowered varieties closely resemble dicentras in their delicacy. The blue-flowered varieties are a bit trickier to grow than the yellow *C. lutea*.

Dicentra formosa and *D. eximia*: The trouble-free dicentras have a delicate fernlike texture in their blue-green leaves. Flowers are normally rose, although some are white. These two varieties are mound forming and bloom much later and longer than the common bleeding heart, *D. spectabilis*.

Heuchera: Coral bells were a sweet little cottage garden plant that had little fanfare until the early 1990s when new varieties with brilliant foliage burst on the market. The

A delicate underplanting of ferns, Thalictrum *and* Persicaria bistorta *'Superba'.*

fabulous wine red leaves of 'Purple Palace' started things going, but now no end of choices exist, from silver-veined leaves to speckled pink and white leaves.

Hosta: They come in a zillion sizes and colors that range from blue green to gold lime, with lots of variegated choices as well. All have terrific foliage. Hostas are one of the easiest plants to grow, but they do need a vigilant slug patrol.

Lamium and *Lamiastrum*: Get past the ugly common name of dead nettle. These two closely related spreading plants are beauties. Well, the flowers aren't much to brag about, but grow them for the crinkly leaves veined and spattered with silvery white.

Pulmonaria: Lungwort is a beautiful clumping plant that is greatly underused. It has long-lasting blue or white flowers throughout spring and charming freckled foliage that remains attractive as long as it stays in the shade. The leaves scorch in sun.

The following are suitable understudy plants where you have a bright sunny border. Some plants, such as lady's mantle and bergenia, will do fairly well in either sun or shade.

Cranesbill geranium: Did I say lady's mantle is the perfect petticoat plant? Well cranesbill geraniums (the true perennials, not the pot plants) are in close competition for that appellation. These loosely rounded plants have lovely flowers in whites, pinks, mauves, purples and blues. It's common for the flowers to have exquisite veined patterns, depending on the variety.

Dianthus: Plant carnations and pinks with the caveat that they are not crazy about our acid soil. If they are to thrive, you need to add lime to the soil. Still, their blue-green, grassy leaves and spicy scented flowers may be worth the effort.

Euphorbia cyparissias: This is a low-growing euphorbia, just a foot high, but it has the same chartreuse flower bracts and gray-green leaves of taller varieties. It has a tendency to spread.

Lirope muscari: Lilyturf has a grassy leaf and somewhat resembles grape hyacinth. It flowers late in the season and is another of those plants with a wandering habit.

Persicaria bistorta 'Superba': Just to confuse you, this little plant with lavender drumstick-like flowers was sold previously as *Polygonum bistorta* 'Superbum'. It's a spreader, so plant it where it has room. Although a sun plant, it needs slightly moist soil.

Sedum: Many of the small succulents have a nice carpeting effect. 'Ruby Glow', just as the name suggests, is a beauty for color.

Tradescantia x *andersoniana*: Look for the 'x' indicating this is a hybrid spiderwort because the hybrids are not as invasive as the American native *T. virginiana*. Most flower nearly all summer in the blue-purple range and have attractive grassy foliage.

APRIL 16, 1998

SOWING SATIN AND LACE

An interplay of textures will add to the beauty of your garden, so pair heavy broad-leaved plants with fine and filmy foliage

IN OLDEN DAYS, WHEN DRESSES MERITED THE name gown, designers knew a thing or two about embellishment. A bit of airy lace was just the thing to accent and lighten the elegant but heavy drape of a magnificent gown.

Even the most fastidious gardener can sometimes suffer an invasion of the beautiful but noxious weed Spanish bluebells.

Think of the great broad-leaved plants as the sumptuous satins, the heavy brocades and the dark velvets of the garden. Now, let us tuck a tat of lace here and there to offset all this weightiness. There are certain plants that have the delicacy and filminess of lace. Some simply have deeply dissected leaves, while others are down-right thready.

Alone, the great broad-leaved plants are important. On their own, the delicate lace-leaved plants are pretty. Combine them and you have the makings of a great garden. The interplay of textures is sublime.

Ferns — of which there is a wide variety — are an obvious foil for large-leaved plants. They are vastly underused in Northwest gardens, perhaps because they are so common outside our gardens. But if ferns are an obvious choice to embroider dark corners, what about some other finely textured foliage that may not be so obvious?

There are several plants that you might not think of as foliage plants, because they generally are listed among perennials and judged on the merits of their flowers. Meadow rue (*Thalictrum*) is a perfect example. It has a froth of spring flowers, usually purple, that are nothing to write home about. But forget the flowers. It makes a perfectly splendid stand of airy leaves in sun or part shade.

T. aquilegiifolium, which grows to 2 or 3 feet, resembles the foliage of columbines. *T. rochebrunianum* is an understudy for maidenhair ferns and grows 3 to 5 feet. The similarly sized *T. speciosissimum* has bluish-green foliage.

For a lower growth of lacelike delicacy, there are several choices. Bleeding hearts (*Dicentra*) have charming flowers. But they could earn their place for their foliage alone. The most common, *D. spectabilis*, has the arcing wands dripping with the hearts that give the plant its name. A shade lover, it sometimes dies back during summer but will return the following year.

The flowers of the *D. formosa* are not as elegant, but its soft mounds of foliage are sturdier. It is also an Oregon native. The hybrid, *D.* 'Luxuriant', has especially lovely dark blue-green leaves and, for those who must have flowers, blooms all sum-

> *Think of the great broad-leaved plants as the sumptuous satins, the heavy brocades and the dark velvets of the garden.*

mer. All of the bleeding hearts are fond of moisture and grow between 1 and 2 feet tall.

Corydalis lutea is a cousin of the bleeding hearts and is a great mimic of maidenhair fern. It grows in low, soft, pillowy mounds and sends up dainty yellow flowers, although there is a rare, blue-flowered version to die for. (Check specialty nurseries for the latter.) It self-sows prettily in shady areas.

For a change of pace, and a thready, filmy quality, you'll find a star performer in the herb garden. Take common fennel (*Foeniculum vulgare*) out from among the herbs and plant it next to lilies or some other sparsely leaved plants. Look for the variety 'Purpurea' or bronze fennel. What a combination with white or pink lilies! Be warned: it self-sows. Pull young seedlings out early or they send tap roots to China. Fennels are sun-lovers and grow upright 3 to 5 feet.

If you want to be the first on your block with an offbeat plant, look for the fernleaf poppy (*Paeonia tenuifolia*). Its finely dissected leaves are as filmy as asparagus fern. It also has purple to red flowers and will do well in sun or part shade. It will reach about 2 feet.

Astilbes should be on anyone's list of great flowers. It also makes most lists of great foliage, making it one of the most perfect plants around, especially for shady gardens.

APRIL 15, 1994

❧

WRONG PLANT, RIGHT GARDENER

If a plant isn't robust where you've planted it, move the wimp or guillotine it

I HAVE ALWAYS HAD TROUBLE WITH THE WORD robust. In college, I covered a lecture on the French Revolution for the school paper. I subsequently wrote an article quoting the lector talking about some guy called Robust Pierre. A professor thought this was pretty funny and sent it into *The New Yorker*, so I can't say I've never been published in a major magazine.

Later, in an early job, I edited the word robust out of a technical report, thinking it referred only to personal health, not realizing it was also an economic term. I even, to my everlasting embarrassment, wrote a smug note in the margin saying improper use of term.

So it's no wonder that antipathy with the word carried over into my gardening. It took

> *There is a flip side of robust, the good side.*

me several years to figure out that the word robust in a plant description was a euphemism for invasive, thuglike and the creature that eats your garden.

I am reminded of this every year when we go through the annual rite of spring, pulling up the ribbon grass (*Phalaris*).

But I am increasingly aware that there is a flip side of robust, the good side. And that reminds me of a comment I heard on a visit to an English garden several years ago, which I have recounted before. Nevertheless, it is a point that bears repeating.

We were admiring the beauty of the garden, and one of our party asked the hostess how she went about the design. She smiled and said, "I simply put plants where they are happiest." For me, this was one of those little light-bulbs-going-on-in-your-head moments.

I realized then that a garden full of plants at their healthiest, or most robust, will look grand regardless of less-than-perfect design. Similarly, a beautifully designed garden will never reach its potential if the plants aren't at their best.

That's possibly why there is a collection of books and articles focusing on right plant/ right place themes. Such books are helpful as guides to what does well in assorted soil types, light conditions and climate zones. Still, they may not be detailed enough because each individual garden has microclimates and assorted conditions that can affect a plant's health. At times, temperatures can vary by as much as 20 degrees within an urban plot if, for example, conditions range from an exposed windy area to a south-facing stone or stucco wall. Most of us don't have those extremes, but even a few degrees can make the difference in survival for one of those tropical glamour plants we've become so fond of.

Over the years, I've had a growing suspicion that we'd be better off if we looked less to books for design and more to our own plots to help us with design. Instead of imposing a plan rigidly, we should listen to what our garden is telling us about where plants are happiest.

Admittedly, the whole process can be baffling. You'll have a plant so beautifully robust in one place that you go out and buy another of its kind. Then you plant it in another place that for all the world appears to have similar conditions, and the plant turns out to be a total wimp.

There may be a logical reason. The second plant might have come root-bound or diseased. But often it's infuriatingly mysterious. Your plant just doesn't like That Place. For this reason, I'm big on moving wimpy-looking plants around until they do find their spot. Sometimes all this moving just makes a weak plant weaker, but other times there's a Clark-Kent-to-Superman transformation.

Personally, I've become increasingly ruthless about plants. Robust stays. Wimpy goes. This may sound revolutionary, but Pierre would be proud of me.

APRIL 28, 2005

ALL FOR ONE
Collecting new hybrids grows quickly into obsession

MY NEIGHBOR ROSEMARY IS COLLECTING cultivars of coneflowers (*Echinacea*) this year. I like it when she gets into something new because I enjoy the hunt. The other day I spotted an *Echinacea* 'Green Envy', which I bought for her. Five minutes later I went back to the plant table because I thought what if hers turns out really great? I'll regret not having one. So of course I had to buy another for me.

If the plant comes true to the picture on its label, it will have light green petals with a flush of pink near the cone. Remember when coneflowers were just purple? Today they come in several hues, including bright red and yellow (witness new introductions 'Tomato Soup' and 'Mac 'n' Cheese').

Often, when hybridizers take a common plant and suddenly produce uncommon hybrids, the need to try them all takes over. This happened to me with those homespun coral bells that I first grew for their flowers. Then, one day a purple-leaved coral flower appeared on the market.

It wasn't the first new hybrid, but

There's no such thing as too many hostas.

dilettante who toys with one fad or another. True collectors really focus on a species, do their homework, keep records and know that taxonomy has nothing to do with April 15.

In England, both public and private gardens host what are known as "national plant collections." These are sponsored by the National Council for the Conservation of Plants and Gardens, which was established in 1978. These gardens have areas devoted to a single genus, with a display of the multiple species and varieties. There are now about 650 national collections.

I don't think we have anything similar in the United States in terms of a sponsored system, but there are collections in some gardens, usually botanical gardens. For example, the U.S. National Arboretum has an azalea collection. And, of course, there are rose gar-

Heuchera micrantha 'Palace Purple' was the one that started the "purple rush." Suddenly nursery shelves were bursting with redder and blacker hybrids, and some with marbled leaves. Next came golden, chartreuse and orange leaves.

Before I knew it, I wanted them all. But I couldn't keep up, and the golden varieties didn't do as well in my garden.

But I am not a true collector, simply a

> *I am not a true collector,*
> *simply a dilettante who toys with*
> *one fad or another.*

dens, but those don't count because, well, rose growers aren't always aware there are actually other plants.

Years ago I attended a lecture by Joe Eck,

who, along with Wayne Winterrowd, owns and writes prolifically about their garden at North Hill in Vermont. Eck recalled a visit by a world-famous gardener. She took one look at their garden and sniffed, "Well, I guess you can have too many hostas after all."

Of course, the perfect response was to say, "It's a collection."

Finally, if you want to know where you stand on the collection issue, you can use the measuring stick created by my friends Dick Bach and Virginia Burney. They say: One is a find, two is a pair, three is a set, four is a collection and five is an obsession. Ah, thank goodness we just have four cats.

APRIL 16, 2009

READ BETWEEN THE LINES
Know what those plant tags are really saying to keep garden bullies at bay

T HERE SEEMS TO BE A SERIOUS OMISSION IN most plant descriptions on nursery labels and in botanical books. It's easy to find out about a plant's mature size, cold resistance, light and water needs, flower color and other important characteristics.

But few descriptions reveal much about a plant's general decorum. Does a plant have wandering ways? Is it a bully that will trample its neighbors? It's important to know whether a plant is mannerly or if it's an out-and-out thug.

Of course, thuggery is in the eye of the beholder. One gardener may call a rampant spreader a beast, while another may find the same plant salvation for a difficult hillside.

A cottage gardener may adore the way certain plants self-sow, while someone with formal beds may view the same plants with alarm. Similarly, the gardener with room for generous borders will appreciate a fine drift of yellow loosestrife (*Lysimachia punctata*). But someone with a tiny city garden would find this robust perennial threatening.

Invasive nature is not in itself a crime. But failure to adequately inform gardeners of a plant's wanton disposition possibly is. I'm reminded of this each year as we perform our annual rite of digging up ribbon grass (*Phalaris*).

This is not a treatise against aggressive plants. Many can be stunning and important additions to a garden. It is, however, a plea for information that allows us to select and use aggressive plants properly. For example, a plant that will run roughshod in the garden could make a spectacular accent in a pot.

RED-FLAG WORDS

These shouldn't necessarily scare you off when you see them on a tag; the idea is to use them as signals to do further research.

rampant grower
aggressive
spreading
tendency to . . . creeping
robust
generous self-sower
noxious (this should scare you off)
pernicious (ditto)
prolific (when not referring to bloom)
vigorous
naturalizes
colonizes
suckering
runners
weedy
creeping habit
seeder

PLANTS WITH WANDERING WAYS

Aegopodium podagraria — bishop's weed, ground elder

Angelica archangelica

Bamboo (only running types)

Convolvulus arvensis — field bindweed, wild morning glory

Fallopia japonica — Japanese knotweed (formerly *Polygonum cuspidatum*)

Hedera helix — English ivy

Houttuynia cordata 'Chameleon' — chameleon plant

Linaria vulgaris — common toadflax

Lysimachia punctata — yellow loosestrife

Lythrum salicaria, L. virgatum — purple loosestrife (avoid this noxious plant)

Mentha — mint

Petasites japonicus — giant butterbur

Phalaris arundinacea — ribbon grass

Ranunculus repens — creeping buttercup

PLANTS WITH UNRULY TENDENCIES

These have a tendency to spread or self-sow, but most are garden-worthy if kept in control.

Acanthus spinosus — bear's breeches

Achillea millefolium — yarrow

Alchemilla mollis — lady's mantle

*A classic example of "Do as I say and not as I do," this border features the pretty but highly invasive bishop's weed (*Aegopodium podagraria*) as a variegated ground cover.*

Borago officinalis — borage
Campanula persicifolia — bellflower
Centranthus ruber — Jupiter's beard
Convallaria majalis — lily-of-the-valley
Euphorbia cyparissias — cypress spurge
Euphorbia dulcis
Euphorbia griffithii
Foeniculum vulgare — fennel
Galium odoratum — sweet woodruff
Iris pseudacorus — yellow flag iris
Lunaria annua — honesty, money plant
Lysimachia clethroides — gooseneck loose-
strife
Macleaya — plume poppy
Myosotis scorpioides — forget-me-not
Persicaria bistorta — knotweed
Persicaria virginiana — tovara
Physalis alkekengi — Chinese lantern
Stachys byzantina — lamb's ears
Symphytum — comfrey
Verbena bonariensis
Viola — violet

APRIL 5, 2001

❧

FAITHFUL FOLIAGE
Leafy interest carries on as flowers bloom and fade

At this time of year, it's difficult to think about foliage, what with May flowers about to burst and the largess of June just around the corner. But let me make a case for foliage plants.

When I started gardening, my fantasy was an English cottage garden. That, of course, was in the Dark Ages, back before we'd been educated that we could have our own "natural" or Northwest style. Anyway, I managed a reasonable triumph by June. The roses rip-

ened, the poppies popped and the delphiniums soared in that beginners' luck way that has never, ever happened since.

Then after about three weeks, I found my garden slumping, although it recovered somewhat when high summer and the daylilies emerged. In each down period, my knee-jerk reaction was to race to the nearest nursery and load up on annuals. Does this sound familiar? By July, of course, the pickings were mighty slim, and for a while I became the nicotiana queen.

That's when I began to pay attention to what I was seeing in my trips to England. Gardens there were heavily into foliage plants. So I came home and began inserting more leafy interest into my own plantings.

It made sense because, like England, we in the Northwest enjoy a luxuriously long garden season — February through October at the least. That's great, but it can also mean our gardens tend to emulate a Trail Blazers season, with alternating hot streaks and nasty slumps. After all, the average perennial flowers only about 10 days.

Enter attractive foliage. What better way to hold a garden together through the thick and thin of flowers? I certainly don't limit myself to foliage plants, but I do place far greater emphasis on plants with interesting leaves these days. That doesn't exclude many great flowering plants. A number have handsome foliage, with iris, peonies and astilbe cases in point.

But foliage offers more than consistency. In particular, it has given me a great appreciation for the importance of texture in a garden. Leaves come in all sizes and shapes — swords, rosettes, paddles, threads, hearts and many more. A plant with big, broad leaves can give focus to an otherwise fuzzy jumble

*Japanese forest grass (*Hakonechloa macra 'Aureola'*) with the ornamental onion* Allium christophii.

of plants. Similarly, lacy foliage is a fine foil to broad leaves.

And some supremely architectural plants, such as New Zealand flax and cannas, amount to living garden sculpture.

FAVORITE FOLIAGE PLANTS FOR TEXTURE

Acanthus mollis (bears' breeches)
Alchemilla mollis (lady's mantle)
Asarum (wild ginger)
Canna
Ferns
Geranium renardii
Grasses/sedges
Gunnera
Hosta
Kirengeshoma

Ligularia
Petasites
Phormium (New Zealand flax)
Rodgersia

FAVORITE FOLIAGE PLANTS FOR COLOR

Athyrium niponicum 'Pictum' (Japanese painted fern)
Berberis thunbergii f. *atropurpurea* (barberry)
Carex elata 'Aurea' (golden sedge)
Cotinus coggygria (smoke bush)
Hakonechloa (Japanese woodland grass)
Heuchera (coral bells)
Iris laevigata 'Variegata'

APRIL 24, 2003

WATER WISE
Minor watering adjustments won't cramp gardening style

UH OH, THAT UGLY WORD "DROUGHT" IS starting to sneak into gardeners' conversations. I overheard it just the other day. "Should I even start a new garden this year?" asked one person. "Maybe this isn't the year to invest in a lot of new plants," another said. "Am I limited to one of those dryscaping gardens that looks as if it should be in New Mexico?" wondered another.

It's too early to panic. I, for one, am not about to restrain my annual bout of plant lust, at least not too much. Nor am I about to limit my plant choices to drought-resistant plants. And I'm certainly not ready to replace my vegetable patch with a cactus farm.

But I'm going to be sensible. We don't know if there will be restraints on water use this summer. But we do know that it is always smart to be water-wise. Conserving our resources makes sense, in good water years and bad. These 30 water-wise tips are a great place to start.

WATERING TECHNIQUES

1. Except for new plants, hold off beginning your watering regime as long as possible so that roots are forced to go deep for water. Deep-rooted plants resist drought.
2. When you do begin watering, water deeply and less frequently to maintain deep roots.
3. Water in the morning or evening when you won't lose so much water to evaporation, and don't water when it's windy.
4. Match watering equipment to watering areas to avoid overlap or, worse, watering sidewalks.
5. Put in drip irrigation where mass sprinkling isn't needed.
6. Put in automatic timers, because everyone forgets to turn off the water on occasion.
7. Use shut-off nozzles for hand watering and washing cars. A running hose uses about 100 gallons of water every 20 minutes.
8. Don't use water like a broom. Sweep driveways, terraces and sidewalks.

PLANT CHOICES

9. Add more native plants. They have proved they can withstand the region's weather extremes.
10. As a general rule, plants with silver or bluish foliage and felty leaves have Mediterranean origins and thrive in low-water conditions.
11. Aromatic herbs are generally drought-resistant. This would be a great year to start an herb garden.

12. Plants with fleshy leaves such as succulents need relatively little water and make great pot plants during dry summers.
13. In general, hardy ornamental grasses are good choices to withstand drought. They may die back in extreme dry conditions, but usually come back once moist conditions return.

LAWNS

14. Lawns need about 1 inch of water a week (or every three days in very hot weather). The Portland Water Bureau recommends the tuna can method as a test. Place empty cans at various places to gauge how long it takes to water to a depth of 1 inch. (Our cat, The Perp, recommends you put out a full can of tuna, but ignore her.)
15. Keep lawns dethatched and aerated to promote water absorption.

FLOWER AND SHRUB BEDS

16. Add lots of organic material to the soil. Water goes twice as far when the soil is loose and friable.
17. Use mulches to control evaporation and maintain even temperatures.
18. Keep beds weeded because weeds compete for water.
19. Use balanced fertilizers that include potassium to promote deep root growth.

POTTED PLANTS

20. Put potted plants inside another pot for insulation and to cut down evaporation.
21. Use nonporous containers, especially on small plants and hanging plants, to cut down moisture loss.
22. Group potted plants together to increase humidity.

23. Use a few big pots instead of lots of little potted plants. The smaller the pot, the more often it must be watered.
24. Add a commercial wetting agent (polymer) to potting soil to retain moisture.

LANDSCAPING

25. Limit lawn to play and walking areas. Substitute ground covers, which are less thirsty, in other areas that normally would be lawn.
26. Incorporate "hardscaping" into your design, such as attractive paved and decked areas. Gravel is an inexpensive alternative in work and play areas.
27. Use the oasis planting method. Group thirsty plants in one area so that you can water efficiently.
28. Plant trees that give dappled, not heavy shade. Lawns and even most flowering plants do well in dappled shade and need far less water.
29. Wind is drying, so put windbreaks around areas that need frequent watering, such as vegetable gardens. These can be fences or living barriers, such as hedges.
30. Keep half to two-thirds of your pond covered with floating plants to hold down evaporation. This is also great protective cover for fish.

APRIL 26, 2001

❧

TWEAKS BY THE YARD
Minor adjustments get the garden back on track

I HAVE FRIENDS WHO HAVE A LITTLE COURT-yard off their kitchen. It's no bigger than the average condo terrace. The area was pretty but not exciting. But then they installed a three-tiered fountain in the courtyard.

If I'd seen the fountain by itself, I'm sure I would have thought it too big for this very small area. I would have been wrong. Yes, the fountain dominates, but entirely successfully. It's a marvelous focal point viewed from the house. When the French doors are open, you hear the lovely music of cascading water. In one stroke, the space has gone from merely pretty to spectacular.

If your garden is looking a little tired, don't jump to the conclusion that you need to re-landscape or embark on a major project. Sometimes all it takes is a single — albeit bold — stroke, such as my friends' fountain, to transform a space. Not all changes have to be costly. Here are some ideas to perk up a garden that's gone a bit limp.

Practice paint power. I've seen gardens turned instantly charming by the addition of purple paint on a gate or sky blue on planter boxes or barn red on trellises or those wooden tepee-like plant supports. Robin's-egg blue is particularly smashing on formerly white wicker or gazebos.

Add cluster clout. If you like one ornament, get several more, but keep the number odd so the grouping looks natural rather than symmetrical. Clustering adds pizazz to pots, ornaments and, sigh, even pink flamingoes.

Get a little edgy. Defining edges is an instant way to pull a slightly out-of-focus garden back into focus. You can edge planting beds and paths with anything from bricks to boxwood. Rocks work in woodsy gardens, and those cute low fences are at home in cottage gardens.

Make a grand entrance. The folks across the street from me have replaced their straight cement front walk with a gently curving path

A grand entrance is one option, hinting at a secret garden beyond.

paved with stone. It's transformed the entire front, turning it from a yard into a garden.

Apply true grit. Got an ugly cracked cement patio or walkway, but can't afford stone paving? Just edge the area with stones or bricks and cover the concrete with soft crunchy gravel. A good size is quarter-minus.

Lighten up. If camellias and rhododendrons have gotten out of hand and now amount to big dark blobs when not in bloom, turn them into small multi-stemmed ornamental trees by limbing them up. Remove lower branches and some stems, but leave a number of stems proportionate to the top of the shrub.

Discover an island. If a big, hulking tree dominates your yard and doesn't really relate to anything else, make it a focal point by mounding an island around it. Pile on good topsoil in a natural shape around the tree, but keep the area around the trunk clear and at its original soil level. Plant your new island bed with shade plants.

Rearrange the furniture. Think of garden furniture as functional ornaments. A bench, a couple of chairs or a small table and chairs can create an instant intimate space. The secret is not to put them in the obvious place, on the back deck. Look for a sheltered place under a tree, carve out a small space in a flower bed or tuck them under an arbor.

P.S. This works better if you're not using stackable plastic chairs.

Break the mold. Contrast adds drama. If your garden is a series of pleasant mounding shapes, change the pace by adding a striking columnar shape (perhaps a conifer) or a stand of springy grass or an architectural plant with fantastic leaves.

Lose some weight. If something's a continual challenge, such as a tree that nothing grows under or a shrub that's too big for its space, grit your teeth and get rid of it. It's remarkable how some deft editing can make a difference.

APRIL 18, 2002

❧

LIST SPROUTS TO MORE THAN TWO DOZEN

The old standbys are personal choices for an ideal garden

REMEMBER THE GAME IN LIT CLASS? IF YOU could take only 10 books to a desert island, which would you take?

Well, forget the desert island. If you were on a nice fertile bit of island, which 10 plants would you take?

Gentle Reader — as Miss Manners so politely puts it — I'd love to hear your choices.

I tried mine. I flunked. I couldn't hold the list to 10. I couldn't even get down to 20. The best I could do was 24. In looking over my list, I learned something about myself. I'm as common as garden dirt.

Oh, I like "collectible" and rare plants, but when push comes to shovel, I'll take mostly the old standards to my island. Here is my list, in alphabetical order.

Alchemilla mollis: Edge paths with the perennial known as lady's mantle for an instant English-garden look.

Allium giganteum: This bulb looks like ET before it blooms. Then one day it bursts into a giant purple ball of stars.

Astilbe: The feathery plumes of this perennial ignite the shade with color. They also dry beautifully to a burnished russet and last into autumn.

Callicarpa: Beautyberry shrub decks itself out in striking, opalescent purple berries throughout the winter.

Cornus kousa: If you could have only one tree, it should be a dogwood, with its graceful shape and apple-green leaves. Oh, yes, don't forget the spring blossoms and autumn color.

Cotinus coggygria: Named smoke bush for its midsummer cloud of frothy hairs. Choose 'Purpureus' for its smoldering burgundy leaves.

Delphinium: I have a rule. Anything that needs lots of attention doesn't grow in my garden. The stately blue spires of delphiniums, which need staking, are the exception.

Dicentra spectabilis: The arcing stems of

Astilbe *'Bridal Veil'*.

the perennial bleeding heart are the epitome of old-fashioned grace.

Digitalis (foxglove): This biennial may be my favorite flower. It's also the murder weapon in one of Agatha Christie's mysteries.

Fritillaria meleagris: The checkered lily is a delicate woodland bulb with extraordinary veining that gives the flower a distinctive checkered pattern.

Helianthus annus: Come on, now; you can't have a garden without a sunflower.

Hemerocallis: Some call the daylily the perfect perennial. It thrives in sun or shade, hard clay and with dire neglect.

Hosta sieboldiana: The giant quilted blue-green leaves will turn you on to foliage.

Iris pallida: Who cares if it flowers (which it does very prettily); the fine-striped foliage is a show in itself.

Jasminum nudiflorum: Nothing is cheerier on a blustery January day than the butter-yellow stars covering the bare leaves of winter jasmine, a small shrub.

Lavandula: A garden without lavender has no soul.

Lonicera: Nothing sweetens the summer air like the common honeysuckle. Hummingbirds love it.

Macleaya cordata: The plume poppy is the strangest member of the poppy family. Imagine 8-foot stalks topped with feathery plumes that don't need staking.

Malus: Long before the crabapple's blossoms pop open, they hang pendulous like ruby-tinged tears.

Nandina domestica: Heavenly bamboo isn't a bamboo at all. It is a winsome small shrub with delicate leaves and great clusters of berries that make wonderful sprays in Christmas wreaths.

Nicotiana sylvestris: This is the most dramatic of the flowering tobaccos (annuals), a 5-foot-tall candelabra of flowers.

Ribes sanguineum: Flowering currant blossoms with luminescent rose-tinged clusters in early spring.

Rudbeckia fulgida: Billowing mounds of old-fashioned black-eyed Susans take summer into autumn.

Saxifraga x urbium: Legend has it that this starry-white rock-garden flower was the first thing to sprout in bombed-out London after World War II. That's why it's called London pride.

APRIL 23, 1993

FLOCK OF FOLLIES
Flamingos strut into my garden

I AM OFFICIALLY ANCIENT. NO, I DIDN'T HAVE another birthday, and no, I didn't just get my first query from a waitress asking if I wanted the senior menu. That happened long ago. What finally put me over the hill, if ever I was at a peak, was losing my glasses.

Oh, I've misplaced them plenty of times, but always found them after exploring the usual places. This time, they were missing in action for more than 24 hours, and it was my husband, Ted, who found them. Worse yet, they were practically under my nose.

This — officially being ancient, that is — has gotten me to thinking how aging has changed my attitudes about my garden. I'd like to think that I have maintained my sense of adventure and flexibility to change. But deep in my heart of hearts, I suspect I may have just gotten more foolish.

Remember my gnome phase? Well, I've

gone and done something even more over the top. The other day I bought pink flamingos at a nursery. Not just two, but eight! I, who have maligned the poor creatures over the years as the epitome (or do I mean the nadir?) of unnatural selection.

I blame my purchase on the internationally famous Atlanta-based garden designer Ryan Gainey. Years ago, I saw a picture of his garden. He had a whole flock of flamingos. Somehow a flock seemed pretty funny, whereas a mere two seemed tacky. So that is my defense, although I realize it probably won't stand up in the Court of Good Taste.

Somehow a flock seemed pretty funny, whereas a mere two seemed tacky.

So where will they go? We have a little spot against the back fence deeply shaded by large rhododendrons. Not much grows under there, so Doug the Wonder Guy cleared out a little space and put a bench there. The flock will be grazing in this area, and I'm hoping the shade will tone down their raging pinkness. Right now they are stacked on a bench looking neon bright, and I'm sure anything that florid must be emitting radiation.

We will call the little area something like the Dell of Dubious Taste or the Grotto of Ghastly Excess, just so everyone knows the intent is humor. Wink, wink. And, yes, I know if you have to explain it, it probably doesn't work.

I was with my friend Denise when I picked them up. She takes me to my chemo treatments, and on the way home we reward ourselves with a visit to a nursery. We have been friends for at least 40 years, so I knew she wouldn't be overtly judgmental. But as we neared my house, she asked very carefully what DTWG would think of them, so I sort of had a clue that she was thinking maybe I'd gone over the top. She's right, of course.

When we hauled them out of the car, Jimmy the painter kind of chuckled. DTWG, on the other hand, had his usual stoic, polite face on as he helped me carry them to the back. But once back in the Shelter of Shame, I noticed he had gathered all the faux frogs from the garden and positioned them to stare at the bench.

So, I thought, ha, he's not one to talk about taste. Even Jimmy said he didn't feel comfortable sitting on the bench with all those frogs staring at him. I, on the other hand, felt quite at home with all this foolishness. It's a comfortable bench back where it is shady and moist and dark. I think it will be quite lovely to sit there on a hot day surrounded by beasts faux and real.

I do realize that many of you will not buy all this rationalization and are thinking, "Good grief, first the woman had gnomes and now flamingos. What next?" I'm kind of wondering that too, and it's a little scary.

MAY 21, 2009

SIREN CALL
Turn away from spring's temptations

IT'S EASY TO BE SEDUCED. THOSE NURSERY plants with nodding bells of flowers, rays of daisy petals and tender little rosettes are beckoning. It's sooooo. . . . But wait, it's only May, and there are at least five, count 'em,

Who can resist a delicately-colored iris, even if it doesn't fit your garden plan?

five magnificent months of garden weather ahead. The clever gardener will start selecting plants for the well-paced garden that has something going for it month after month.

Alas, this takes a substantial degree of planning and discipline, qualities that aren't easy to conjure up in the throes of plant lust.

Left to our own devices, most of us can barely resist planting the spectacular May or June garden. After all, didn't we grow up on pictures of the picket-fenced plot brimming with fragrant roses, heartbreakingly blue delphiniums, spunky poppies, cheerful foxgloves, stately iris and . . . need I go on?

In gardening-challenged regions of the country, which is most everywhere outside the Northwest, this sentimental May-June focus makes sense. There seem to be about five minutes between the last snow storm and the onset of the kind of heat and humidity that drives people indoors to dark, air-conditioned corners where they sip iced tea and dream of Alaskan cruises.

But ours is a gloriously long gardening season, which is why we must resist the urge to load up on every blossoming beauty we meet. We need to be strong and take a sec-

ond look at the ugly duckling, flowerless seedlings we were about to pass up. They may look drab now, but chances are they will blossom into swans in July, August, September, even October.

To plan for a long blooming season, check out the accompanying list. But treat it as a rough guideline of what blooms when. Gardens are like babies; they don't all walk and talk at the same time. Varying conditions and just plain idiosyncrasies can affect bloom schedules.

For example, my mother lives in Portland's southwest hills, and her flowers bloom as much as three weeks later than those in my Southeast Portland garden, even though they sometimes have been divided from the same mother plant. The difference is altitude.

On the other hand, I have friends in hilly areas whose plants mature earlier than mine. That's because in terracing their gardens, they filled in with loads of loose, compost-rich soil. So, despite the elevation, the soil warms up earlier than my own icky clay, which seems to neutralize any compost I add.

It's also a good idea to keep notes of what's abloom and when. This will help you figure out if bloom gaps exist so you'll know where to concentrate your plant selection for next year. My gap used to be the whole month of July. After the great flush of spring bloom, I'd have a few weeks of down time until the rudbeckias, and asters kicked in.

Once I figured this out, I zeroed in on plants that bloom in July as well as plants that provide foliage color. Now, I'm working at selecting plants that push the garden into October, because (gloat, gloat), it's not unusual for us to have fine weather at a time when the rest of the country is scraping frost off windshields.

MID-SUMMER BLOOMERS

Perennials: *Acanthus, Achillea* (yarrow), *Astilbe, Astrantia, Aruncus* (goat's beard), *Campanula, Coreopsis, Eryngium, Filipendula, Gaillardia, Hemerocallis* (daylily), *Kniphofia* (red hot poker), *Liatris* (gayfeather), *Ligularia, Lilium* (lily), *Lychnis* (campion), *Macleaya, Malva, Monarda* (bee balm), *Penstemon, Phlomis, Phlox, Rodgersia, Salvia, Verbascum, Veronica.*

Shrubs and vines: *Cistus* (rock rose), *Clematis* varieties, hardy fuchsias, *Hebe, Lavatera, Lonicera* (honeysuckle), *Passiflora* (passion flower), *Philadelphus, Solanum* (potato vine), *Spiraea japonica.*

LATE-SUMMER BLOOMERS

Perennials: *Crocosmia, Echinacea* (purple coneflower), *Echinops* (globe thistle), *Eupatorium, Helianthus, Heliopsis* (false sunflower), Japanese anemone, *Lobelia cardinalis* (cardinal flower), *Rudbeckia* (black-eyed Susan), *Solidago* (goldenrod), *Verbena bonariensis.*

Shrubs and vines: *Abelia, Caryopteris, Clematis* varieties, *Hibiscus syriacus* (rose of Sharon), *Hydrangea, Hypericum, Perovskia* (Russian sage).

LATE-SUMMER INTO FALL BLOOMERS

Perennials: *Aconitum* (monkshood), *Aster, Boltonia asteroides, Chrysanthemum, Cimicifuga* (bugbane), *Helenium,* hardy hibiscus, *Kirengeshoma, Sedum, Tricyrtis* (toad lily), several ornamental grasses.

Shrubs and vines: *Clematis*

MAY 15, 1997

UPSTART SHRUBS

Stage a daring border raid

CONVENTIONAL WISDOM USED TO BE THAT shrubs were for giving our gardens structure and backbone. The idea was that they would fade gracefully into the background to frame the "important" plants, which of course were perennials and annuals.

Not so in today's bolder garden. With new and newly popular cultivars available, it's hard to think of shrubs as mere background. Today's shrubs, with their dazzling colored and variegated foliage and sculptural leaves, aren't about to move meekly to the back of the bed.

This presents some challenges. Shrubs aren't as easy to move as flowers, so it pays to put a little thought into placement. Using shrubs artfully is more than a matter of plunking them down where you have space or, as is most traditional, girdling the foundation.

Here's how to use them to your best advantage:

As mixers and fillers. The mixed border, shrubs combined with flowers, is definitely more interesting, possibly because it replicates the layered look of nature. But select rounded or vase-shaped shrubs that are soft and billowing. Stiff, woody shrubs generally don't mix well unless they are intentionally and skillfully used as a sculptural statement

To create harmony. When shrubs with similarly colored foliage are repeated throughout a garden, they provide consistency, pulling disparate colors together. A repeated theme may be just the thing for giving an otherwise slightly confused garden polish and sophistication.

To emphasize color. Shrubs with variegated leaves and colorful stems and veining

Flowing spirea combines well with strappy daylilies.

make brilliant echoes for the colors of neighboring flowers. Imagine gold-rimmed leaves next to a golden flower or a crimson-stemmed shrub as a foil for red flowers.

To bridge seasonal gaps. With the Northwest's long growing season, it's hard to keep flower beds looking prime month after month. Most perennials bloom only two or three weeks. Shrubs, particularly those with colored foliage, will make a constant display.

> *Using shrubs artfully is more than a matter of plunking them down where you have space.*

To provide focal points. A columnar shrub, such as certain conifers, or a topiaried shrub, such as boxwood, can be a delightful exclamation point in an otherwise run-on-sentence of flowers. Just don't overdo the punctuation.

As sculpture. Use an elegantly shaped shrub, which has come by its shape naturally or by judicious pruning, as a piece of living sculpture. Place it where it will be a focal point and can be enjoyed from more than one side. Sculptural shrubs can be stand-alone specimens in lawns.

To suggest transitions. A pair of small ball-shaped shrubs at each side of an entry to a path make a welcoming gateway. A conical shrub is graceful way to mark the corner of a flower bed.

TEN CHOICE MIXER SHRUBS

1. *Berberis thunbergii* 'Bagatelle'. Barberry with deep red leaves, small shrub
2. *Buxus sempervirens* 'Graham Blandy'. Boxwood with green, columnar form
3. *Cotinus coggygria* 'Royal Purple'. Purple-leaved smoke bush
4. *Hydrangea macrophylla* 'Preziosa'. Red-tinged leaves, small shrub
5. *Hypericum inodorum* 'Elstead'. Shrubby Saint John's wort with red-tinged leaves
6. *Lonicera nitida* 'Baggesen's Gold'. Golden-foliaged box honeysuckle
7. *Physocarpus opulifolius* 'Diablo'. Ninebark with reddish leaves
8. *Sambucus nigra* 'Guincho Purple'. Elder with deep purple leaves
9. *Spiraea japonica* 'Goldflame'. Gold leaves
10. *Viburnum opulus* 'Nana'. Green, crinkly textured leaves

MAY 18, 2000

SPRING FLING
Discipline takes a back seat when traveling by plantmobile

MY FRIEND CARLENE ANNOUNCED THE other day that we had to go to the nursery because she needed a clematis. After all, she said, she only had four. "Needed" is the operative word here, as in "needed" chocolate.

Those of you who have been infected with plant lust will understand perfectly. Where I work, there has been a lot of "needing" this past spring. We have needed to go to the nursery on our lunch hour several times, and we have needed to make journeys to plant sales on weekends.

> *Those of you who have been infected with plant lust will understand perfectly.*

My friend Cheri, who was married in my garden last year, just bought a new house and is especially needy. This is pretty evident in the way she bounds out of Carlene's plant-mobile at a nursery and fairly flaps her wings in euphoria, squealing, "Oh, I have to have this." This, from someone who is a perfect lady at the office.

Another friend, Judy, put her house with a charming-but-small yard up for sale and found an acreage in the country because she needed more room to plant. Christy, a new friend, has joined us in the plantmobile excursions and has needed plants so much that the fact that she has to carry them home on MAX has not deterred her.

Our needs have been so paramount that last year Carlene talked her husband, Mike, into buying a plantmobile about the size of the Queen Mary that has come equipped with plant racks in the back. I suppose the dealer thinks of them as something silly, like racks for grocery bags, but we know better.

Even the magnificent plantmobile has not met all our needs lately, despite the fact that Mike obligingly removes the back seats so we can cram in more plants. When we went to the Clackamas County Master Gardeners' plant sale, for example, we actually needed to have to other friends come along in a pickup. This was fortunate since it turned out we all bought trellises (this is what clematis can lead you to).

Obviously, what is needed here is a set of rules to bring order to those of us with no discipline. I decided to jot down what I thought would be reasonable rules for buying plants, and I recommend them highly.

1. Do not buy any new plants until you have planted all the ones you bought on your last outing.
2. Do not buy more plants than will fit in your car.
3. Know where a plant will go before you buy it.
4. Never get in line at the cashier station, then turn around to go fetch a new plant that you saw in someone else's cart.
5. Never delude yourself that you are really taking that second plant for a friend.

Do I follow these rules? Let's just say that if this were a pass-fail test I'd be stuck in first grade.

Fortunately, plant lust is seasonal, holding us in its thrall mainly in the spring. In fact, the other day, just before going out with a friend to visit some open gardens, I made the following statement to Doug the Wonder Boy, who was slaving away in my garden. "You will be happy to know that I am through buying plants for the season."

Being a polite young man, he merely rolled his eyes. "No, really," I said. "I'm a clump buyer. I buy lots of plants in spring, but that's it." A couple of hours later he had the discretion to hold his face fairly immobile when I returned with two flats of plants.

All I can say is that only two of them were clematis.

MAY 30, 2002

SOCIAL CLIMBERS
Showy vines will grab your attention

VINES ARE HOT. YOU CAN TELL THAT BY the growing clumps of clematis at our favorite nurseries. Mysteriously, they have migrated forward where they can trap you. It's hard to walk out without one or two or, heaven help me, three or four. I am running out of posts.

The thing is, lovely as clematis is, we've got to remember there are other vines. Wisteria, of course, is a must if you've got the room, because, as we all know, wisteria can eat up the house. Well, not literally, like English ivy, which I swear leaves actual teeth marks. It's more like a boa constrictor that swallows its quarry whole.

But I digress into gory details. The point is, there are plenty of divine vines out there, and if, as they say, variety is the spice of life, we definitely ought to look beyond the starry

Clematis *'Durandii'* blooms from June to September.

charms of a 'Nelly Moser' and her clematis sisters.

For anyone who has shade, I can't say enough about *Akebia quinata*, which is called chocolate vine supposedly because its small flowers are a chocolate purple. Frankly, as an expert on chocolate, I have to say this is a stretch. It flowers early and has delicately divided leaves.

My akebia adorns a copper arbor in fairly deep shade. I marveled at how it was just the right proportion, not overpowering for a small arbor. Then one day I took a look at the two-story-tall plum tree next to the arbor and noticed the akebia had grown to the top. But if you don't have a nearby tree for it to climb, it's easy enough to control with pruning because the stem isn't thick.

There's one more thing I should mention. Last summer, my akebia sprouted mysterious-looking pods for the first time. So you should not watch certain science fiction films about pod people if you want to be totally comfortable with your akebia

Another great vine that's gaining popularity is the potato vine (*Solanum crispum* 'Glasnevin'). I brought one back from England years ago before they were readily available here. Mine gave up the ghost one cold winter, and for a while, I gave up trying to grow it.

But then I noticed all my friends have luscious potato vines that have weathered many winters, so I think our home-grown specimens may be better adapted to our climate. I've planted a new one with high hopes. Solanums are fabulously fast-growing and famously long-flowering, with small yellow-centered purple flowers. Just to be safe, I recommend growing it on the sunny south side of a house. It can get to 20 feet.

If you're looking for a vine that is spectacularly showy in shade, look no further than the climbing hydrangea (*Hydrangea anomala*, syn. *H. petiolaris*). Not only will it thrive on a north wall, but it also will smother itself with large, flat, lacey flowers. This vine is robust, eventually getting to 50 feet. However, it is a slow starter, so don't expect flowers for three or four years.

The ornamental kiwi (*Actinidia kolomikta*) has to be one of the most decorative foliage plants, and it grows to a well-behaved 15 feet or so. When mature, its leaves look as though they've been dipped in pink and white paint. It's a sun plant but will scorch in hot afternoon sun. Also, I read in a book that cats are strangely attracted to it, but my extensive research of cats has not confirmed this.

This year I'm trying a golden hops (*Humulus lupulus* 'Aureus') for the first time. It is a staple of English gardens and is grown principally for its chartreuse gold foliage, although it has interesting cone-like flowers. I'm told that it shouldn't be allowed to stay too dry in summer but that it does need good drainage. It's a sun plant, although it will tolerate a bit of shade and will get to 20 feet at maturity. Finally, you'll be hard put to find more beautiful foliage than the burgundy-leafed grape called *Vitis vinifera* 'Purpurea'. Grow it for ornament because the grapes are decidedly bitter. Nevertheless, they look quite wonderful in the autumn garden, as they hang in clusters. It's relatively small at 10 feet, and while grapes are supposed to be grown in sun, mine is very happy on a fairly shady arbor.

I realize most of these vines reach a pretty hefty height at maturity, but several are slow-growers. I have to be honest and admit I don't have 20 feet of space to spare for my new golden hops, but as Miss Scarlet said, tomorrow is another day.

MAY 16, 2002

❧

LESSONS FROM THE EAST
A visit to the Japanese Garden can reveal lessons for the home landscape

IN PORTLAND WE HAVE AN OFTEN OVERLOOKED local treasure: the Japanese Garden in Washington Park.

Locals tend to reserve it for when the folks from out of town visit. Meanwhile, the rest of the world has been discovering this garden and has hailed it as the finest example of its genre outside Japan.

It's hard to pick up a new garden book that shows examples of garden styles without Portland's own as the premier example of Japanese style. Obviously, the national press is on to a good thing.

So maybe it's time to take a fresh look at this moss-covered bowl in Portland's Southwest hills with fresh eyes. What, for example, can it teach the gardener with a quaint little Cape Cod and picket fence who has no interest at all in anything with bamboo in it?

First of all, it can teach us that green is okay. Once the ornamental trees have stopped blooming (and they were fabulous this year), flower color in the garden becomes scarce. Notable exceptions are the iris, which are coming into bloom now. But even they seem to have been selected as much for their foliage.

Yet, even devoid of flowers, the garden is interesting, exciting, even exhilarating. This is a lesson for those who live in shade or those who don't want the maintenance of flowers but still aspire to beauty. The thing that takes the place of flower color is texture. The Japanese Garden combines the velvet of mosses, the feathery softness of laceleaf maples, the brush-stiffness of conifers into a tactile crazy-quilt that stirs the senses much as color does.

How the Japanese Garden got its texture doesn't have to be a mystery. The garden's ticket office sells a list that gives both common and botanical names and provides a map to help locate plants.

The garden's extraordinary texture is enhanced with the use of hardscape — rocks, gravel, granite slabs — that are treated just like plants. You won't see a moss-covered rock edging a path like a cute gnome. Instead, it is half buried looking, as if it grew there.

Green can be exhilarating all on its own.

And hardscape is treated with the same exquisite quilt mix as the plants. In an English garden, a path typically is either brick, gravel or some single element. In the Japanese Garden, a stone path will be punctuated here and there by a slab of granite or marble. It's as if a use was found for all the builder's leftovers. Indeed, the mythical builder has made superb use of leftover ceramic roof tiles. Stood on end, they form crisp path edgings.

Next is the lesson of how the Japanese Garden is planted: It has the spareness of a Haiku. Space is planned so that the visitor sees not a mass of green, but distinct, individual plants. The plants themselves seem to have been selected for their form, so that they present themselves like living sculptures.

That effect is enhanced by pruning that has been raised to art form. Every city gardener should make a trip to this garden before ever laying hands on clippers. Trees and shrubs have been opened up so that their natural shape stands out with clarity.

Water, like stone, also is an integral part of the garden. Westerners already have begun catching on to the water idea thanks to liners that have turned ponds into something that can be built in a weekend. But the heroic Japanese ponds with their fat koi and waterfalls aren't something one can copy without a windfall at the lottery. Instead, the ideas to take home are the tiny water features — scooped-out stone basins or rain-worn rocks with their water-collecting indentations.

Finally, look at the map of the garden that comes with the price of a ticket. Notice that the garden is laid out for strolling. From no location can the visitor see the entire garden at once. Even a small garden can bor-row some ideas: paths that curve to make the stroll seem longer and small secret spots with a bench for restful meditation. Perhaps the nicest ideas of all to copy are the beautifully crafted covered benches (they look like artistic bus stops) so that one can enjoy the garden with a steamy hot cup of tea on a rainy day.

MAY 15, 1992

PLANTS IN SUPPORTING ROLES
They round out the perfect garden and never hog the spotlight

IT'S NOT UNUSUAL TO SEE SOME FINE ACTORS in movies or television shows for years and years and not know their names. That's because they're supporting players, not stars. As an example, when John C. Reilly was nominated for an Oscar for best supporting actor this year, many people wondered who he was. Yet he had been in three of the five Oscar-nominated films for best picture.

That's the way it is with certain plants — supporting players, never stars. They won't draw your attention the way a rose would, or a glorious red smoke bush or a sky blue delphinium. Yet in their way, they help make the "perfect" picture.

They rarely steal center stage, but they are utterly reliable in their role. Some are simply handsome background plants, some excellent fillers and some, like the geranium listed below, add a delicious bit of spice.

There are dozens of such plants, and, in a category that's hard to narrow down, here are my nominees for best supporting plants.

Geranium 'Ann Folkard': If ever there

were the perfect bit player, this is it. The rangy Miss Folkard is a loose woman, but in her it's a virtue. Her tendency to ramble and weave through other plants is what makes her special. Her flowers are a violet-magenta that stops just short of being strident. Stick her among other plants, particularly purple-leafed heuchera, and let her weave her way around. She'll bloom all summer. Sun, part shade.

*Solomon's seal (*Polygonatum hirtum*) with the enormous leaves of* Petasites japonicus.

Berberis thunbergii 'Atropur-purea Nana': This little red ball of barberry is certainly not as spectacular as a smoke bush. But wherever you want a small dash of wine red, this is the shrub. It's sometime sold as 'Crimson Pygmy'. It has a nice soft globe shape and grows only about 20 inches in diameter, which makes it a perfect accent for even the smallest garden. 'Bagatelle' is an even smaller version. Both are great foliage plants for combining with perennials. Sun, light shade.

Thalictrum aquilegiifolium: For the life of me, I can't imagine why meadow rue, which isn't a rue at all, isn't more popular. Imagine the leaves of the most attractive maiden's hair fern, then add soft purple fuzzy flowers. It grows straight up to about 3 feet. There are other *Thalictrum* cultivars, and they're all winners. Moderate shade, moist soil.

Alchemilla mollis: Low mounding lady's mantle is perfect for softening the edges of beds and paths, whether in or out of bloom. It's famous for its pretty foliage with a waxy coating that makes dew or raindrops ball up like little pearls on its leaves. Then comes a fuzzy abundance of soft yellow-green flowers that bloom for about month. After they bloom, just shear the plants down, and fresh leaves will quickly emerge. It does have a tendency to seed around, but not outrageously so. Or, at least I still have friends who will accept baby plants, unlike the case with daylilies. Sun, shade, moist soil.

Macleaya cordata: Here's a handsome guy for the back of the border. Years ago, I bought a trio of these plume poppies with no idea what they'd do. A friend just said I had to have them. Well, they soared to about 8 feet and don't need staking, an attribute I find immensely endearing. Despite their size, plume poppies (which don't look anything like a poppy) don't take up much room because they are tall and thin. They have large sculpted leaves and, in midsummer, are topped with feathery plumes that resemble

> *If hostas are the stars of the shade garden, Solomon's seal is their best supporting player.*

astilbe blossoms. The clump expands each year, but it's easy to pull out new shoots if you get to them early. Sun, light shade.

Artemisia lactiflora 'Guizhou': If, when you think of artemisia, you think of silver leaves, here's a surprise. This artemisia has dark purple ferny leaves, and sends up billowy white blooms. It's a 5-footer, so stick it in the middle of the border where neighboring plants will help support it. It will bloom its little heart out all summer. Sun, moist soil.

Knautia macedonica: So, okay, this flower will never win best of show. Its little purple-red tassels of flowers are modest, but plentiful. They rise on thin stems that poke up through other plants, and go on for weeks and weeks if regularly deadheaded. The leaves are nothing, but you can and should tuck this plant between others where they won't show much. Sun.

Polygonatum hirtum: If hostas are the stars of the shade garden, Solomon's seal is their best supporting player. *P. odoratum* 'Variegatum' is a very pretty variegated cousin. I'm afraid I'm beginning to sound like a press agent for this plant because I've written about it earlier this year. But I'm downright evangelical on the subject. It forms a nice little clump of slightly arching stems that drip with scented little bells in spring. The rest of the time it is, well, merely incredibly graceful. Part to full shade, moist soil.

MAY 15, 2003

IT'S MY GARDEN
And I'll grow what I want to

POSSIBLY YOU'VE JUST COME THROUGH A BOUT of plant lust, and there are several little plants sitting on your deck with no place to go.

One way to make room is to take the advice of Irish garden writer Helen Dillon. She suggests you regularly walk around your garden and demand of each plant that it justify its existence.

To that end, here are 10 questions you ought to put to your plants. My plant examples are purely subjective. A nonperformer for me may be a star for you.

1. **Deep down, do I really like you?** I planted *Phlomis fruticosa*, but eventually took it out because it was stiff and a bit weedy. Then I replanted it when I saw it looking fabulous in someone else's garden. Alas, I still don't like it in my garden.

2. **Do you let yourself go?** Even before *Buddleja* (butterfly bush) was declared a noxious weed, I'd taken mine out. It was glorious in flower, but I can't reach up to remove those lingering dead blooms. I also took out a 'Gertrude Jekyll' rose. It was perfectly gorgeous with its multiple petals, but once it got wet (which was most of the time), those petals rotted and stuck to each other in a horrid moldy mass.

3. **Do you come on too strong?** I planted a lavatera shrub and was amazed at how long and profusely it bloomed. But after time, those florid pink blooms started to get to me. It was just too Pamela Anderson.

4. **Are we really right for each other?** My neighbor Rosemary and I brought *Galega orientalis* seeds back from England one year. It turned out to be raggedy and rangy in our borders, so we both took it out. But it would look fabulous in a meadow.

5. **Are you a diva?** Anything that demands too much attention — staking, constant

Blue hardy geraniums are indispensable.

deadheading or vigorous watering — is a candidate for dismissal. Ligularia is a case in point. It's so water-needy that it droops by midday even if it's had a morning watering.

6. **Are you over the hill?** Not all perennials are long-lived, but some take a long time to expire. Take heuchera, for example. If you have some, you know how in just three or four years they can get those high woody centers that look so ratty.

7. **Are you just making a cameo appearance?** A plant that flowers only a week and doesn't have particularly interesting foliage isn't worth my affections. That's why I replaced my Siberian iris with longer-blooming Japanese iris.

8. **Are you just spiteful?** Everyone else around me seems to be able to grow penstemon and eryngium, but I have no luck with them. Then there are those stubborn bushes that refuse to bloom. I had a non-blooming *Philadelphus* for five years before I finally caught on that it would never bloom for me. I'm certain I heard it laughing behind my back.

9. **Has the spark gone out of the relationship?** For inexplicable reasons, I am bored with nandina, which I used to love. True, that's a subjective call, but it's your garden, and you don't need to justify yourself.

10. **Were you just a passing fancy?** One too many bananas have broken my heart. I'm moving on.

MAY 5, 2005

SIMPLE PLEASURES
Single-petaled flowers add timeless elegance to modern gardens

I GREW UP IN THE 1950s, A PERIOD OF TASTE-less but largely benign excess characterized by such icons as pink Cadillacs and mink coats. Mind you, as an adult I would never consider a fur unless it is alive and kicking, but this was the '50s, before we were all socially conscious. Thankfully, even then I was not into pink Cadillacs.

One day I saw a picture of a celebrity in one of my mother's fashion magazines. The woman was wearing a coat that was cloth or leather with a bit of the lining peeking out, just enough to show the lining was mink.

Oh, wow, I thought, this person is so rich and so secure that she doesn't actually have to flash her mink. That was one of my childhood epiphanies. It was the dawning realization of the art of subtlety.

This memory came back to me the other day when I was making much ado over a rose at a nursery. The plant in question was *Rosa* x *odorata* 'Mutabilis', an old-fashioned China rose, small and bushy. It blooms from spring until frost and doesn't seem to get black spot even when crammed in with perennials and other shrubs.

I turned to a companion and told her she should buy this rose because it's wonderful and hard to find. She showed little interest because it didn't look "like a real rose." By that, I surmise, she meant it didn't look like a pink cabbage. The thing is, 'Mutabilis' has only single-petaled flowers.

But subtle doesn't equal plain. 'Mutabilis' sets nearly red buds that open to a copper-washed pink and eventually a yellow-coral. You'd miss most of this changing color in a tightly petaled rose. Similarly, you'd also miss the lovely golden-tasseled centers of peonies if you only selected the fancy-pants, multi-petaled varieties.

These days, subtle isn't considered a selling point. If you open a plant catalog, you're likely to see the word "double" in big letters,

A single-petaled rose is as quietly elegant as a mink lining.

I know I am not the only one who is falling for simplicity.

heralding a new cultivar. Sometimes the new variety is a sensation, but often as not, bigger really isn't better.

I find myself returning to the classics. In their simplicity, single flowers remind me of that coat lined with fur. They have an elegance and purity. Think of the sweet beauty of a dogwood blossom or a Japanese anemone, or the sublime grace of a calla lily.

I know I am not the only one who is falling for simplicity. I see a lot more of the little alpine or bell-shaped clematis vines for sale. I am not immune to the showy beauty of those big purple starlike clematises, but I no longer grow them to the exclusion of the delicate little nodding flowers.

I have also come to prefer plain tulips to the ruffled varieties known as Rembrandts. I like the satiny smoothness and elegant line of the simple petals. The same is true for poppies. I don't want can-can petticoats. I love the single petals with the translucency of tissue paper.

But I am not a purist who would eschew all flash. I do have my weak and possibly tacky moments. When it comes to dahlias, all logic goes out the window. I feign no sophistication here. I prefer hands down the big shaggy blooms to the tight little pompons. And every time I see these dahlias bloom, I think of Dolly Parton and realize there will always be a place in the world and in every garden for a bit of over-the-top charm.

MAY 27, 2004

Part 3

SUMMER

Perfect Partners, Pot Ploys and Parterres

Clematis *'Anna Louise' is stunning against the chartreuse of a flowering euphorbia.*

SANITY BREAK

Take a break from your chores to savor the garden

JUNE SHOULD BE THE REALIZATION OF ALL THE prep work you've done this spring. The moment of triumph. The glorious time when all the plants are in place, and there isn't a speck of bare ground to be seen.

What a fantasy. If you're like me, you still have flats of plants sitting on the deck waiting to be planted. You still stare at bare spots and wonder what grew there and why it disappeared. Let's not even talk about weeds and spittlebugs.

The danger of late spring is getting into such a snit that we burn out too soon. By now, we should start enjoying the garden we've been working so hard to prepare. Part of the fix is adjusting our attitude, and part is learning just how much garden we can handle.

By attitude, I mean learning to live with imperfection. So what if the hostas have a few slug bites? So what if an occasional dandelion pops up and waggles its fronds at you? So what if you're in the middle of a project and can't get it done before company comes?

On the other hand, there are some things you can't say "so what" to. I can't blow off the black spot all over the roses. Gardens are like teen-agers. It's OK if they look a bit unkempt and shaggy. It's not OK if they look unhealthy.

Beyond adjusting your attitude, here are ways to ensure your garden doesn't devour you before the Fourth of July.

If you have bad luck with certain plants, forget them. If your roses get black spot and fungus before they even bloom, you're not alone. Unless you enjoy the special care they require, learn to live without hybrid tea roses. If your delphiniums are as wimpy as mine are, look for triumphs elsewhere. Repeat plants that you have luck with. After all, repetition is a strong design element and gives a garden consistency.

Banish high-maintenance plants. Floppy plants that need girdling, such as Shasta daisies, don't live in my garden. I hesitate to plant flowers such as rose campion (*Lychnis coronaria*) and coreopsis. They are long bloomers, but they need constant deadheading to look decent.

Cut back on the number of annuals you plant, and replace them with perennials. It's labor-intensive to replant everything each year, and perennials in 4-inch pots don't cost much more than annuals. Confine annuals to pots for easy color spots.

Make plants with pretty foliage, rather than flowers, the backbone of your garden. Yep, I know I sound like a broken record about this, but it works.

Avoid invasive plants, especially ones that spread by root runners. They're really hard to dig up. Plants that spread by self-sowing aren't quite as bad. Be careful when buying certain ornamental grasses and plants that like moist soil. These tend to be spreaders.

Don't use pruning to keep large plants in small spaces. Anyone who has ever pruned a laurel hedge to try to keep it the size of a boxwood hedge knows whereof I speak.

Set plants closer than recommended to keep weeds down. You'll also get a quick, lush look, and if things end up too crowded, plants are fairly easy to move.

Finally, I had someone pass on a great idea from writer Ann Lovejoy. According to my informant, Lovejoy advises sticking a shovel upright in any area you haven't done anything with. Visitors to your garden will look at the shovel and kindly assume you're working on it.

JUNE 1, 2000

UNDERSTUDIES
Annuals can fill the gaps left by early blooming perennials

JUNE, CROON, MOON, SPOON. SUCH A ROMANtic month. For many, especially the rose growers, it is the zenith of the gardening year.

Alas, June seemed to have happened last month.

With the unseasonably warm and dry March and April, flowers peaked early. May, the month of promise, became the month of delivery. The peonies, old roses, iris, delphiniums, alliums and several of the clematis have come and gone.

So has that perfect-moment-in-the-garden when all the delphiniums stood up straight and the roses had not yet begun to disgrace themselves with black spot.

Perhaps you are feeling a letdown now, the gardeners' equivalent of postpartum depression.

Normally it occurs in July, but everything is early this year. A symptom is that panicky feeling that you have gaps in your garden and you're running out of time to plant.

And there seem always to be spaces, even in a garden that just weeks before was packed to the hilt. The spring bulbs, poppies, bleeding hearts, lilies and other early bloomers have died back.

But all is not lost. It may be too late to get robust growth from perennials this season unless you buy a large and expensive plant, but there are other less-expensive and fast-growing fillers that can freshen up a garden nicely.

So, before you say, "I can't stand those stiff little bedding plants like marigolds or those sticky petunias," loosen up. There are some very loose annuals that blend beautifully with natural gardens. Two of my favorites for filling gaps are cosmos and nasturtiums (*Tropaeolum*). They have a soft, billowy quality that blends well with perennials.

But my all-time favorite late filler isn't a flower. Annual purple fountain grass (*Pennisetum setaceum* 'Rubrum') is a spectacular filler. It will look especially smashing if planted where it will be backlit by the sun.

If your clematis has bloomed itself out, grow morning glory (*Ipomoea*) up trellises and over the clematis. You'll wake up to flow-

Do you find yourself missing the freshness of spring flowers and foliage while waiting for lush summer flowers to bloom?

ers every morning. No, I'm not nuts, because this pretty flower isn't the rampant morning glory called *Convolvulus*, which is also known as bindweed and (imaginatively) devil's entrails. I promise, *Ipomoea* is a well-behaved annual.

If you've got spaces in containers where bulbs have flowered and died back, stick in a really glamorous plant that needs a container to show off. The aptly named pineapple flower (*Eucomis*) is great in pots. So is the exotic love-lies-bleeding (*Amaranthus caudatus*). Both would get lost planted in a bed, unless, of course, you stick the pot itself in the bed. That can make a nice accent.

Other exotic creatures to stick in pots include the giant leafed caladiums for shade and taro (*Colocasia*) for sun. There also is a growing selection of small (about 2 feet high) cannas grown for their exotic flowers rather than their leaves.

Finally, think about vegetables as fillers. Nothing puts the stamp of "summer" on a garden quite like healthy vegetables, and there's no reason they have to be consigned to a "patch." For color, try purple eggplants, scarlet-stemmed chard, red and gold peppers, blue-green artichokes, purple lettuce and big chubby blue-gray cabbages.

You'll hardly miss those delphiniums and roses.

JUNE 10, 2004

❧

FEATS OF CLAY
With some compost, these plants can thrive in water-sucking soil

I AM GOING TO VIOLATE ONE OF THE INTERNAtional rules of horticultural ethics today. I expect the plant police to arrive at any minute and take me away.

Instead of lecturing you about how you should add organic material to your soil, I am going to tell you about plants that do fairly well in clay. Now don't get me wrong. You still need to add organic material, forever and ever. It's like dieting: You can never be off a diet.

But let's face it. All of us have some corner of the garden where, no matter what we add, our clay swallows it up, burps and remains stubbornly clay. Others of us have to support families and dogs and cats and cannot devote our lives to putting in the endless amounts of composted organic material necessary to sustain those delicate plants that come with labels that say "good drainage is essential."

I don't know about you, but when I see that phrase, I get cold shivers. It's like opening some device and seeing the words "Some assembly required" or getting a letter that says, "We're coming to stay with you."

If you live in the Willamette Valley, chances are you have clay soil. Exceptions generally are areas along rivers and creeks and in floodplains where you will find sand.

Clay soil isn't all bad. It is exceptionally rich in nutrients. I rarely fertilize my own garden. It is slow to dry out, and, at least in this part of the country, it is on the acid side, which makes it hospitable for a wide range of plants. That's why rhododendrons, azaleas and camellias do so well here.

On the other hand, it retains water like a camel, and it is slow to warm up in spring, which means that, despite our mild climate, we get a late start on annuals and vegetables.

The big problem, of course, is the water retention. Most people think the plants that die over winter succumb to cold. The fact is, most of the goners simply drown. When roots sit for extended periods in soggy soil, they rot.

Fortunately, there are some plants that seem to be relatively impervious to clay soil, and not only appear to thrive but come back year after year. I use the term "relatively" because even these stalwarts cannot overcome impossible conditions.

Soil that has never been amended is not likely to produce. If you have no weeds, that's a sign that nothing will grow unless you change your soil. If you're moving into a newly built house where heavy equipment has compacted the soil, you'll just waste your money putting in plants until you amend the soil.

No, the clay-surviving plants are for people who have at least tried and who are at least willing to throw some compost into the hole when they plant.

Among perennials and biennials, the closest you'll come to sure things for clay soil are daylilies (*Hemerocallis*), iris, foxgloves (*Digitalis*), campion (*Lychnis*), bergenia, lady's mantle (*Alchemilla*) and forget-me-nots (*Myosotis*).

Close seconds in the survival contest are astilbe, montbretia (*Crocosmia*), hosta, coneflower (*Rudbeckia*), Christmas and Lenten rose (*Helleborus*), Oriental poppies (*Papaver orientale*), London pride (*Saxifraga umbrosa*), masterwort (*Astrantia*), meadow rue (*Thalictrum*), phlox, aster, rhubarb and Joe Pye weed (*Eupatorium*).

Other reliable clay survivors include lungwort (*Pulmonaria*), bee balm (*Monarda*), peony (*Paeonia*), Japanese anemone, sneezeweed (*Helenium*), goldenrod (*Solidago*), *Verbena bonariensis*, Jacob's ladder (*Polem-*

Thalictrum *is perfectly happy in clay soil.*

onium), bear's breeches (*Acanthus spinosus*), ligularia, rodgersia, monkshood (*Aconitum*) and meadow sweet (*Filipendula*).

Some invasive plants are useful in areas with heavy clay, because they're tough enough to make it and the clay will hold them somewhat in check. Plants in this category include purple loosestrife (*Lythrum*), yellow loosestrife (*Lysimachia*), and knotweed (*Polygonum*).

There are other tip-offs that will help you expand your repertoire. Look around your neighborhood and see what's growing in gardens where people make minimal effort. Your soil will be similar, and probably even better if you've worked it at all. So if they are growing coral bells, so can you.

Another sure sign that a plant will do well is if it self-sows in your garden. If, for example, you can't get forget-me-nots or lady's mantle to self-sow, that is a sign from the goddess Flora that you should give it up and order a trainload of compost.

JUNE 9, 1996

❧

MATCHMAKER, MATCHMAKER
Pairing up perfect partners in the plant world can take special care – or be a happy accident

I'M ALWAYS ON THE LOOKOUT FOR PLANTS THAT act as foils; that is, plants that bring out the best in their neighbors. Take the new coral bells (*Heuchera*), for example. I have lost all discipline and am buying up every new cultivar I can find.

There's nothing this plant doesn't pair with. By itself, the flower is merely pretty, but tuck a purple-leafed variety such as 'Purple Palace' next to a scarlet or purple posy, and you've got a stunning couple. Or marry a frosty-leafed variety such as 'Snowstorm' to a white blossom, and you've got the proverbial marriage made in heaven.

Some foliage plants make such great companions that they might as well hang out signs that say, "matchmaking service."

Not all great pairings are planned. In my own garden they invariably happen by accident. A couple of years ago I planted a *Hydrangea serrata* 'Preziosa'. It's a small shrub, long blooming, and is one hydrangea that is happy in sun. But I digress.

> *Some foliage plants make such great companions that they might as well hang out signs that say, "matchmaking service."*

A stand of sedge (*Carex elata* 'Bowles Golden') somehow had cozied up next to the hydrangea. As often occurs, I have no memory of planting it there. When the broad flowerheads of the hydrangea are still in the bud stage, which lasts quite a long time, they're a brilliant yellow-lime, almost exactly the color of the neighboring carex. When the flowers open to a rosy pink tinged with lime, it's still a smashing combination.

You might think I'm extraordinarily artful, if it weren't for another accidental pairing. A clump of orange crocosmia also mysteriously found its way to the foot of the hydrangea. I have spent the spring begging friends who have come to dig up plants to take the offending crocosmia away, but it's not a big seller.

The upshot of these accidental wins and losses is that I pay more attention to intentional plant pairings. Here's what I look for in good companions:

Plants with variegated leaves are a natural. Tuck leaves with yellow rims or stripes next to yellow flowers, or white rims or stripes with white flowers. Golden *Euonymus fortunei* 'Emerald 'n' Gold' is perfect with yellow roses. White-rimmed euonymus (look for names such as 'Silver Pillar' or 'Silver Queen') is equally pretty partnered with a white rose.

There is no end to the variegated hostas waiting to serve as escorts. And the same goes for grasses. Just avoid spreaders like the nasty green-and-white ribbon grass *Phalaris* (as in Fear of Phalaris) that's into hostile takeovers. There are plenty of polite clump-forming variegated grasses and sedges, such as *Carex morrowii variegata*. I especially like this carex shoulder to shoulder with a green and white hosta.

Not all leaves have defined variegation. Some seem to have a wash of a second color over the leaf, such as on purple sage (*Salvia officinalis* 'Purpurascens'). Imagine purple alliums growing through purple sage. One of the most glorious shade combinations I've seen was a bronze-tinged *Rodgersia podophylla* cozied up to a rosy astilbe.

I've also started to pay attention to veining in leaves and colored stems. Some plants have wine-red veins or stems that will pick up and accent a neighbor's flowers or foliage. *Rosa glauca* (also sold as *Rosa rubrifolia*) has glaucous blue leaves and scarlet stems and veins and looks sublime next to a wine-red smoke bush (*Cotinus*).

Then there are the yellow veins of the green-leaved cannas such as 'Striata' or 'Bengal Tiger' that are a dramatic matchup with the sun-yellow flowers of high summer.

Chartreuse or lime-gold foliage is an electrifying combination with blue flowers and divine with wine (the color, that is). Golden spirea 'Goldflame', the Japanese forest grass *Hakonechloa macra* 'Aureola', lime-colored hostas and common oregano (*Origanum vulgare* 'Aureum') all make great partners.

Silver foliage is a pretty complement to white, blue and pink flowers. When you want a bit of heft in a border, billowing *Artemisia* 'Powis Castle' is the thing. On the other hand, ground-hugging silver *Lamium maculatum* in varieties such as 'White Nancy' or 'Beacon Silver' is perfect at the toes of white flowers. *Cynara* or cardoon (an ornamental artichoke) is a spectacular large-leafed plant for a white garden, and, if you don't mind their spread,

lamb's ears (*Stachys*) can carpet the front of the border.

Glaucous blue leaves — examples include grassy *Festuca glauca*, *Hosta sieboldiana*, *Ruta* and *Rosa glauca* — are exquisite with purple and pink flowers, as well as white and soft buttery yellows. Bluish leaves also are spectacularly companionable with burgundy-colored foliage as well as flowers.

Red or bronze leaves not only look sensational with blue, but also make fine accents with red and purple flowers. The first red-themed garden I ever saw had a great reddish-leaved banana plant at its center.

Red and bronze foliage is at its most luscious when partnered with peaches and corals. Think of great shaggy cantaloupe-colored spider dahlias against a backdrop of wine-red canna leaves. Other companions to look for are red-leaved varieties of barberries (*Berberis*), smoke bushes, astilbes, bergenias, bronze fennel (*Foeniculum*), lobelias, New Zealand flax (*Phormium*) and grapevine (*Vitis vinifera* 'Purpurea').

I hope many of these suggestions will distract you while I am buying up all the heucheras in town.

JUNE 4, 1998

❧✕☙

POND LIFE IS DUCKY
After the pea soup, it's clear sailing

I'M FREQUENTLY ASKED HOW I'VE SOLVED THE raccoon problem in our pond. The truth is, I didn't solve it, or the blue heron problem, for that matter.

It's not for lack of trying. I've experimented with nearly every remedy recommended, from netting (blue herons spear fish right through it) to predator scent. Do you know how embarrassing it is to go in a store and ask if they have red fox urine?

The one thing I haven't tried is putting up an electronic fence, because I have a spastic cat (really) who hangs around the pond. One jolt would send him flopping into the water. This is a cat of very little brain, mind you, and I can't count on him having the wherewithal to find his way out.

We finally gave up on fish, and the raccoons have given up using our place for wild parties. We know they're still around because we see them scuttling across the yard, which sets Hector the dog yapping frantically. This merely annoys but does not frighten the raccoons. But at least they're not knocking over the pots in the pond, champing the leaves and destroying the pump the way they did when we had fish.

Still, for all the problems and mistakes (and they've been legion), we love our pond. The frogs are back, and Luciano and Placido sing their arias nightly. We are hoping that next to show up will be Kiri rather than Jose because we'd rather have tadpoles than three tenors.

While we still have our difficulties — this spring we had another leak — the good news is that maintenance gets easier each year as the pond matures. Early in the pond's life, we battled the pea soup look. But with established plants, things have stabilized and now it takes almost no maintenance to keep the water clear.

Indispensable are oxygenating plants such as Canadian pondweed (*Elodea canadensis*) and the partially submerged parrot feather (*Myriophyllum aquaticum*). These are great plants for gobbling up nutrients and starving out algae, which creates the pea soup look.

The flag iris in the pond enjoy a light spring rain.

We've never been scientific about how many plants we toss in (without planting them, by the way). It started with half a dozen strands, and by the end of summer they had multiplied into a mass resembling Medusa's hair. In fall, we rake most of the oxygenators out, leaving just a few to carry over through winter. The discards may be smelly and slimy, but they're great on the compost pile.

Pond experts recommend covering one-third to two-thirds of a pond's surface with plants to keep algae down, insulate the water and keep temperatures from fluctuating widely. Plants also are touted as a way to protect fish from predators. But raccoons give no credence to this theory, and neither should you.

Since our pond is in shade, water lilies and lotus are out. But shade doesn't seem to limit most of the common water plants. If you're just discovering water gardening, here are some great starter plants.

YELLOW FLAG IRIS (*Iris pseudacorus*): Here's a perfect pond plant if you have room. Each year our stand of iris expands and threatens to take over the planet, and we have to beg friends to come over and hack some of it off for their ponds. Of course, we don't tell them how it expands, just like the people who gave us our first bit of flag iris didn't tell us (thanks, Dick and Ginny). But you've got to love a plant that is so easy to grow that it doesn't even need to be potted. You just throw a rooted clump in the water, whereupon it immediately flops on its side in a dead faint. Not to worry. After a couple of weeks it sends shoots straight up, and you've got an island of iris.

PICKERELWEED (*Pontederia cordata*): Another plant that's close to maintenance-free. Needs to be potted, but pots can be left in water over winter with no problems. Elongated heart-shaped leaves and elegant purple flowers in midsummer which, unlike many water flowers, actually hang around for a while.

FLOATING PLANTS: A quick way to cover a lot of surface. I prefer cute little water lettuce (*Pistia stratiotes*) over the fleshy water hyacinths (*Eichhornia crassipes*). Why? If you throw half a dozen of each in your pond in spring, by fall you'll have only 8,000 water lettuces as opposed to 8 million water hyacinths. Believe me, you'll be glad both are annuals. If you buy any water plant, chances are some duckweed (*Lemna minor*), a tiny floater, will come in as a free passenger. It has its charm but will carpet a pond surface on the first hot day, so keep a skimmer handy.

PAPYRUS (*Cyperus papyrus*): The "in" plant for ponds, but unless we have a tropical winter, it will need to be lifted out of the water and wintered over in a protected area. But its luscious tropical look is worth some effort. Mine survived winter in an unheated, uninsulated greenhouse, but shoots have been slow to emerge. Better to regard it as an an-

nual, and if it somehow survives, regard it as miracle.

Availability of water plants is finally catching up with the proliferation of ponds, set off by the introduction of pond liners and molded pond forms. Today, specialty water nurseries are popping up, and general nursery centers carry a greater variety of water plants and pond accessories than a few years ago.

JUNE 11, 1998

ON THE ROCKS
A rock garden take your yard to new heights

BY GARDENING STANDARDS, ROCK GARDENing is new after just 200 years. It got its start in the late 1700s, when wealthy Europeans were swept up in the fad of beating the Joneses by getting the rarest plant on the block.

Plant explorers pushed out to ever more exotic regions in search of new supply to meet the demand. One of those new places was simply up. Plant explorers scurried up mountains in the proverbial four corners of the globe, and there they discovered a wonderland of new plants.

Here were strange and exotic species growing in the most improbable places, tiny jewel-like plants in outcroppings of rock with little or no soil. They had strange shapes, hugging the ground to escape the merciless winds. They survived in the most extreme conditions, smothered by snow in winter and exposed without protection to sun in summer.

And because the short growing season left little time for a seed to germinate and flower to maturity in one season, they were perennials. Best of all, nature made up for what the plants lacked in stature. She cloaked them in masses of brilliant blossoms, so that they made vibrant paint strokes of color against the otherwise barren rock.

These plants — and there are hundreds of species — became known as alpines, after the Alps, where many were discovered.

Soon, gardeners in the flatlands were building special rock gardens, called rockeries, to house their new acquisitions. Some went overboard and created miniature Matterhorns, but the beauty of the plants seems to have survived the silly stage, and today's natural rockeries are finding more and more homes in the Northwest.

The Northwest, somewhat surprisingly, is a particularly good place to grow alpines. While it hardly has the temperature extremes of high altitudes, the region does duplicate one condition necessary to the alpines' survival. The summers are nearly always dry. The plants do not take well to the humidity that is prevalent in the summer throughout much of the rest of the country.

There are really two reasons to have a rock garden. One is that it duplicates the natural conditions alpines enjoy. The other reason is that a rockery is an ideal place to display those small but exquisite plants whose delicate charms would be lost in the exuberance of a flower border. Consider the charming primrose or the dainty dog-tooth violet or the exotic checkered lily. Each would be overlooked among tall, showy flowers. It would be like trying to find a tiny ballerina in a line of high-kicking cancan girls.

Here were strange and exotic species growing in the most improbable places.

Rock garden plants then, to use a practical definition, are either alpines that grow naturally in rocky outcrops, or simply small and dwarf plants that look best when displayed in the scaled down landscape of a rockery.

Because rock garden plants are low growing, the gardens themselves tend to be small, frequently gardens within gardens. A spectacular exception is the Ohme Garden, which is open to the public. It carpets several acres of rocky bluffs overlooking the Wenatchee Valley in central Washington.

Most frequently, a rock garden is a sunny patch set aside to display tiny plants. It can be an irregular island carved out of a lawn, or it can be tucked into a small area with already defined edges, such as the strip along a driveway. It is almost always best to set aside a rockery, that is, to define it as a separate space, because rock garden plants do not make a graceful transition into other garden areas such as flower beds and shrubberies.

Siting should balance both growing and aesthetic needs. The first requirement means a fairly sunny site and — this is essential — one with good drainage. Alpine plants like and need regular watering, but they cannot tolerate standing in water. The survival mechanism that led them to hug the ground also made them vulnerable to rot should the ground remain wet. On the other hand, the ability to survive quickly draining conditions is what makes them excellent for rock walls, another popular form of the rock garden.

From an aesthetic standpoint, the rockery

should be sited to allow close-up views, either off a deck or terrace, along a retaining wall or as a delicious surprise one comes across at the end of a path. These plants are not built to be enjoyed in distant vistas and panoramas.

As far as designing the rockery, the key is to duplicate the basic conditions that nurture growth, not to duplicate the alps. Raised beds, either gently mounded or rimmed with rocks, are an excellent way to ensure drainage and define the rockery.

Keep island rockeries irregularly shaped. Unlike perennials and herbs, rock garden plants do not display well in geometric beds. Soil should have lots of compost, sand and even gravel. A lot of rock garden plants also like the acidity peat moss provides.

It is even possible to create different moods with planting. You can duplicate the serenity of a Japanese garden, without copying its style, with a spare selection of plants set apart by gravel.

Each plant can be admired individually like a tiny jewel for its shape or color. Or you can plant more closely and more colorfully for the Persian carpet look of an alpine meadow.

Finally, rocks aren't even necessary, but if you use them, here are some guidelines.

- For a natural look, use native stone.
- Err on the side of understatement. One dramatic, well-shaped boulder will be more pleasing than a lot of little rocks.
- If you are going to use several rocks or boulders, get assorted sizes and cluster them in groups rather than going for a polka-dot effect.
- Imbed rocks in the earth, sometimes covering as much as two-thirds of the surface. Rocks in nature don't just sit on top of the ground.
- In a flat garden, angle stones as they would appear in nature in an outcrop. Be sure they all slant in the same direction.
- When the rockery is built on a slope (excellent for drainage), place the stones horizontally so that they form a terraced effect.
- If the garden is large, use flat stones for paths. This will allow you to move within the rockery and have easy access for planting and weeding.

JUNE 8, 1990

TEST YOUR GARDENING I.Q.

Know your slugs from your bugs? Dig into this quiz and find out.

IT'S HARD NOT TO HAVE A GREEN THUMB IN the Northwest. Plants just seem to grow by themselves. But so do slugs and weeds.

So knowing something about local dirt and the stuff that grows there is important if you want to keep your garden looking good.

How are your garden smarts? Here's a quiz to test your everyday planting savvy.

TRUE OR FALSE

1. The terms organic and natural on labels are interchangeable.
2. When selecting seedlings, it's best to pick the biggest you can find and the one with the most blooms.
3. It's a bad sign to see leaves beginning to sprout when you buy bare root plants.
4. On a hot day, it helps to water at midday to keep the lawn from burning.

5. If some fertilizer is good, twice as much is even better.
6. The best time to dig a new flower or vegetable bed is in early spring.
7. Dormant spray means that the ingredients in the plant spray will release slowly over time.
8. You can grow plants that are not hardy in your climate zone.
9. Some perennials have short lives.
10. Mulch is added in late fall to keep plants warm over winter.
11. To encourage better fruits and flowers, use a fertilizer that's high in nitrogen.
12. Folk remedies work just as well for killing slugs as anti-slug applications you buy in stores.

ANSWERS

1. False. Minerals that are essential to plant growth are not organic, but they are natural, that is not synthetic or man-made. Organic materials are those that come from living materials, such as plants or animals (manure, leaf mold, bonemeal, etc.)
2. False. The smaller the plant, the better chance it has to transplant and "take" in your garden. Look for seedlings that are compact and bushy.
3. True. Sprouting leaves or white thread-like rootlets are a sign that the plant is no longer dormant. Once out of dormancy, survival chances of bare root plants are questionable.
4. False. Midday watering is wasteful because much of the water evaporates. Because there is less water to sink in, it stays near the surface and encourages shallow roots. Shallow-rooted lawns are most likely to burn.

Whatever method you use, be sure to protect your hostas from slugs.

5. False. Fertilizers were formulated and tested by scientists, and it pays to read directions. They are a lot like medications: too much of a good thing can be dangerous. Excess fertilizer can burn and even kill plants.
6. False, especially in the rainy Northwest. Not only is autumn drier, making digging easier, but it pays to dig in compost and fertilizer and let it sit over winter to settle and decompose. Then in spring, there's no worry about fertilizer burn for new seedlings.
7. False. Dormant spray refers to the time of year spray should be applied. In the Northwest, it is commonly applied to trees and shrubs in January and February.
8. True. Within a climate zone, there are

microclimates. Areas that are sheltered, have a southern exposure or are next to a heat-soaking wall will be warmer, and you can usually grow plants that are considered marginal in this climate.

9. True. Perennials are plants that normally live more than two years; after that, they have varying lifetimes. Daylilies will be around 50 years or more. But if your delphiniums didn't come back after three or four years, don't feel guilty. They're short-lived perennials.

10. False. Actually, it's just the opposite. Mulch is applied to keep plants cold. It's the thawing, then refreezing that causes most of the winterkill. West of the Cascades, winter mulches shouldn't be applied until after Thanksgiving, or else they will keep the ground too warm, and plants will not go dormant.

11. False. Too much nitrogen will encourage foliage growth at the expense of fruits and flowers. Potassium is the nutrient that encourages flower and fruit production.

12. True, or at least maybe. Everybody has an opinion on this. Some people swear by pans of beer, others salt slugs and still others bravely get up at dawn and apply a killer trowel to emerging slugs. Store-bought anti-slug measures help, but can pose safety hazards to children and pets if not applied carefully.

WHAT DOESN'T BELONG IN THE FOLLOWING LISTS?

A. Stonefruits Apples Berries Citrus
B. Aphids Lacewings Spider mites Mealy bugs
C. Douglas fir Rhododendron Oregon grape California poppy
D. Fungicide Herbicide Fertilizer Insecticide
E. Species Cultivar Hybrid Sport
F. Calcium Nitrogen Phosphorous Potassium
G. Corn Beans Lettuce Tomatoes
H. Diatomaceous earth Pyrethrum Rotenone Malathion

ANSWERS:

A. Citrus are the only fruits in the list that are not hardy in the Northwest.
B. Unlike the others, lacewings are helpful bugs that help control harmful insects.
C. The rhododendron was not introduced to the Old World by Scottish botanist David Douglas. The other plants were as well as flowering currants, several pines, white dogwood, lupines and many more.
D. Herbicides kill plants; the other products were formulated to help them.
E. The word "species" before a plant name indicates it is a plant in its original or wild form. The other terms refer to plants that have changed either through crossing parent plants or mutations.
F. While some calcium is important, it is not considered one of the three essential nutrients in fertilizers. When you buy a fertilizer, you will see three numbers (e.g., 6-10-8). They refer to the percentage of nitrogen, phosphorous and potassium.
G. Lettuce is a cool-weather crop that does better planted early or late. If you plant it in summer, choose varieties that can withstand heat.
H. Only malathion is a non-organic insecticide. Organic insecticides still must be used with caution as they can be dangerous if ingested by children or pets, and they can kill good insects, such as bees, and fish. Their advantage is that they break down into non-toxic substances rapidly.

SCORING:

Score 1 point for each question you answer correctly. 16-20 correct: Genius with a green thumb. 11-15: Good work. Keep digging. 6-11: Nice try. Hire a gardener. 1-5: You have the brain of a slug.

JUNE 9, 1991

❧

HEAD TURNERS

On garden tours, there are always those plants that provoke questions

I'M ONE OF LIFE'S UNORGANIZED PEOPLE. IF I tell company to show up for dinner at 6 p.m., you can bet that at 5:45 I am jumping out of the bathtub, brandishing a hair dryer, putting the biscuits in and slapping the dishes on the table. By 5:59 p.m., you'll find me cleaning up the hairball that just appeared on the entry hall carpet.

So, you can imagine my horror when at 10 a.m. three weeks ago a very large bus pulled up in front of my house. It had arrived from Eugene for a garden tour, and it was exactly one hour early.

I looked out my kitchen window at the bus. The people on the bus looked out their windows at my house. They were incredibly polite; no one got off the bus. This state of affairs went on for about 10 minutes. Finally, I broke down, walked out and invited them in.

I babbled that I had intended to deadhead the roses (it had rained earlier that morning), and the nice people offered to deadhead the roses if they could come in early. I very nearly took them up on the offer.

During the course of the day, about 500 people trooped through my garden and the garden of my neighbor Rosemary. All were exceedingly nice, as nice as the Eugene early birds who had been ready to wait on the bus for an hour.

Later, Rosemary and I compared notes. Oddly enough, we discovered that despite the myriad plants in our gardens, most of the questions focused on just 10 plants. So I thought I'd share the crowd pleasers with you.

1. *Viburnum opulus compactum*: This small (3 1/2 feet, rounded) shrub nestles just outside my front door. If there's such a thing as a perfect shrub, this is it. It has sweet white flowers in spring, red berries in autumn, and elegant maple-like leaves from early spring to autumn. Its shape is gently billowing, and it never needs pruning. Maybe that was the attraction.

2. *Petasites*: The real show-stopper was a plant I wrote about a few weeks ago, but it belongs in the "you have to see it to believe it" category. The huge oval leaves of petasites looming over the back shade border are hard to ignore. I measured the leaves, and they were a whopping 30 inches across. Some sources say this is an invasive plant. I have not found it so,

The eye-popping Petasites japonicus.

but my two plants are in fairly deep shade.

3. *Aconitum lycoctonum*: The common aconitum, of course, is the indigo blue monkshood, a late bloomer. But the much daintier, early blooming *A. lycoctonum* has delicate, serrated leaves and a profusion of tiny cream-colored flowers on multiple stems. It's far prettier than the common aconitum.

Allium christophii *opening its starry flowers.*

4. *Macleaya cordata*: At Rosemary's, the world's tallest poppy — about 8 feet high — drew oohs and aahs. I have this plant, too, but mine is in a shadier area and not quite so spectacular. Macleaya sure doesn't look like a poppy, but it has unusual scalloped leaves and long-blooming plumes that resemble flowers of astilbe. Best of all, although tall, it doesn't need staking.

5. *Thalictrum aquilegiifolium*: The pretty meadow rue, which isn't a rue at all, garnered its share of comments for its delicacy. It has fuzzy purple-blue flowers and blue-green leaves that resemble those of a tall maidenhair fern.

6. *Tovara*: I first spotted this plant on a tour of someone else's garden. It was part of a red theme garden. Although the leaves of tovara are apple green, each is decorated with a blood-red chevron. The flowers are insignificant; you grow it for its foliage, which forms a neat mound.

7. *Hydrangea* 'Preziosa': People stopped often to admire a pretty, small hydrangea with yellowish flowers, bronzy leaves and deep red stems. This hydrangea is unique because it's quite happy in full sun and is as desirable for its burnished foliage as for its flowers.

8. *Phlomis russeliana*: I knew people would ask about this odd plant, with yellow whorls circling square, stiff stems. It's not really pretty, but certainly interesting.

9. *Lamiastrum*: The heavily variegated green and white leaves of this fine ground cover got their share of attention. It's a shade lover that is perfect for lining the edges of paths. The heavy white veining gives the plant a silvery sheen.

10. *Allium christophii*: Of all the flowers people gasped and gaped at, this particular allium was the big winner in both our gardens. Alliums are dependable and spectacular, and you plant them in autumn just like any other bulb. I have never met an allium I didn't like, but *A. christophii*, with its airy lightness and huge spherical heads up to a foot wide, is my favorite. One would never guess they are related to the lowly onion.

JUNE 19, 1997

POT PLOYS
Quick tricks for containers help a busy gardener

WE ARE BEING DELUGED WITH BOOKS, magazines and classes dedicated to container gardening. No doubt part of the interest can be attributed to all the downsizing to condos, where the only garden space available is a balcony or small patio.

But plants in pots also are catching on in larger gardens, where in some cases they are used as art. A fabulous plant in a fabulous pot may not be cheap, but it's a lot less expensive than an original sculpture and can be very effective.

I am not a particularly good container gardener. When you have a big garden to take care of, it's hard to find the time to assemble a perfectly balanced garden within a container with the requisite spiky thing, surrounded by bushy things and anchored with some trailing thingies. So not having the patience to do all this, I have found some quick tricks to make pots work.

Use substantial pots: They can go longer between waterings, they display plants better, and they have the heft to stand out in larger gardens.

Use more perennials: They start poking up at least by the time I'd be getting around to adding annuals. Perennials that work well include hostas, eucomis, cannas, phormium, yuccas, agaves, hardy fuchsias, ferns, agapanthus, heuchera and many more.

Emphasize foliage: There's a great deal to be said for not having to deadhead, and, with the wonderful assortment of foliage color available, you can get a lot of drama.

Go for a single dramatic plant: Use architectural plants that hold interest by themselves and don't need companions in the same pot. This is a great way to use tropical plants since they will be easier to move to winter protection if they're in a container.

Avoid the polka-dot effect: Rather than scattering pots about, either use a single significant container as a focal point or cluster several potted plants of varying heights and sizes together to make a mini-garden.

Hide bare soil: Cover with pretty mosses, polished rocks, colored-glass chips or whatever looks interesting. Not only does it look nicer, but it acts as mulch so that pots don't dry out as rapidly.

Tuck in a bit of whimsy: Often I don't have enough of that nice lime-green moss to cover all the soil, so I add little decorative objects to help cover. I've used glass balls, decorative tiles and ornaments such as a stone or pottery bird. Unfortunately, sometimes a

Cats love pots. Orville is particularly fond of them.

cat believes itself sufficiently decorative and uses the pot for a napping place.

Be uplifting with your containers: Put a plant on a pedestal to make it more important. Last year, a large purple phormium in the back border was all but lost by midsummer as other plants around it filled out. This year, we've got it on a pedestal. You can even use an upside-down pot as a lift, especially if it will be hidden by other foliage.

Limit container colors: There are a number of beautiful glazes now, and every time I go into a garden center and see red pots, I want to buy them. But I'd already gotten started on a watery-blue glaze. Since glazed pots are expensive, you can use them as occasional accents with terra cotta, which goes with almost anything.

Match plant with pot: I have two Japanese maples back in what we call our Zen garden, and I found a pair of tall narrow pots that show off the trees better than the usual rounded shapes. The pots are a plain earthy color with no decoration. Given the Asian feel of the space, I want the pots to disappear so what you see are the trees. But where you want an ornamental pot to stand out, use plain foliage, such as a hosta. Flowers could make the whole thing too fussy.

Be winter-wise: If you don't have a greenhouse or a place to protect containers over winter, select very thick pottery or even terra-cotta-stained concrete. Otherwise, plan on moving pots to protection. And, unless you've seen something I haven't, don't get a fake terra-cotta-style pot. No matter how hard you squint, they still look fake. I know, because I have a couple.

JUNE 23, 2005

REAL LIFE
Make the most of imperfection

SOMEONE SENT ME AN ARTICLE BY THE DEsigner John Saladino. In it, he said, "My rules of thumb? Never plant things in amounts of less than three dozen."

Oh get real, John. Most of us don't have a grand estate and a staff of gardeners in little starched green aprons. We don't have block-long borders, ponds large enough for rowboats, walled Italian gardens or sweeping copper-beech hedges.

Our homes aren't set, as so many garden books show, in storybook landscapes with the "borrowed scenery" of Capability Brown-inspired parks and the ubiquitous church steeple just over your hedge. For most of us, the borrowed scenery is the peeling paint on the neighbor's garage.

Someday, a brilliant designer will do a design book especially focused on the broad, shallow gardens common to American housing built in the past half-century. Oh sure, there are books on "small" gardens, but the

> *For most of us, the borrowed scenery is the peeling paint on the neighbor's garage.*

vast majority of these show the narrow-but-deep plots common to English and East Coast row houses. In the meantime, I will fearlessly leap into the breach with the usual highly opinionated advice.

My No. 1 piece of advice is to face the fact that driveways are not invisible. Ever since the emergence of the two-car family, houses have been designed with double garages fronting the street, which means there's the ubiquitous slab of concrete out front. Not a garden-friendly picture.

With the emergence of stamped concrete and other faux surfaces, you can get an attractive surface without the expense of stone and brick. It's still an expensive undertaking, but putting in a new driveway usually costs less than a new deck.

My next bit of advice is, just as there should be no bare ground, there should be no bare garage walls or barren fences, unless the latter are highly decorative, such as pickets or cast iron. Affix lattices and smother them with vines so you have a green backdrop. I have neighbors who have made a faux cottage out of their neighbors' garage wall. They've put up a door (which doesn't open, of course) and window frames filled with mirrors, and now it looks charming.

Continuing with the advice, I would lose the lawn once the kids are too old to do somersaults and have moved to tossing baskets into the hoop on the now nicely paved driveway. This will give you room to make a natural landscape with small ornamental trees, shrubs and occasional accent flowers, plus nice little graveled or paved spaces for tables and chairs.

Alternatively, if you have a small yard, turn the entire thing into a garden room. One of the best small garden designs I've ever seen was at a North Portland home, where the owners simply made the entire backyard into a courtyard. The area was paved, with just enough land around the periphery to soften edges with plantings. A three-tiered fountain centered the courtyard, and large pots of architectural plants gave a lush feeling.

It reminded me of gardens in Provence, where you step out of the house into a large garden room suitable for dining and entertaining. Beyond the walls are the rose gardens, olive groves, vegetable rows and swimming pool. In the case of the Portland garden, there was no "beyond the walls," but you could imagine it.

And the last bit of advice for the small garden is to make it perfect, perfectly groomed, that is.

That's your advantage over all of us. I have three-quarters of an acre, and by the time I've finished weeding one end of my garden, the weeds on the other end have started back up. It's then that I stop fantasizing about a country garden with room to plant three dozen of something and start fantasizing about a really, really small — but perfect — garden.

JUNE 30, 2005

❧

A ROSE IS A ROSE IS A TROUBLESOME ROSE
Roses are red, gardeners are blue, black spot disease is something to rue

NORMALLY, I CAN COUNT ON ABOUT 15 MINutes of perfect roses. That's the time between the first bloom and the first sinister sign of the dreaded black spot disease. This year, the black spot hit even before the blooms.

I don't know about you, but when my roses go bad, I feel a singular sense of failure. After all, I live in the Rose City, one of the world's capitals of rose growing. I ought to be able to grow roses, for goodness sake.

But, if there's a bug, virus, fungus, rot, wilt, canker, blight, nutrient deficiency or chain-saw murderer out there, it's headed for my roses — at least the hybrid teas. Some people have wisely given up on hybrid teas,

Clinbing roses can lift your spirits — and your eyes when they clamber this high.

returning to the old-fashioned, disease-resistant roses.

I have those too, but I'm having a difficult time weaning myself entirely of hybrid teas. Okay, so the bushes are ugly, but nothing is their equal for cutting flowers.

The trouble with hybrid teas is that one of their parents is practically a hothouse flower. I'm talking about Chinese tea roses. When Europeans first came upon the tea roses, they were swept away by their continuous and prolific bloom.

But tea roses were too delicate for even temperate climates, so breeders crossed them with a hardy European rose to get our modern hybrid teas. They may be winter hardy now (sort of), but they still seem delicate and fussy when it comes to other problems.

I sense I'm not alone in my frustration with hybrid teas. No one really wants to admit they live in Portland and don't have championship roses. It's like living in Switzerland and having to confess you can't ski.

But I can tell there are others out there who are battling the evil forces trying to destroy their roses. Recently, I mentioned a homemade insecticide using Fels Naptha soap. I foolishly did not specify a formula, and a number of alert readers called or wrote.

Actually, there's no hard and fast formula. You just mix the soap with enough water so that it's thick enough to give the leaf a coating. Getting too much on won't hurt, since it's not toxic and will wash off. The idea is that the soap coats the leaf so nasty aphids can't dig in.

But aphids aren't the No. 1 enemy, according to letters. The dreaded black spot tops the list, followed by powdery mildew, both fungal diseases. Nothing will cure black spot or mildew once they set in. But that doesn't mean you can't save your rose.

The first thing you have to do is a Gypsy Rose Lee act. Yes, you have to strip the bush of all its infected foliage. There's no getting around it. And, whatever you do, don't put the infected foliage in the compost pile, where it will start an epidemic. Bag it up and put it in the trash.

> *The first thing you have to do is a Gypsy Rose Lee act.*

One more thing, which I know is going to sound extreme: Be sure to wash your clippers before cutting into healthy stems or going to another plant. Fungal diseases spread that easily.

Now, you've got a thoroughly naked and embarrassed rose bush that's going to take a little time before it's attractive again. But you've got a fighting chance. Think of it as having a kid who caught ringworm at school. Sometimes the only cure is shaving the little one's head.

Next comes the prevention program, so

The delicacy of a rose is unsurpassed.

that the new foliage that sprouts is healthy. You can go to a garden center and get chemicals. If you want to go that route, you can read the labels and don't need me to read them for you.

But many of us want to take a more environmental route, hence we look for organic recipes, such as the Fels Naptha. I am what is known as a pseudo-environmentalist. That means I go the organic route, except when it comes to slugs. There, my environmentalist leanings break down into abject hypocrisy, and out comes the Deadline.

But back to roses. Here's another organic measure to try, and it shouldn't cost much, if anything at all. A few years ago, I was treated to a personal tour of Great Dixter by Christopher Lloyd, the owner and a renowned English garden writer. Actually, he mistook my small party for another visiting American group, which had actually paid for the privilege of a guided tour. When he realized the mistake, he was quite peevish and retreated into his manor for a "lie down" as the English say.

But, during the time he actually thought we were money-paying rich Americans, he gave us his secret for keeping roses disease free. He has his gardeners put grass clippings around the bottoms of his roses, but not so they're smothering the stems. As the clippings decompose, according to Lloyd, the heat of their composting kills any lurking fungi or insects.

For some reason, I never got around to trying this, but Margaret Willoughby, another Portlander who was present at the illicit Lloyd tour, passed this tip on to her daughter. This year, her daughter has trouble-free roses, even though they are offspring cuttings of Willoughby's own roses, which had black spot and other problems.

I personally haven't tried it, but there's nothing to lose since grass clippings are free and certainly plentiful.

ROSES THAT EXCEL HERE

According to the venerable Portland Rose Society, almost any rose will do well in the maritime Northwest, given proper care. Still, there are some hybrid tea roses that tend to outperform others and that are especially good in a damp climate. The society lists the following roses for the Portland area.

'Blue Nile', mauve
'Chicago Peace', pink blend
'Color Magic', pink
'Dainty Bess', pink
'Electron', pink
'Folklore', orange
'Fragrant Cloud', orange
'Heirloom', mauve
'Helmut Schmidt', yellow
'Honor', white
'Just Joey', apricot
'Keepsake', pink
'Las Vegas', orange
'Medallion', apricot
'New Day', yellow
'Olympiad', red
'Paradise', mauve
'Pascali', white
'Peace', yellow
'Peter Frankenfeld', pink
'Polarstern', white
'Precious Platinum', red
'Princess Margaret', pink
'Pristine', white
'Red Devil', red
'Savoy Hotel', pink
'Silver Jubilee', pink
'Touch of Class', pink
'Tiffany', pink
'Voodoo', orange

JUNE 23, 1996

BEAUTIFUL BORDERS
Continual blooms are nearly impossible, but certain tactics can brighten beds

THE HOLY GRAIL OF GARDENING SEEMS TO be the continuously blooming border. Pursuit of this perfect border is the very essence of gardening for many, the challenge that drives them. For others it ranks just under slugs and black spot in the frustration department.

The challenge of maintaining uninterrupted bloom is a problem in areas such as ours where green things poke up in mid-February and don't wind down until mid-November. It's no big deal for gardeners where the ground doesn't defrost until May and by July everyone is headed indoors to escape the humidity.

With everything compressed into about three months, it's a piece of cake to have a sublime garden. Here, the strategic planning behind a long-blooming border could put Desert Storm to shame.

Not only do you have to arrange plants so that as one finishes blooming another one

A lovely border should lead to a resting place or a secret around the bend.

starts up, but you also have to balance shape, texture, size and color.

That's all well and good if you have the space, time, inclination and possibly a staff of gardening elves tucked away. But intrepid Northwest gardeners are meeting the challenge of a long growing season with different approaches.

- **The Big Bang Approach.** This is where you build to one splendid crescendo, say a romantic spring garden with old-fashioned roses or a pull-out-all-stops autumn focusing on trees and shrubs that will put on a dazzling color show. The advantage is that you have a chance to reach perfection. The downside is that it's short-term.
- **The Moving Target Approach.** There's no rule that says every part of the garden has to bloom at the same time. If you have a large enough space, you can focus on different areas at different seasons. For early spring, there might be a rock garden with jewel-like alpines. By late spring, the focus would move to the rose garden, and still another section could have a sensational border of late-blooming asters, rudbeckias, autumn sedums and ornamental grasses. By focusing on different areas, you can group plants that peak together for heavy-duty impact. The downside is that areas of the garden not peaking will be essentially green, which isn't all that bad.
- **The Twin Peaks Approach.** There's a natural garden rhythm in this part of the country. A whole slew of flowers naturally crest in June, then peter out. Then there's a wave that hits in August and lingers into September. That's when the rudbeckias, coneflowers, sunflowers, asters, sedums and other late bloomers take over. Because

this follows a natural pattern, it is relatively easy to achieve. There's no disadvantage if you leave for vacation in July when the garden is in its slump.

- **The Two Party Approach.** You can avoid the slump by planting lots of annuals early enough so they take over as spring's flowers swoon. Besides continuous bloom, you can literally change your look, enjoying a soft pastel garden for spring, then moving on to hot colors with marigolds, dahlias, zinnias, salvia and other bold-as-brass annuals. The disadvantage is that planting masses of annuals each year, as opposed to just using a few to fill in spots, is labor-intensive.
- **The Foliage Filler Approach.** You can bridge the July slump beautifully if you have a good backbone of colorful foliage and interesting textures. Red and golden barberries, golden and silver euonymus, burgundy smoke bush, silver cardoons and artemisia, smoky blue rosa glauca — these are just a few examples of reasonably sized shrubs that will add color to your garden between flowering peaks. As for texture, grasses and large-leafed plants come into dramatic focus when flowers die back. The advantage is that it's an easy alternative, plus a mixed border (shrubs as well as flowers) is a handsome look in itself. There's really no disadvantage, unless you're a flower purist.

There's no single correct approach. The size of your garden and the time you have to spend on it may dictate which of the following angles works best for you.

JUNE 25, 1995

WARNING SIGNS

Garden burnout strikes early

L AST WEEKEND, A LOCAL GARDENER WHOSE garden was hours away from being open for a tour developed a self-styled mini-nervous breakdown.

"I was standing on the edge of my deck watering some plants," she explained, "and suddenly I started snuffling. My daughters said, 'Mom, you'd better come inside.'"

Even Ernie seems to be losing interest.

Across town, another woman whose garden was on the same tour was having her own malaise. A friend had even come over to help with last-minute weeding and deadheading. Certainly, she should have been in the garden cleaning up.

But, no, she absolutely could not face it one more minute. So the pair of them took off to see the other gardens on the tour. Now, both of these women are normally pretty tough, able to squish aphids with their bare fingers. It doesn't take a high-priced expert to diagnose a severe case of garden burnout.

It's probably happening all over town. We are, it seems, creatures attuned to our climate. One of the pleasures of gardening is that we grow cyclic, in sync with the seasons. By autumn we are pleasantly worn out, ready to hang up the trowel and retire for the year. Come late January, the juices start stirring again. By February, we are revved up and madly plotting changes. As March hits, we are like racers lined up for the starting gun.

The downside of being in tune with these cycles is that when the seasons are off kilter, as is the case this year, so are we. This year, our hearts and souls feel as if we've already had summer.

We're through, done, kaput. We don't want to pull another weed, snip another deadhead, zap another bug.

Gardeners suffering from burnout need to know they're not alone; it is absolutely normal to feel this way.

You are not a bad person — despite what your kids say.

You may well be a victim of garden burnout if you have one or more of the following symptoms:

- The last plants you bought, you just stuck into bare spots, pots and all.
- In the morning, you find garden shovels, trowels and weeding implements strewn all over the yard — where you just dropped them the night before.
- You notice that your feet hurt and your knees are dirty and the dogs think you smell great. You knew all of that, but it didn't bother you before.
- You realize that being able to find only one garden glove, a left-handed one at that, is a justifiable excuse not to work in the garden.
- Nothing looks right. You are buying lottery tickets so you can afford a landscaper

to come in and just redo the whole darn thing.

- You could care less about compost. You are tired of hearing recipes for it. You never want to think about it again.
- You fantasize that you have a nice apartment over the garage and a nice couple will move in and cook and garden for you.
- You actually hope it will rain on the weekend.
- You begin to think of the weedy areas as meadow.
- You have decided to grow (or get) long fingernails in the middle of the summer.
- You don't care if the lawn does go brown.
- You have agreed to let your spouse set up the hammock, even if it does have a big ugly metal frame.
- You have to come in for a dish of ice cream after just an hour in the garden. It used to be a reward for a day's work.

> *Sometimes going to a nursery and buying an unseemly number of plants seems to help.*

- You have been reading real estate ads about condos with great views and no yards.

Because there isn't a lot of experience dealing with garden burnout this early in the season, it's hard to make a prognosis. Perhaps we'll all get a second wind.

Sometimes going to a nursery and buying an unseemly number of plants, for which you have no space, seems to help. Other times, visiting other people's gardens raises a glimmer of inspiration and drive.

Chocolate ice cream helps, too. Just take two scoops, and call someone in the morning.

JULY 3, 1992

OUTSIDE THE COMMON REIGN

There's a world of quick-and-easy options beyond geraniums, marigolds and petunias

JULY HAS ALWAYS BEEN A CHALLENGING MONTH for me. Spring is tingling anticipation. June is magnificent fulfillment, and August is the bountiful month of vegetables and fruits, while September brings the first hint of foliage fireworks.

So, what does July have to offer? The once-blooming roses and shrubs are over. Many of the garden-book plants that are supposed to bloom this month actually did their thing in June, thanks to our milder climate.

The lady's mantle (*Alchemilla mollis*), which I let trample the garden with abandon, needed cutting back and has left bare spots. The tree mallow (*Lavatera*), which was a champion July bloomer, grew misshapen and had to be dispatched. So, what to do?

Aha, annuals to the rescue, but not just any old annuals. Let us overthrow the dictatorship of stiff little geraniums, mustard-bright marigolds and sticky petunias. Oh, I admit to seeing many agreeable gardens with these perky annuals, but, alas, these plants, while suited to pots, do not mix well with perennials and shrubs.

My favorite annual for filling bare spots in a border is actually a grass, purple fountain grass (*Pennisetum setaceum* 'Rubrum'), to be precise. While it doesn't have flowers, it provides a color punch with its mahogany leaves and fuzzy plumes. Plant it where the sun will catch it, and it will positively glow.

Castor bean (*Ricinis communis*) is another dramatic foliage plant with sculpted glaucous leaves and red veins. And, yes, it is terribly poisonous and should not be planted where children or pets might nibble it. It's a vertical plant that will grow tall but not wide. *Perilla frutescens* has no such scary reputation. It's an Asian annual herb that resembles basil, but with bronzy-red leaves. It can grow into a 3-foot bush in a season.

As for flowers, plain old cosmos are my favorite filler plants. They grow fast and full in a ferny cloud that covers many sins. They're great around lilies to hide the browning stems once the lily has done its thing.

Other good annuals for mixing with perennials include tobacco plant (*Nicotiana langsdorffii* and *N. sylvestris*), gentian sage (*Salvia patens*) and a variety of sunflowers (*Helianthus*). Then there are the stars of late summer, dahlias, which come in forms from subtle to, well, Dolly Partonish. If you didn't plant tubers in spring, you can get potted dahlias now, although the selection is much more limited.

For color punches on the terrace, there are flowering maples (*Abutilon*) for sun and, in shade, coleus (*Solenostemon*). Both are best potted up. Abutilon will winter over if taken into an unheated garage or placed against a south-facing wall. Coleus likely won't winter over, but it tends to look lost if it isn't stuck in a pot.

I can't say enough about flowering maples. Not only do they have elegant flowers, primarily in soft corals and yellows, but they also have lovely maple-like leaves, sometimes very prettily variegated.

As for coleus, I never thought I'd be recommending them, but they have made a comeback, thanks to the many spectacularly colored hybrids. The key to making coleus work is to keep pinching them back so they don't become leggy like my mother's plants used to get, which is probably why I had a bias against them.

JULY 5, 2007

CULTIVATE ART
Outdoor decor digs in

GARDEN DECOR IS BIG BUSINESS THESE DAYS, whether it's actual art or a found object. There are entire books, and now stores, devoted to garden decor where plants are quite secondary. Anyone who has seen my garden knows that I am doing my part in this area to help the economy.

July, when plant lust has quieted down, is a good time to think about adding something besides plants. It's not a perfect substitute for buying plants, but it helps those of us who can't quite stop puttering in our garden.

There's certainly a lot to choose from, and some are pretty pricey, such as sculpture, fountains, Italian pots and those giant concrete pillars and gunnera leaves by Bainbridge Island-based artists Little and Lewis that I fall asleep dreaming about.

But most of us have budgets considerably smaller than our dreams. So we have to make do with more mundane objects that perhaps stretch the meaning of "art." Fortunately, that seems easier to do outside than inside. A rusty object clearly has more flair in the garden than in the living room.

Birdhouses are always charming garden ornaments.

From what I can tell, gardeners have definitely risen to the challenge of filling their gardens with winsome but low-cost "found" objects."

But there's more to creativity than finding the ornament. Siting and placement come into play, too, and can turn something ordinary into something utterly charming. Here are some tips for enhancing an ornament.

Consider background: Modern-looking objects look terrific against big broad leaves, while rustic objects, such as old birdhouses, are most at home with cottage-garden plants. A fussy, ornate object needs a plain background, or it will get lost.

Don't let it all hang out: A goddess or nymph rising up out of foliage, her bottom third hidden, has more mystique than if you can see the whole statue. Similarly, a small beastie just peeking out from under leaves is more interesting than if the whole critter shows.

Go for surprises: Not every decorative object needs to be a focal point. Tuck some ornaments away in little places so that people can make charming little discoveries as they walk about your garden. For example, we have a wire sculpture of a cat crouching in a tree.

Make it more important: A pedestal or platform, whether it's an elegant pillar or a pile of slate, can elevate an ordinary object figuratively as well as literally. Even a mossy rock can be a platform for something like a tiny frog, which would otherwise get lost.

Make good marriages: Placing objects that relate to each other together can add drama. Put a cobalt blue pot next to a clump of iris of the same color. Place a faux bunny next to the lettuce. There's a pottery dog looking up at the bottom of the tree where we've placed the wire cat.

Go for cluster power: Okay, so you can't afford one great piece of art; get equivalent impact by putting a lot of small objects together — a whole clump of ceramic mushrooms, a flight of glass dragonflies, a collection of birdhouses, a line of elephants all in a row crossing your grass.

Concrete leaves mounted on small posts forms a grouping of "mushrooms"; a ceramic bowl decorated with grape leaves sports a tiny frog.

Add a dash of whimsy: Throw birdseed underneath a flock of pottery birds. Place fish on stakes rising out of grass that looks like ocean spray. Sit a kitty sculpture in a birdbath.

If you're going tacky, be in-your-face about it: Ryan Gainey, an Atlanta-based designer, gets away with pink flamingos because he has a whole flock of them. One much-photographed garden in Oregon is famous for its cluster of blue gazing balls. I recently rounded up all my various bunnies and stuck them in the vegetable garden.

But don't stretch the tacky too far: I might be softening a bit on flamingos (if you have a whole flock or a sign that says Flamingo Lounge). I might even have a gnome. But I still can't abide those cutouts of chubby ladies bending over showing their bloomers. Possibly it hits too close to home.

JULY 1, 2004

THE BEST IDEAS JUST TRAIL OFF

A feast for the senses, the thrill of discovery can entice strollers down a twisting path

WITH HIGH SUMMER UPON US, IT'S TIME to go down the garden path — literally. Put down that trowel, back out of that flower bed and take a hard look at the entire garden.

Can you really walk around your Eden with a cup of tea? Or is it just something you see from the deck?

There's a difference between a garden and a garden view. Any garden worth its salt should have strolling possibilities that fill all

A garden is all about mystery and secrets, discovery and revelation.

of the senses. Walk in a garden to take in the scent of perfumed flowers, to feel the dew as you brush by, and to hear the symphony of buzzing bees, chattering squirrels and chirping birds.

Nothing can perk up a tired plot as much as a well-placed path. A typical rectangular city lot feels bigger when a horseshoe-shaped path runs along the sides and back of the property. If there's room, increase the sense of space by letting the trail meander a bit.

And a path can cut across the lawn. In a formal plan, a trail shooting down the middle and ending up at a focal point, such as a statue,

> *A trail can offer a magic carpet ride with a sense of discovery at each twist and turn.*

can be more interesting than an enormous expanse of lawn. In a less-formal garden, an off-center, curving path works best to bisect large areas.

Perimeter paths open up gardening opportunities. Many urban and suburban yards are ringed with shrubbery, often overgrown and bushy rhododendrons.

An interesting option is pruning the bottom branches of large rhodies, leaving enough stems and foliage on top to make attractive multi-stemmed trees. Underplant with exquisite small woodland plants, such as trilliums, dog-tooth violets, fritillaries, ginger and epimedium.

Normally you'd never see these tiny jewels from the deck or house, but a trail can offer a magic carpet ride with a sense of discovery at each twist and turn. Paths also divide a garden, giving the effect of rooms. Increase the effect by adding an arbor as you make the transition from one space to another. A path also can be used to transform that impossible narrow space between your house and the neighbor's. Just run a snaking path down through the space, bracket it with soft plantings such as ferns (these are usually shady places) and suddenly you have an intimate garden.

And here's an easy trick that's guaranteed to add instant pizazz. Where you have a long shrub or flower border, interrupt it with a small path, just a few feet long, that cuts right into that border and ends up at a bench, ornament or water basin.

A friend cleared out a narrow path just where the flower bed turns a corner of the property. She ran it up to a tree where she plopped down a rough bench. It was barely visible through the arching branches of surrounding shrubs. With the simplest of steps, she had created feeling of a secret retreat.

While these strictly ornamental paths can be narrow, most paths should be practical as well as pretty. An excellent rule of thumb is to make the path wide enough to take a wheelbarrow through the garden.

Straight paths look best with a focal point, such as a statue, birdbath, sundial or lovely gate, at the end. Curved paths are at their most sublime when they are lined with shrubbery so you can't tell what's just around the corner. The element of surprise is enticing.

If you want to make a path look longer than it is, you can add another dimension by making the beginning of the path slightly wider than the end. But unless the change is subtle, it will look silly.

JULY 2, 1995

SPREAD A DEEP, DARK SECRET
These plants flourish in shade

THE TROUBLE WITH MOST GARDENING BOOKS on shade plants is they don't get into real shade. They describe that namby-pamby dappled shade or light shade or half-day-of-sun shade. It's time to square up to deep shade.

If you live in the Northwest, chances are there is a tree in your life. And chances are you've heard it's hard to grow things in deep shade. That's probably true if you're looking at a big fir tree that rains needles down like, well, Oregon rain.

But if you have a big, fat deciduous tree, you may be surprised at just how much you can grow under it. I know whereof I speak. The area along our back fence is shaded almost constantly by trees about the size of the Empire State Building in the neighbor's yard.

Then, in our own yard, there's a large silver maple that anchors one corner. The area also is lined with large old rhododendrons. About five years ago, I limbed them up so they'd look like small multi-stemmed trees rather than shrubs. Then I decided to weave a meandering shady walk along the back, cosseted with plants on each side and the occasional critter (real and faux) poking out á la the French painter Rousseau.

I approached the problem with my usual scientific precision. Which means I chugged over to a few favorite nurseries, grabbed up every plant that was remotely described as a shade grower, came home and threw them all in the new shade area willy-nilly.

Today, my shade walk is by far the most exuberant part of my garden. Not only do plants thrive in shade, real shade mind you, but several even seed on their own (see accompanying list of shady characters).

That is not to say that gardening in shade is without its challenges. The biggest is water.

Conventional wisdom is that soil retains moisture in shady conditions. But when you get into really deep shade, such as what you'd expect right under a silver maple, you get the opposite effect. Dry shade. That's because big trees slurp up all the moisture much in

Hydrangeas bloom better with more sun but given a modicum of shade, the leaves stay fresh and gorgeous through fall without burning.

the manner certain dogs attack their water bowls.

To compound the dryness problem, when it does rain, the heavy canopy of a good-sized tree acts as an umbrella, so the ground immediately underneath doesn't benefit. Still another challenge is that slugs regard shade as the promised land. They are about a million times more active in shady spots. This is almost a scientific fact.

None of this should deter you, because shade offers some terrific advantages. When you're not overly concerned with flowers, you tend to pay more attention to plant texture and foliage shape and color. Shade plants tend to be lusher, with bigger and more interesting leaves. A shade garden is a restful garden. And, it's virtually maintenance-free, except for those slugs, of course.

SHADY CHARACTERS

The following perennials and flowering shrubs can stand fairly deep shade. Some of the bloomers might not flower profusely or at all in deep shade, but they will have healthy and interesting foliage.

Aconitum (monkshood)
Anemone japonica (Japanese anemone)
Aquilegia (columbine)
Asarum (wild ginger)
Astilbe
Athyrium niponicum (Japanese painted fern)
Convallaria (lily of the valley)
Dicentra varieties (bleeding heart)
Epimedium
Fuchsia magellanica
Galium odoratum (sweet woodruff)
Geranium phaeum
Hakonechloa (Japanese grass)
Helleborus (hellebore)

Hemerocallis (daylily)
Hydrangea
Hypericum (shrub forms)
Iris pseudacorus (yellow flag)
Lamium (dead nettle)
Ligularia varieties
Lysimachia nummularia (creeping Jenny)
Oxalis
Persicaria varieties
Petasites
Podophyllum (May apple)
Polygonatum (Solomon's seal)
Pulmonaria (lungwort)
Rodgersia varieties
Saxifraga
Tiarella (foamflower)
Trillium

JULY 1, 1999

INDULGE COLOR WHIMS
Let your choices follow the seasons

IT'S NOT JUST THE COLORS YOU USE BUT THE intensities that make color combos work. One reason Monet got away with pink and orange is that he used an intense pink. Similarly, a buttery yellow flower will hold up next to a red bloom, while a pale, creamy yellow will wash out.

I've struggled with color ever since I started gardening. The problem has always been indecisiveness. When I started gardening, I was pretty sure I wanted a soft pastel English look. After all, like many of my generation, I grew up on the romantic notions of *The Secret Garden*. I loved the pinks, violets, blues and creamy yellows that are always shown in picture books on a misty morning.

For a while, red simply didn't have a place in my garden. I can't say, however, that I achieved perfection in my pastel scheme because there were those Oriental poppies the color of juicy oranges that bloomed like brilliant flags each spring. It took me 10 years to work up to getting rid of them. Then there are still the ubiquitous daylilies. At least they are a softer cantaloupe color, so I am able to rationalize their presence.

But every time I would go over to my friend Virginia Burney's house, her garden's vibrant primary colors would knock my socks off. I always thought of hers as a Fourth of July garden, with flowers in firecracker red, true blue and bright white. She did have a little yellow, but it was always a bold taxi yellow, not a wimpy yellow like mine. When the occasional pink flower popped up in her garden, she gave it to me.

After each visit, I'd go home wanting to tear up my garden and start over. I'm sure many of you know the feeling. But through the years, I've been experimenting with color and finally have gotten part of it right — right for me, that is, since color is a very personal thing.

My great discovery, which I'm sure legions of gardeners figured out long before I did, is that you can have more than one color scheme. Thanks to our long growing season, you can start out with pastels in spring and move into more vibrant colors as the season matures.

Light is a good guide. Spring days are often bright but overcast, and the soft green-gold of new foliage and pinks and violets pop out in this light. As the calendar moves on and the sun rises higher, soft pastels wash out. It's time for more vivid colors. By autumn, the light is again lower and slanting and has a honeyed tone that is a perfect foil

Who can resist the ubiquitous but heart-stopping Crocosmia *'Lucifer'?*

for the burnished reds and golds of autumn foliage.

So now my garden starts out pastel but moves into stronger colors as summer deepens. I'm still not comfortable with bright red, so I tend to select deeper mahogany reds. Dark red lilies, knautia, penstemon and, eventually, dahlias replace the pinks and violets of spring's alliums, irises and roses. Golden sunflowers and rudbeckias echo the summer sun. And I love the apricot colors of tawny daylilies, verbascum, cape fuchsia and many dahlias.

Mind you, this progress from the violet end of the rainbow to the warm end all sounds better on paper. This is, in theory, what I want my garden to do. I still haven't gotten past the fact that some terrific pink Japanese anemones or the delicate purple toad lilies bloom late and I have to have them, wrong color and all.

But at least I've moved on from the color mishmash of what I refer to as my "Circus Period."

HANDLING COLOR

The artist Claude Monet had pink roses and orange poppies side by side, and somehow it worked. But most of us don't have a painterly eye. Here are some hints for working with color.

Practice restraint. A limited palette, with repeating colors, makes the garden look more unified. This isn't the same as a monochromatic scheme. Personally, I find one-color gardens a bit boring.

Indulge in blue. Snap up every blue flower you can find. A touch of blue enhances any garden, even an all-white one. Blue is equally comfortable with pink, apricot, orange or red. It's a color you can't have too much of.

Introduce colored foliage. Colored foliage — particularly wine and golden — is the best way to bridge the ups and downs of a long growing season.

Pay attention to hues.

JULY 12, 2001

GET THEE TO A ROCKERY!
Alpine plants provide a jewel box of discovery

UNTIL THIS SUMMER, ABOUT THE LAST TYPE of plants that came to my mind at this time of year were rock garden plants, those brilliant sprays that paint the city's rock walls neon colors every April. This summer I had that silly notion soundly dispelled.

Earlier this month, we completed one of our projects — a terrace of split basalt. We set the stones on sand and swept compost-rich soil into the cracks to hold them in place. We spaced stones somewhat irregularly so we could tuck in little rockery plants.

"We" doesn't mean that I lifted a single one of those heavy stones; my contribution to the project was to hie myself off to nurseries to load up on little fuzzy green things to begin filling the cracks. I expected to come back with creeping thyme, tufts of fescue, hens and chicks (*Sempervivums*) and other bits of foliage. As for flowers, I was sure that would have to wait for spring.

What a surprise to find a whole jewel box of rockery plants that flower in summer. I suppose purists would say they aren't true rock garden plants because they're not alpines. But as far as I'm concerned, if it fits in a nook or cranny, it's a rockery plant.

It's a whole new world to explore.

What cuties they are, too, with a host of new names I've never come across before. What fun.

It's a whole new world to explore.

Here's what I collected in my little red wagon with just a couple of nursery stops. In my first foray, I stuck with more familiar plants. All are summer-bloomers and winter-hardy. One end of my terrace is sunny, the other has afternoon shade, so I plucked out a combination.

Alchemilla erythropoda. Lady's mantle, one of my favorite plants, comes in this dwarf form. (There's also a tiny *Alchemilla alpina*, but I didn't run across it.) It has the same exquisitely sculpted leaves and froth of yellow-green flowers in summer, only in small scale. It'll do for either sun or shade. The question is, will it also seed as freely as its full-size cousin? I guess I'll find out. (8 inches)

Allium senescens 'Glaucum'. Ornamental onions really get around. This summer bloomer has pink globular flowers and blue-green strappy leaves and definitely prefers shade. (6 inches)

Campanula 'Birch Hybrid'. Nothing beats these mounding blue bellflowers (8 inches) when it comes to profuse, all-summer bloom

packaged in a no-care plant. Similar to *Campanula carpatica* (10 inches), which has both blue and white forms.

Dianthus x *gratianopolitanus* 'Tiny Rubies'. A sweet miniature pink that flowers most of the summer in full sun. Foliage is a thick grassy tuft of emerald green. There's a whole world of dianthus suited for rockeries; I just happened to pick this one. (10 inches)

Dicentra formosa 'Alba'. Considered a spring bloomer, but this white bleeding heart also flowers sporadically throughout summer. Foliage is a pretty mound of laciness, much like a delicate fern. (8 inches)

Dierama dwarf hybrid. A happy find I came by locally. Earlier this year I wrote about a wand flower with great, arching stems dripping with pink bells over a tuft of grassy foliage. What I didn't know is that there's a dwarf form. This one needs sun and good drainage. (foliage 1 foot, stems longer)

Geranium cinereum 'Ballerina'. This low-growing hardy geranium with lilac-pink flowers blooms all summer. *Geranium dalmaticum*, another dwarf summer bloomer, has pink flowers. (both 6 inches)

Laurentia fluviatilis. Blue star creeper's sapphirelike flowers bloom happily in sun or shade from May through September. An indispensable plant for filling in crevices, it spreads, but not invasively, in a soft, matlike carpet. (2 inches)

Potentilla nepalensis 'Miss Willmott'. Ellen Willmott, who lived in the late 1800s and early 1900s, was by all accounts a crabby woman. Nevertheless she was a great plantswoman who dropped her name on a number of cheerful plants. This cinquefoil has rosy flowers in summer and pretty leaves brushed with rouge. (1 foot)

Primula capitata. Surprise — not all primroses are for springtime. This one has purple flowers from July to September and felty, grayish leaves. Thrives in shade. (1 foot)

Sedum lydium. Stonecrop is a mat-forming succulent with tight rosettes of bright green leaves with red tips.

JULY 30, 1998

❧

A 'SCENTIMENTAL' FOOL
Fill those languid nights with fragrance

SCENT SEEMS TO STUMP GARDEN WRITERS. They stumble around trying to describe it and ramble off into romantic reveries quoting long-dead English poets and Greek philosophers.

Either that, or they get into biology and go on about essential oils and the sex life of plants and how bugs fertilize flowers. Before you know it, the whole thing starts to sound like an X-rated movie.

I tend to fall in the first group. I know I'm a sentimental fool because I just can't bring myself to use the word "smell," unlike Vita Sackville-West, who insisted that smell was a perfectly good word for describing attractively scented plants.

For me, there are two seasons in the garden when scent is the dominant pleasure. One, oddly enough, is late winter when the likes of witch hazel, winter jasmine and viburnum produce tiny, exquisitely perfumed blossoms on bare branches.

I believe winter scent comes as such a powerful and pleasurable surprise because the garden is otherwise relatively bare. Later in spring and early summer, there are so many visual pleasures that scent takes a back seat.

But now comes a second season for the scented garden. It is the languid nights of high summer when the air is so sweet and warm that we linger on our porches and terraces and door stoops long after dark. This is the magic time, when the honeysuckle, lilies, heliotrope and other aromatic flowers loosen their magic and make us dream of being in an Arabian Nights garden.

While scented plants generally require no more care than unscented plants, there are some things you can do to enhance their aroma. Here are some tips for adding fragrance to your garden:

Select strategic sites: Place plants near places you pass through or relax by — a doorway, an arbor, an open window, an outdoor sitting area or a strolling path.

> *But now comes a second season for the scented garden. It is the languid nights of high summer . . .*

Go for waft, not wind: A gentle breeze helps spread scent, but wind will simply dissipate it. Exposed gardens need windbreaks to get the most out of scented flowers.

Stick to originals: When selecting plants for scent, it pays to look for old-fashioned varieties. Plants that have been hybridized to produce multipetaled blossoms, assorted colors and other desirable characteristics often lose most or all of their original scent.

Evoke a special place: A sunny, well-draining hillside is a natural for a Mediterranean-theme garden redolent of the heady scents of Provence and Tuscany. Include lavender, santolina, rosemary, artemisia, caryopteris and *Perovskia* (Russian sage).

Combine two senses: Not all fragrant plants release their scent into the air unaided. Scented leaves, especially, need to be stroked. Plant an herb garden with fennel, rosemary, basil, sage, chamomile, artemisia, mints and other pettable plants. Set thyme underfoot.

Try theme collections: Group plants of similar scents, such as lemon geraniums, lemon verbena, lemon thyme, lemon balm and perhaps a potted lemon tree that can be taken indoors for winter. Other scent themes to try could be cloves and rose, although, given my proclivities, I ought to be lining up chocolate-scented plants.

14 FRAGRANT PLANTS FOR HIGH SUMMER

Brugmansia x *candida*. With its huge trumpet flowers, this shrub is in vogue now. Definitely exotic, it must have winter protection.

Centranthus ruber. Red valerian (also called Jupiter's beard) is a spring-blooming perennial that usually has a second midsummer bloom.

Cosmos atrosanguineus. Here's the plant to start my theme garden. The chocolate cosmos is said to be a perennial, but its hardiness is iffy.

Dianthus. Most perennial carnations and pinks have a distinctive spicy scent like cloves.

Heliotropium. *H. arborescens* is a terrific annual pot plant with a scent reminiscent of vanilla.

Hosta plantaginea 'Grandiflora'. Now here's a hosta with both showy and sweetly scented flowers. Also a perennial.

Jasminum officinale 'Grandiflorum'. This cultivar is somewhat more winter hardy than other summer-blooming jasmine vines.

Lilium. Top scented lilies include *L. candidum* (Madonna lily), *L. regale* (regal lily) and *L. speciosum*.

Matthiola. Annual stock is one of the most fragrant flowers. *M. bicornus* has so-so flowers but possesses the most powerful scent, especially at night. *M. incana*, the common stock, has lesser scent but showier flowers.

Nicotiana sylvestris. This tall variety is the most fragrant of tobacco flowers, but *N. alata* and *N. affinis* are nice as well.

Pelargonium species. There's a scented geranium for nearly every kind of scent. Garden writer Barbara Damrosch produced the following list: *P. graveolens* (rose), *P. tomentosum* (peppermint), *P. crispum* (lemon), *P.* 'Clorinda' (eucalyptus), *P.* 'Mrs. Kingsley' (mint), *P. denticulatum* (pine), and *P. fragrans* 'Showy Nutmeg' (nutmeg).

Philadelphus. This summer-blooming shrub covers itself in white flowers. Other varieties are suitable for a scented garden, but 'Belle Etoile' is particularly choice.

Reseda odorata. Mignonette is an old-fashioned annual.

Rosa. You'll want to select repeat-blooming roses for midsummer scent. There's a lot to choose from, but since the English (David Austin) roses are popular now, here's a fragrant list from Heirloom Old Garden Roses in St. Paul: 'Belle Story', 'Charles Austin', 'Chianti', 'Ellen', 'Gertrude Jekyll', 'Mary Rose', 'Othello', 'Prospero', 'Sharifa Asma', 'Tamora', 'The Countryman', 'The Prince', 'Wenlock' and 'William Shakespeare'.

JULY 16, 1998

FIGHTING CLAY WITH CLAY

Leftover pots help solve a hard problem

WHAT DO YOU DO WITH A LITTLE GARDEN space that has lousy soil? Most of us have a problem area like that. Our patch is tucked between the east fence and a boxwood hedge framing the vegetable garden. It has been, alternately, an herb garden and a white garden, neither of which was very successful.

The thought of amending more soil was almost more than I could bear, but then Doug the Wonder Boy came up with a perfect solution. We had some leftover terra cotta pots that we left off the terrace this year for a more open look. Doug grouped some of the pots, along with shards from broken pots and a couple of Moroccan tiles, in the problem space.

He tilted some of the pots, and laid others on their sides in that artsy-tartsy way you see in magazines. Some of the pots are quite small, so he knocked out the bottoms and partially buried them so roots of tough plants could work their way down into the real soil.

> *The thought of amending more soil was almost more than I could bear.*

We planted the pots with succulents and herbs: thymes, sages and other gray-leafed plants.

Doug, who is becoming decidedly assertive as our gardening becomes more and more collaborative, decided he'd like to add some flowers, but only white ones would do. So we found some little silver-leafed rockery beauties. We've sprinkled the ground with gravel to give it more of The Look.

We named it the Mediterranean garden. If this sounds a bit over the top, believe me we don't mean it seriously, since the space is quite unpretentious. The English often give elegant names to parts of their gardens, names such as the tea garden, the meditation garden and the Italian garden. If we gave truly descriptive names to our spaces, they'd be more like the soda-pop garden, the mindless repose garden and the Gresham garden, which is on the windy side of the yard.

Anyway, we're having fun, and it seems to be an idea that would be quite adaptable to those little spaces with rock-hard soil that lie between houses and driveways, or that are too small to really dig into or even ones that have no soil at all. I'm thinking of our old Eastmoreland house that had a pool with a concrete surround that went smack up to the fence.

I recently visited a garden with what looked like a lush herbaceous border in a very narrow space, less than 2 feet wide, between a garage and a walkway. It wasn't until you got right up to it that you saw all the plants were in pots. This particular border was in deep shade, so the pots were filled with large-leafed plants of different textures, and it looked quite dramatic. The key for a natural look is to stagger pots of different sizes.

Of course, the folks in condos and townhouses with those little terraces have been way ahead of us in using pots creatively. Those of us that have real dirt sometimes forget that we can solve soil problems (read: clay and more clay) by plopping pots down instead of breaking our backs digging.

Then there are those difficult spaces under trees where nothing seems to grow. A cluster of potted plants, even houseplants vacationing outside for the summer, would surely beat stringy annuals trying to grow in shaded soil full of tree roots.

My own little Mediterranean garden gets lots of sun and has no tree roots, although we do wage battle daily with morning glories that perversely thrive in areas of particularly bad soil.

And you do need to water potted plants more frequently.

Other than that, the only problem is that I have to get over the habit of announcing I am off to buy plants for my pot garden. It has gotten me some funny looks.

JULY 11, 2002

THINK OUTSIDE THE POT
Creative containers pick up where the garden leaves off

IF I WERE TO WRITE A CHRONICLE OF MY GAR- dening career, there would be a sizable first chapter called, "The early years: Marigolds and petunias in pots on the back deck." Certainly it was some time before I got out of the rut of thinking that pots automatically meant annuals or, as they are coyly called, color spots.

That's why it's so exciting to see all the clever perennials and even small shrubs gardeners grow in containers. Planting pots with perennials definitely seems to be an idea whose time has come. Makes sense too: It's both economical and labor-saving, because you don't have to replant every year.

The one caveat is, if you don't plan to move pots into sheltered positions for winter, the plants you select need to be truly hardy. Roots in pots get several degrees colder than those in the ground.

That said, here are some good reasons for looking beyond annuals for container plants. Architectural plants need elbow room to strut their structural beauty. They often show better in a pot than crowded into a flower border. Popular accent plants include New Zealand flax, bear's breeches, yucca and canna. These plants make terrific focal points and, combined with great pots, work as living garden sculptures.

Not all foliage plants are architectural, but they still make attractive container plants that are relatively carefree (compared to dead-heading those sticky petunias). Great candidates include hosta, heucheras, fancy ferns, small conifers, many grasses and plain old boxwood, which looks anything but plain when properly pruned into a neat shape. Flowering perennials work too if they have strong foliage, such as striped irises, agapanthus and calla lilies.

Some plants need to be admired up close. I just bought three little poppies that will have chartreuse flowers on stalks less than a foot high. They would be swallowed up if I stuck them in the border. *Cerinthe*, with its hauntingly beautiful sapphire flowers, is typical of small, jewel-like plants that look best in pots. *Clematis integrifolia*, a nonvining clematis that grows to a floppy 3 feet, is another prime pot candidate. So is eucomis, a plant with pineapple-shaped foliage.

Tender perennials are ideal in pots because they can be moved into shelter for winter. Then buy tropicals such as ensete, musa (the bananas), angel's trumpet and abutilon without fearing frost.

Those must-have-good-drainage plants thrive in containers. If you don't have a gravelly rock garden, think pots for succulents such as agave, aloe, echeveria, sempervivum

An old cast iron fountain with urns piled one on another makes a gorgeous multilevel planter for sedums and succulents.

(hens and chicks) and many little alpine plants like my late lewisia, which apparently succumbed to soggy feet this past winter.

Even small gardens can host invasive plants in pots. Bamboo springs to mind. A pot tames the pretty variegated plant called *Houttuynia cordata* 'Chameleon' with the pink, green and yellow leaves. Mints (*Mentha*) and grasses with runner roots mix well with pots, too.

Handy potted plants can plug holes in the garden that emerge. I grow lilies in pots, then stick them in the border when they are about to bloom to fill in where needed. After blooming, their stems and leaves turn brown and ugly, so I just remove them and put them in a holding space until they're ready for duty the following year.

Finally, pots are the answer if you want to grow plants susceptible to soil-borne diseases. In our neighborhood, we have lost several maples, including my street tree, to verticillium wilt. I'm seeing dieback on some of my Japanese maples, including the beautiful laceleaf by our pond.

Small, slow-growing trees can be very happy in pots for several years. That's why two new little Japanese maples that have come to our house are now tucked in pots and will stay there until we know the disease has run its course.

JULY 18, 2002

❧

STRANGER DANGER
Unsuitable plants beckon alluringly from nursery aisles

IT TURNS OUT I HAVE THE DISCIPLINE OF A CAT. I should have retired from plant buying in spring.

Instead I've spent much of July hopping from nursery to nursery. I blame my friends, because in my circle, someone is always saying, "Let's go to a nursery." What I need is an intervention. What I have are friends who are enablers.

I do find that my approach to summer shopping is different. Instead of buying en masse as in spring, I am more focused on special plants. That doesn't mean I'm saving money. I may be buying fewer plants, but the ones I'm falling for tend to be more expensive.

Take *Melianthus major*, a gorgeous shrub with blue-green leaves. After killing three of these plants in as many winters, I pledged "no more." But every time I saw one at a nursery, I could feel little stirrings of lust. Finally, I saw a good-sized one at the Lake Oswego Farmers Market and broke down and bought it.

Then, after killing a banana last winter, I announced that was it for bananas. But I hadn't counted on some gorgeous red-veined varieties showing up in local nurseries and waving their big paddle leaves at me. So now I have not one, but two. They look terrific stuck in pots.

I have rationalized that, although the two cost $45 each and probably won't live through the winter, a lot of people will spend as much on annuals. So why not treat them as annuals? This is my new perspective, which is designed to soften the blow if the bananas go belly up next winter. I'm planting them in pots so they can be moved into the greenhouse. I'm hoping that will save the bananas, but I'm not counting on it since the previously deceased banana went toes up in the greenhouse.

Each year, I try a few new things that I

know nothing about, which I suppose is just another rationalization for buying more plants. Recently, I spotted a ferny little beauty stuck in one of those "seduction alleys" that nurseries have set up near their entrances to tempt you with new offerings and the latest combinations. Even knowing it's a setup doesn't prevent me from being roped in.

But it also said the tree may dazzle you with its elegance.

This is what happened to me with a gorgeous little tree with ferny leaves in a rich reddish-brown. I believe it actually stuck out a foot and tripped me. Turns out it is a mimosa (*Albizia julibrissin* 'Summer Chocolate'), which I always associated with warmer climes. Nevertheless, its little tag insists it is hardy in Zones 6-9. Also, I believe that anything with the name chocolate in it is a sign from heaven telling me to buy it.

When I got home, I Googled the tree and found mixed reviews on mimosas, which is not what you want to find when you've spent nearly $100 on a plant. One Web reference said mimosas may wilt, may seed all over, and the sap (I'm not making this up) may erode the paint on your car. But it also said the tree may dazzle you with its elegance. This particular cultivar also was listed in *Garden Design* magazine's "100 Hot Plants," so it can't be all bad. I just won't park my car under it.

When I picked up the mimosa, I also picked up a sweet little evergreen conifer with the mysterious name *Sciadopitys verticillata*. It looked very cute, round and squat with long soft needles. I thought it would make a nice little accent plant for texture.

Then I got it home and looked it up in the garden encyclopedia *Flora*. It turns out that it is also known as the Japanese umbrella pine and will grow 70 feet high and 20 feet wide. The tag said only "slow growing." I now realize this is code for "you are buying a monster, and this is our way of softening the blow."

Now I'm wandering around trying to figure out where to put both the paint-eating mimosa and the someday-to-be-giant pine. This is terrible. I have no room for anything more. It is way past prime planting time, and I'm still buying plants, even ones with dubious traits. The awful truth is staring me in the face. It's time I admitted it. I am a plant glutton.

JULY 28, 2005

IDLE TIME
The appeal of low-maintenance gardening grows with age

WITH AUGUST ABOUT TO ARRIVE, IT IS AN excellent time to expound on the joys of sloth. August is a relatively lazy month, too late for much planting and too early for harvest and cleanup. In general, we gardeners are in an enjoying mode, rather than a working mode. It's a time for hammocks, barbecues and sitting on the porch.

The older I get, the more the idea of low maintenance seems to appeal as a year-round approach to gardening, not just for August. I really made the big leap into laziness the day I got rid of all my hybrid tea roses. I don't advocate that for everyone, and I mightily admire those who nurture these lovely creatures to perfection.

But for those of us who don't want to do quite so much work, this is a big step. I have found I am taking more and more of these steps. With the exception of delphiniums, I avoid any plant that needs staking. It is a job that I find particularly disagreeable, and it is difficult to stake a plant in a way that is natural looking. Really it is an art, and one that I don't possess.

I am also ridding myself of floppers. These are plants whose foliage seems to swoon once they've bloomed. In this vein, I have been gradually replacing my Siberian iris with Japanese iris (*Iris ensata*). Even after blooming, the Japanese iris leaves stand straight and stately, as do several of the stiffer-leafed iris such as *Iris pallida*.

Daisies, of course, are out.

Daisies, of course, are out. They flop at the merest thought of a nap. I am giving stern lectures to the asters to behave, or some of them may be dispatched as well. I find that you can avoid the flop syndrome on several plants by shearing them in midgrowth. This will make them bushier and more likely to behave. It works wonderfully on chrysanthemums.

Anything that gets powdery mildew also is out, which certainly includes *Euphorbia dulcis*, some cultivars of pulmonaria, certain azaleas and, alas, a favorite clematis. I'm finding hose-dragging a drag as well, so plants that can't last between general sprinklings may also be tossed. Ligularia, are you listening?

As part of my dedication to sloth

as a way of life, I've also replaced deadheading with shearing. Instead of individually cutting off the dead blooms of such plants as lady's mantle and coreopsis, I just shear them down like so many sheep. You can take lady's mantle almost to the ground, and you'll have the freshest little leaves in no time at all.

I also become laissez-faire about certain marginally hardy plants. I used to dig up my cannas and put them in shelter for the winter. It's just too much work. I now leave them in the ground, mulch the crowns, and so far so good. Some winter I'll lose them, but meanwhile I've had a good run.

On the other hand, some plants are just too pricey to risk losing, such as my large phormiums. So, I leave them in pots that can be easily trundled into shelter when the time comes. They don't develop the root growth and get quite as big as they do in the ground, but on the other hand they do live to see another year.

Of course, sloth, or if you are delicate and

What could be more low-maintenance than a few clustered pots?

insist on the term "low maintenance," is a philosophy as much as anything. And as well as cultivating plants, I am cultivating a state of mind that allows for some blinds spots. I am developing a very good blind spot for the little grasses and oxalis that creep up between stones and are so difficult to get out.

Possibly the greatest step you can take to a life of enjoyable sloth is to give up on the perfect lawn. I have a well-developed blind spot for the yellow spots in my grass, and I note that several of my friends have reached this same state. We've all learned to tacitly pretend these spots do not exist, despite the rather large mutts with their tongues hanging out sitting at our feet.

JULY 31, 2003

❧

SENSUOUS SUMMER
It's the time of year when gardens mesmerize the senses

THE PHRASE "HIGH SUMMER" HAS SUCH A romantic ring to it. It evokes all those delightful summer clichés: dragonflies hovering over the pond, the aromas of backyard barbecues, hammocks, red-and-white checked tablecloths, lanterns, corn on the cob, kids jumping through sprinklers, and rocking chairs on the porch.

When it comes to plants, it's the time of sunflowers, dahlias and tomatoes. In other words, high summer is the one season when designer plants take a back seat to the old-fashioned favorites.

If gardens appeal to the senses, then high summer is the apex of that appeal. The sheer abundance of the season is sensuous in itself. Warm nights bring out fragrances, and warm air enhances sounds from the purring of lawnmowers on a Saturday afternoon to the melancholy wail of trains in the night.

The lush summer garden is more tactile. It's hard to walk through a path without brushing against leaves or encountering spider webs, although that's one sensuous experience many garden visitors could do without.

Here are my votes for the things that most make a garden appeal to all senses: sight, sound, touch, smell and taste.

Tomatoes: I don't care if they don't ripen. I grow them for the scent, which always takes me back to childhood.

Ornamental grasses: They rustle in the breeze, brush against you along a path and have an appealing lushness.

Scented flowers: Some of the best are old-fashioned favorites: roses, lavender, honeysuckle, stock, tobacco flower and many herbs.

Grapes: They have a fecundity about them that symbolizes rich harvest. There is something very sensuous about plucking off a grape and eating it right in the garden.

Lilies: I didn't group them with other scented flowers because they are in a class by themselves, for both beauty and scent.

Gravel: I love the satisfying crunch of gravel underfoot. Walking on a gravel path just has a good feel.

Crickets and frogs: Even in parts of the city you can hear this nightly concert that reminds us untamed nature isn't far off.

Anything red: Common red or reddish flowers of high summer include varieties of dahlias, crocosmia, *Helenium*, daylilies and lobelia.

Water: You don't need much space to have the music of water. A little pump in a pot on the terrace will do the job.

The leaves and petals of a lacecap hydrangea glow with backlighting.

Gazebos and porch swings: They are sensuous for the memories they evoke, even if they are only movie memories of old-fashioned romance.

Translucent leaves: Leaves backlit by the morning or late afternoon sun have a sublime, glowing quality. Some of the best are canna leaves, the red, heart-shaped leaves of the little tree *Cercis canadensis* 'Forest Pansy' and, of course, Japanese maples.

Texture: Leaves with a fuzzy, lacy, foamy or needlelike quality are oddly sensuous.

Lawn: Lawns may be out of fashion, but there's no denying that the sweet smell of new-mown grass and the feel of soft grass on bare feet are sensuous experiences.

Cats: Soft furry creatures stretched out in the garden or executing ballet leaps at bugs are certainly a sensuous experience in our garden. Sometimes they push the boundaries of touch, though, when they jump on my back while I'm bending over to weed.

AUGUST 4, 2005

THE WILDLIFE CONNECTION
An often overlooked garden delight is the parade of birds, raccoons and summertime critters that move in and out

WE CAME HOME TO A CRYPTIC NOTE STUCK on the refrigerator by the intrepid Vicki, our weekly housekeeper. "Look under the chair in the front hall for a surprise," she had written.

We looked, and there, alas, was the late Anastasia, a frog princess who had moved into our pond to keep company with Prince Igor, the resident frog. We would like to think that a raccoon did the actual deed, and that The Perp only dragged the body inside. After all, The Perp had been declawed after the shameful incident with the koi.

Fortunately, the death of Anastasia is the only sour note of the summer. One of the joys of these long days is watching the parade of wildlife in the garden. Over the years we added nectar plants, berry shrubs, native plants, bird feeders, bird- and bat-houses and dangling suet cages. But for us, the thing that made the most dramatic difference was the addition of water.

Almost immediately, it increased the numbers of iridescent dragonflies, fluttering butterflies and hummingbirds. It brought a turtle that strayed in from a neighbor's, a large population of water snails and Igor the frog — alas, now a widower.

The raccoons came, too, but so far haven't been able to catch a fish feast because the pond has straight sides. They've confined their mischief to munching the crunchy water hyacinths that float to the edges.

Water, always an attraction, is key during these so-called dog days of summer when even the normally green Northwest starts to resemble a dust bowl. You don't need a pond, however, to have water. In fact, the idea of digging during hot weather repels those of us who would rather be sitting in the shade reading books with words such as "lust" and "unbridled" on the cover.

Bowls, half-barrels and troughs placed strategically throughout the yard will fill the bill, no pun intended. Anything that holds water and doesn't have toxic residue in it will do nicely. In the morning, you'll see the birds splashing in these instant pools.

If your heart is set on a pond, you can make a quickie by copying an idea from a nursery in England, which made a 2- by 3-foot square wall of bricks three or four layers high. They draped a watertight liner over the bricks, then set up a top layer of bricks to hold the liner in place and trimmed the liner so that it didn't show. Voila, a pond.

Those of us who already have rather large ponds are battling the green slime right now. Hot days increase the growth of algae. To some degree, green water is fine. Few natural ponds are clear. Crystal-clear water is not for the fish but for our benefit — so we can see the fish.

If, however, your pond is approaching pea soup and your fish are hanging around the pump where the water is most highly oxygenated, you may have a health problem. The likeliest problem is ammonia buildup from fish wastes and organic material. Be sure not to overfeed fish. If you find food bits floating in the pond after a half hour, you are overfeeding. If you add fresh water, never replace more than a quarter of your pond's water at a time because of the chlorine in city water.

AUGUST 5, 1994

VARIEGATIONS ON A THEME
Foliage that features streaks, stripes, spots and splashes can perk up the green garden

THE PROLIFIC GARDEN WRITER CHRISTOPHER Lloyd once remarked that he hates plants with variegated foliage because they look sickly. Actually, variegation sometimes

Cornus controversa *'Variegata'* is commonly called the *wedding cake tree for its lovely tiered habit.*

is a product of a virus (nonspreading), but more often it's a mutation that can happen to virtually any plant.

As much as I am loath to disagree with such a venerable gardener as Lloyd, I must do so. After all, I am a variegated person and feel obliged to stick up for all of us of the freckled persuasion.

Lloyd has a point in a few cases. The leopard plant (*Ligularia tussilaginea* 'Aurea Maculata') that is all the rage now does indeed look sickly, all blobs of pale yellow. Likewise, I find newly available variegated forms of *Tovara* and *Aquilegia* on the anemic-looking side. This does not mean I won't try these plants as soon as I run across them.

But, to dismiss all variegation in one swoop as ugly or unnatural would be to throw away some plants so lovely and so common that we hardly think of them as variegated. Where would we be without our dogwoods, English holly, zonal geraniums, ornamental kale, coleus, hostas and tricolor sage — all hardly rare, exotic or even remotely sickly.

Variegation is especially useful in shady situations, where a flash of white, gold or red on a leaf can make up for the absence of flower color.

It can also add interest to all-green or limited-color plantings. I recently dined in a lovely garden with a white border. The white roses against dark green foliage were elegant. But I couldn't help thinking it would have been even more interesting with the addition of some plants with variegated white and green leaves.

While some variegated plants are collec-

Podophyllum 'Kaleidoscope' adds great visual interest to the shade garden.

tors' items seldom found outside of specialty catalogs, there are many that are readily available in retail nurseries, and some are quite common.

At this time of year, you can easily find a canna such as *C. generalis* 'Bengal Tiger' with distinctive gold veins running across great paddle-shaped green leaves. Yes, cannas are expensive, but they are dramatic accents either in moist soil or sitting in a pond or water basin. If you leave them in water, make sure they are set so the soil level in the pot is higher than the water. While cannas are considered tender, I have had winters where they survived.

Nothing could be easier to grow or make a better foliage accent in sun or light shade than *Iris pallida* 'Aurea Variegata'. There are five or six other forms of iris with yellow or white striped leaves, and all have the term "variegata" lurking somewhere in their botanical names. All would be worth growing even if they didn't have flowers.

My two favorite variegated shrubs are a

> *Variegation is especially useful in shady situations.*

hydrangea and weigela. What's not to like about a hydrangea? One of the prettiest is *H. macrophylla* 'Variegata'.

Leaves of *Weigela praecox* 'Variegata' have white edging, while those of *Weigela florida* 'Variegata Aurea' are edged in gold. Both have pink flowers and are daintier than their nonvariegated cousins. Give them a little dappled shade or they will scorch in the afternoon sun.

The Japanese painted fern (*Athyrium niponicum* 'Pictum') is a treasure for a shade garden. It is a painterly combination of delicate silver-glazed foliage set off by wine-colored stems. Speaking of shade, *Epimedium*, with its heart-shaped leaves, is one of the most charming of ground covers. I can only imagine it is less popular because it is not evergreen in colder winters. There's a particularly stunning variety, *E. diphyllum*, that has a broad maroon edge to its green leaves.

The purple-leafed varieties of coral bells (*Heuchera*) are all the fashion now, but don't overlook the variegated varieties. 'Snowstorm' has green leaves that look as if they've been dusted with snow. 'Silver Veil' is silver on green, and 'Persian Carpet' is silver on red. Two of my favorites are 'Firefly', which looks as if a fine mist of white paint has been applied to green leaves, and 'Pewter Veil', with its fine brushing of silver on dark blue-green leaves.

Tovara, with its red chevron pattern on apple-green leaves, is not to everyone's taste since it seeds readily, but I like it. In fact, I prefer the red and green version to the more popular and more variegated *T. virginiana* 'Painter's Palette', which has white marbling.

A new favorite plant is one I've seen popping up in local gardens. Frustratingly, it is sold under two names, *Fallopia japonica* 'Variegata' and *Polygonum cuspidatum*. It's bushy with large white areas and very little green, a marvelous plant for flower arrangements. Do, however, be careful. It's reportedly invasive. Perhaps I will rue the day I planted it, but so far it's staying nicely contained.

VARIEGATED PLANTS

Some things to know:

- Since many variegated plants are sports or mutations of a plain-leafed plant, the plant may often send up an all-green branch. Be sure to cut it off, since it will be more vigorous and can take over the plant.

- Variegated versions of a plant tend to be smaller and produce fewer flowers than the all-green version. This is because the plant has less chlorophyll, but it does not mean the plant is not as weather-hardy or healthy.

- Don't bother to collect seeds from variegated annuals such as nasturtiums. The new seedlings will more than likely revert back to the all-green parent.

- Unless you are a collector, don't group a number of variegated plants together or you may get what garden writer Ken Druse calls a "jittery nightmare." Variegated foliage is best used as an accent.

- When forms of the following words are part of the botanical name, they normally denote a variegated foliage plant: variegata (variegated), maculata (blotched), marginata (edging), picta (painted look), reticulata (veined) and striata (striped).

- Forms of the following words will give you an idea of the color of the variegation: alba (white), argentea (silver), aurea (gold), lutea (yellow), glauca (blue-green), purpurea (purple), rosea (rose), rubra (red) and sanguinea (dark red).

AUGUST 11, 1996

❧

HAMMOCK TIME

In an otherwise lazy season, garden predators keep me busy

AUGUST BRINGS THE CRITTERS TO THE GAR- den, some welcome, others not. You can't walk through a garden without collecting wispy strands of spider webs in your hair. Spiders are good guys, eating other insects but not plants. Nevertheless, I am surprised at how many of our visitors are squeamish about them.

Lots of good critters have been stopping by this year — hummingbirds, dragonflies and especially butterflies. I don't think I've ever seen a summer with so many butterflies. I hope it's a trend.

The only things to mar the perfect dog days of summer are the unwanted critters. The slugs and snails are in mortal battle with the dahlias and appear to be winning. There are no baby fish in the pond because the bullfrogs likely ate the eggs. (The bullfrogs are gone now, thanks to Wilbur the cat's dastardly attack right in the middle of our first open garden.)

More ominous is the arrival of predators. Neighbors have spotted a coyote in our neighborhood several times, including in the alley

Fake critters are a lot more tolerable than the real thing.

behind our house. The poor thing has a pup with her, and I'm sure she's hunting for food. We aren't willing to let Wilbur, Orville and Ernie become tender morsels, so all three are rounded up and brought in every evening at nightfall.

And, for the first time, we've had a skunk sighting in the neighborhood. For us, the sighting was distressingly up close and personal. Ernie the dog was thrusting around in the foliage in back. When I went to retrieve him, there was a distinctly malodorous scent, not something you want on a dog that insists on sleeping with you. Into the sink for a bath he went.

We have had one sad event. Goldie, my neighbor Rosemary's koi, which two years ago survived getting shocked when she jumped out of the pond and hit an electric fence, is gone. Rosemary found her little body, or at least the head and tail. Goldie had never been quite right since the shock. Her body was bent, and she tended to stay near the surface of the water, so she was easy prey. But she did survive an amazing two years after the accident.

We don't know if it was raccoons or a heron. In any event, Goldie's remains have been buried in a solemn ceremony attended by Dakota, Fiona and Farley, the Ellises' dog and two cats.

My efforts to control slugs and snails have been pretty useless, as I don't use toxic substances. I go out at night with a flashlight and snip the slimy beasts in two. The first night out I got 125, so the next night I set a target of 100. But by the time my husband called me in for the 11 o'clock news, I'd only dispatched 93. I felt restive and unsatisfied because I'd missed my target.

But then, I thought, "Oh, my gosh, I'm actually setting targets, just like at work." I think it must be time to step back when you start doing it with slugs. What more traps will I fall into? Will I post my third-quarter results for slug slicings? What strategic plan do I have, and what tactics should I employ?

Obviously, it's not wise to mix your career with your avocation. At the office, we are always exhorted to think outside the box. But look where it gets you — a garden full of flamingos. Now if I could just train them to eat slugs.

AUGUST 6, 2009

༄ঔঔ

PARTERRES, PAR EXCELLENCE

These geometric shapes, planted to form symmetrical patterns, can make ornamental beauties out of leafy vegetable patches

SOME OF THE PRETTIEST GARDEN PLOTS I'VE seen this summer have nothing to do with flowers. They're vegetable patches — but not just any patches. These aren't drab rectangles with plants all marching in straight rows.

Taking a leaf from the French, more and more savvy gardeners are transforming their vegetable plots into, if not fine art, at least fine ornament. The champion of all vegetable gardens is the often-photographed kitchen garden at the Château Villandry in the Loire Valley of France. While Villandry sprawls over nearly 18 acres, it offers ideas that can tuck nicely into a corner of a conventional city lot.

The secret is defining and unifying the space, no matter what size, with parterres. Parterres are geometric shapes planted to form usually symmetrical patterns. They can be as simple as four squares.

The most popular shape is four squares with their central corners angled off diagonally to allow a central area that can be anchored with anything from a sundial to a perfectly pruned dwarf fruit tree.

My neighbor Rosemary Ellis has centered her parterres brilliantly with an old-fashioned umbrella-style clothesline that evokes the marvelous image of sun-dried sheets and towels. Her husband Walt gave up trying to get her to remove the clothesline and finally rimmed the base in a circle of bricks and flowers and made her paint the metal a glossy green. The effect is right out of an English cottage garden, a style that has made art out of function.

Parterres work equally well in small gardens or tucked away in small sections of bigger gardens because, even in places like Villandry, vegetable plots have to be small enough to allow someone to bend over and harvest the edibles.

Parterres are frequently raised and framed in wood or brick. Others are defined with short hedges of boxwood or herbs such as parsley, chives and germander. Some of the best borders are simply vegetables such as lettuce and cabbages. Strawberries form another charming edging.

Paths between the parterres can be both functional and decorative. They are a must to help you get to your vegetables. And they can be prettily turned out in fanciful brick or stepping-stone paving. When it comes to paths, small gardens have no disadvantage. Paths should be kept narrow. If the space is too wide, the squares or triangles will simply float individually and won't relate as an overall pattern.

Villandry has another lesson for gardeners with tiny plots. The French make ample use of supports so that twining vegetables,

> *Some people add flowers to their vegetable plots for a conventional prettiness.*

such as beans, can climb and grow in a small space. They also turn supports into ornaments by using pretty copper, twig or lath tepees that can be topped with turned wooden knobs, the kind that can still be picked up in antique malls.

Some people add flowers to their vegetable plots for a conventional prettiness. But vegetables are no slackers when it comes to decoration. It's hard to beat a combination of dark green, lime green and red lettuces blended into a Persian carpet of color. Later in the season they can be replaced with burgundy, blue-green and variegated cabbages. Leafy vegetables not only add color but provide an interplay of textures since some come with round smooth leaves while others are deeply tasseled.

Zucchinis, artichokes, rhubarb and ruby-stemmed chard rival the finest foliage plants. A stalk of Brussels sprouts bearing what appear to be minicabbages is a downright conversation piece. The florets of broccoli and cauliflower are as striking as a flower. And the exotic shapes and colors of eggplants and peppers are dramatic.

Asparagus and, on a smaller scale, carrots add ferny foliage. Onions, leeks and celery add an interesting tasseled effect.

Some vegetables, such as scarlet runner beans and even the plain old potato, have passable flowers. Tomatoes, on the other hand, aren't much in the beauty department. In terms of artistic qualities, they have only one thing going for them — their scent. And it's enough. Forget roses, lilies, lavender and all the rest. There's nothing like brushing against the leaves of a tomato plant to evoke the nostalgic scent of childhood summers. Tomatoes alone are reason enough to find a corner to make a vegetable plot.

AUGUST 12, 1994

❧

IDYLL FANTASY
My ultimate garden is just a daydream away

EVERYONE HAS FANTASIES. FOR SOME, IT'S A villa in Tuscany; for others, winning an Olympic medal; still others, a chance encounter with a dashing pirate who just happens to look like George Clooney.

Not gardeners. We fall asleep to different fantasies. We dream of soil that is crumbly like chocolate shavings; arbors smothered in roses with nary a black spot; velvety lawns that show no yellow spots caused by you know what.

We are masters of little cottages or grand manors with fabulous flowers that are perfectly color coordinated and gloriously healthy. Our tomatoes turn red without fail. The sun shines in daytime; rains fall at night. Weeds do not grow between cracks in ways that cause us to break fingernails pulling them out.

One can almost hear the bees buzzing . . .

Shrubs grow quickly, then stay a modest size. Morning glory does not run amok. We do not (sigh) lose the 10-foot lily just as it was about to bloom because we forgot and watered it with an overhead sprinkler that snapped off the poor lily's head (sob).

Birds, bees and butterflies flutter by. Wasps do not build a nest every year on the front porch. The fish in the pond thrive as predators are thwarted (humanely, of course). The lovely tree, planted with so many hopes, is not slowly dying of a fungal disease. We have at last found the secret of what flourishes in dry shade.

But these are small dreams. Let me tell you about my favorite fantasy. Remember those old sci-fi movies with giant ants and spiders lurking about, before everything was all metal and robots? These critters, the side effects of atomic testing, grew to a huge size; oddly, a size that seemed to change proportion throughout the movie. They had ugly dispositions, a thirst for human blood and the ability to outrun their victims despite their lumbering ways. Woe if you were two teenagers necking on an isolated road; you'd be the first to go.

These beasts were impervious to bullets and fire, so in the end, some stalwart scientist — working alone except for a lovely assistant scientist, Dr. Pointybra — would develop a secret weapon. The Air Force would zoom over and drop a mysterious bomb and destroy the giant ants or spiders, but nothing else. In my fantasy, I'm waiting for the Air Force to fly over, drop something and, poof, all the slugs and snails would be gone.

I think of these silly things as I sit idly in my garden in the dog days of summer. I'm happy to do nothing but daydream for a bit, ignoring the fact that cleanup season is just around the corner. However, just to complete the fantasy, my Jeeves-like butler comes out with a frosty soda and chocolate cookies on a silver tray.

And, good gosh, it's strange how he looks just like George Clooney.

AUGUST 20, 2009

IT'S A DESERT OUT THERE
There are dry spots to deal with — even in wet country

EVEN IN THE WETTEST WESTSIDE GARDEN, there are eastside conditions. You might say it's our little bit of Bend, if not our little bit of heaven.

At our house, the high desert lies just across the driveway, a diminutive triangle of land tucked between the drive and an alleyway at an impossible angle where neither hose nor sprinkling system can reach.

In some earlier energetic incarnation, I envisioned a rock garden there and actually attached hose extensions and clumsily dragged them over for some half-hearted watering. That didn't last long.

We took to calling it the Bermuda Triangle because plants went down like sinking ships. In addition to being difficult to water, the spot takes the brunt of the afternoon sun.

Through the years, however, a few of the rock garden plants survived against all odds, and several more plants that I have no memory of planting appeared mysteriously. And, lo and behold, the triangle flourished, sloppy and meadowlike to be sure, but certainly lush without a bare spot in sight.

From the last spring rain (which admittedly can come in July) to the first autumn shower, the triangle gets no watering at all. This confirms my go-with-the-flow philosophy of gardening, which in this case should be called go-with-the-lack-of-flow gardening.

The idea behind this philosophy is to plant plants that like specific conditions where those conditions exist, rather than fighting Mother Nature.

If you have a wet spot, plant a bog garden rather than fooling around with things such as French drains. (I'm not sure what they are, but they sound ritzy, so I like to drop the name.) If you have a dry, sunny spot, plant a Bend garden. This idea might appear to have been born of logic, but actually, like many great ideas, it was born of sheer laziness.

In spring, the stars of my dry garden are a trio of *Euphorbia polychroma*, two of which seeded from the original I planted. They're small, shrubby perennials with brilliant chartreuse bracts early in the year that make a fine foil for the purples of many early spring flowers, especially the tulips.

Speaking of tulips, some things seem to do better on a neglected, dry site. About 14 years ago, an acquaintance returning from Europe brought me tulip bulbs. Those planted in the triangle come back faithfully every year. Elsewhere, I'm lucky to get three or four good years.

By midspring, a hardy geranium with purple flowers takes over and spreads, bearing flowers into midsummer. I don't know the particular variety. In fact, I don't remember even planting it. But it's pretty until it suddenly stops blooming and needs to be deadheaded.

The summer superstars are the rockroses, small, rounded shrubs that bloom into October. The botanical name of this plant is *Cistus*, not to be confused with *Cytisus* (broom). Another plant with the common name rockrose, or sunrose, *Helianthemum nummularium*, also enjoys the same sunny, dry conditions as *Cistus*.

Other plants that thrive in my triangle on utter neglect include butterfly weed (*Asclepias tuberosa*), yarrow (*Achillea*), mallow (*Malva*), lamb's ears (*Stachys byzantina*), rose campion (*Lychnis coronaria*), snow-in-summer (*Cerastium tomentosum*), Jupiter's beard (*Centranthus ruber*), tickseed (*Coreopsis*) and assorted sedums.

Although I can vouch for these performers in adverse conditions, they are only the tip of the dry iceberg.

Finally, there are a couple of caveats about so-called carefree plants. For our east-of-the-Cascades friends, I should note that although the plants in my triangle thrive in dry, sunny conditions that replicate a Bend summer, some, such as the rockroses, would not take kindly to a Bend winter.

Also, wherever you live, all new plants need at least some tender care and watering. It's only when established that these plants can survive droughtlike conditions. So take care of them when they're babies.

AUGUST 12, 1999

WE'RE HAVING A HEAT WAVE

Four tips on preparing for torrid temperatures

AFTER AUGUST'S RECORD-BREAKING HEAT, I'm tempted to say knock me about if I ever complain about the rain again, but of course I will. After all, there is a plus side to our erratic weather. Just imagine how limited our conversations would be in the Northwest if we didn't have our weather to talk about.

I'd be limited to blathering on about how cute my dog Ernie is, debating whether ice cream or popcorn is the greatest antidepressant ever and wondering aloud if there'll be another mystery in the No. 1 Ladies' Detective Agency series. Just for a little diversity, I'm already training myself to say, "Whaddabout them Blazers?"

But fortunately, just as Bogie and Bergman always had Paris, we will always have the weather. I suspect that, despite our gentle whining, we are secretly titillated by its unpredictability. Surely, it makes life — and gardening — a challenge, but that can be exciting.

It's just that we need to know how to deal with triple-digit heat, something of a foreign concept in these parts. We are used to tips for preparing for freezes, but few of us are prepared for the opposite extreme. Other than water conservation tips, we have little to guide us.

During the recent heat wave, even well-watered plants expired. Drooping leaves are a sign of lack of water, but leaves that have turned brown and crispy are truly sun-scorched. I lost a well-established clematis. Maybe it will come back from the roots, but right now it looks as if the trellis is covered with potato chips. Doug the Wonder Guy's favorite plant, the he-manly gunnera, now resembles burnt popcorn.

It doesn't help much to examine how gardeners in traditional hot areas protect plants in summer. They grow different kinds of plants, many of which would not survive our winters.

Or they take a different approach to gardening. For example, in Italy, summer gardens are often entirely green. Terracotta pots, statuary and clipped boxwood provide accents rather than flowers.

Here are a few meager tips that I've managed to glean.

- Don't prune or fertilize during a heat wave because you don't want to stimulate tender growth.
- Mow your grass higher.
- Don't resort to chemicals if some vegetables aren't producing. Some plants, such as squash, won't pollinate when it's over 85 degrees. Others, such as tomatoes, may get brown spots from the sun.
- Some people prune away tomato leaves in hopes of bigger fruit, but a good thicket of leaves is the best protection from sun.

A panacea for hot weather? A water garden!

• Shade cloth draped over a simple frame may also help keep vegetables from frying.

There are, of course, some silver linings even when there are no clouds. This year the crape myrtles (*Lagerstroemia*), which often don't flower in Portland because they need a lot of heat, are abundant with blooms. For once the tomatoes are red, and early. I'd like to think, too, that the slugs are less active, but that is probably wishful thinking.

In any event, the most important thing to remember is that when our weather folks predict a heat wave, we need to prepare before it hits. Once we get record-breaking temperatures, the last place you want to be is out in the garden under a glaring sun. I personally will be inside reclining like a beached whale and trying to convince Ernie that this is not the time to be on my lap. For once, happiness is not a warm puppy.

AUGUST 13, 2009

[This column originally ran in the Homes & Gardens of the Northwest when there had been a series of 100-plus-degree days.]

❧

A PLACE IN THE SUN
Give each flower bed its chance to be the garden star

GARDENERS SPEND A GREAT DEAL OF TIME pursuing the perfect flower border or flower bed. Often, this means planting an incredibly complicated mix so that you have something in bloom throughout the season. That may make sense in New England, where the season is short. But here in the North-west, it's darned impractical since our season lasts from February to October.

If nothing else, unless you have estate-sized borders, you'll end up with so many different plants that you'll have a polka-dot effect rather than the pleasing sweeps of like flowers.

The alternative to the perfect border is to change focus every few weeks. Instead of trying to get each flower bed to be all things all of the time, give each its own day in the sun, so to speak.

We have, for example, an early spring border, a high summer border and a late summer border. Before you become impressed with such organization, let me assure you that this started out as an accident.

It just happened that the long border in the back was where the delphiniums and poppies were planted, and the long border in the front was where the rudbeckias and asters ended up. After a while, we recognized that the delphinium border looked its finest in June and the aster border peaked in August. Having two spectacles appealed to us, so we began to plant companions that would play up each seasonal peak.

We've applied this same philosophy to the early spring garden. We have a shady side that's lined with large trees. But the trees don't begin to really leaf out until April, which gives us a lot of time — and light — for all the early woodland plants. From February into April, this side is dotted with the dogtooth violets, checkered fritillaries, hellebores, primulas, trilliums and early-species bulbs.

Then, all of a sudden, the show's over. The green canopy has filled out, and there's barely a flower in sight. That suits us fine, because it's nice to have a shady green bower on hot summer days. Now, if we want spectacle, we simply cast our eyes on the other

The midsummer garden at its peak romps with abandon.

side of the yard where the June border is perking up.

If we didn't plan things this way originally, we at least listened to what our garden was telling us. Not only do deciduous trees leaf out, but the sun changes in angles and in intensity as the weeks go by. Different areas of the garden will peak at different times. Obviously, the delphiniums ended up where they did because they did well there. The border in front, where the asters and rudbeckias shine, is still a bit in the shade in spring but enjoys the long afternoon sunshine this time of year.

I eavesdropped on a bit of advice once while visiting a spectacular garden. A guest asked the owner how she went about designing her garden, and the owner replied, "I put plants where they are happiest."

That doesn't mean you shouldn't consider shape, texture, color and size. But when plants are placed where they get just the right balance of sun, nutrients and drainage, they are bound to do their best.

It stands to reason that plants that bloom about the same time share many of the same needs, certainly in terms of light and soil temperature. So a bed or border that is geared to peak during a particular month may achieve a lushness that is not possible in a border that is staggered to bloom over weeks or months.

There's also something to be said for changing focal points. For one thing, it's easier and certainly more realistic than trying to make every corner of the yard look great all the time. For another, the changing patterns make for a more interesting and more natural garden. As they say, for everything there is a season.

AUGUST 27, 1993

THE BRIDE WORE WHITE
The host wore a worried look

ALONG ABOUT THIS TIME OF YEAR, MOST gardeners are beginning to relax. But there's no easing up at our house. My friend and colleague Cheri Larson will be married in our garden in just a few days. For a gardener there is no more pleasurable event.

A garden is such a romantic stage for a wedding, and it is such an honor to host this blessed event. Still, there is a certain amount of Sturm und Drang connected with a wedding or any major garden festivity.

I still recall the first wedding we hosted, for our friends Rick Applegate and Bess Wong back in 1988. It was scheduled in spring, and it turned out to be a particularly wet spring. It poured right up to the weekend.

Then Sunday, the wedding day, dawned warm and sunny, the most beautiful day that ever was in Portland, Ore. You know the kind of day. The first day of pure sunshine after weeks of gray, the kind of day that makes Northwesterners downright giddy. That day when everyone pulls out their shorts from the back of the closet and lines up for ice cream cones.

It was perfect. The guests came in an exhilarated mood. The ladies wore big hats and flowered dresses. We all just knew that Rick and Bess were blessed. The guests parted on the lawn to form an aisle. Here came the bride. Here came our corgi, Guido, who plopped himself behind the bride for the entire ceremony and managed to get in nearly all the wedding pictures.

This year, with a high summer wedding, we haven't had the same worries about rain. Instead, we have a different set of worries, such as how to keep the lawn green and at

What could be more perfect for a wedding than classic blue and pink hydrangeas?

the same time be responsible about conserving water.

We worry that nothing will be blooming. After all, it's a law of nature that when you plan a garden event, everything will bloom unusually early. Conversely, we worry that what will be blooming will be the wrong color. The bride has chosen pink as her theme color. The golden sunflowers and orange dahlias aren't cooperating.

We worry that this is spider season. We like the little guys, but our guests in their dress-up clothes may not relish hacking their way through webs strung across the paths. The spiders set them up faster than we can clear them away.

We worry too that the caterer may have plans for something like salmon pate on the reception menu. I know this is hard to be-

lieve, but our cats have been known to have poor manners at times.

TIPS FOR A MAJOR GARDEN EVENT

Here's how to have a successful party and live through it, too.

1. Communicate with those making arrangements. After our first wedding, we wondered why everyone left us with 200 dirty champagne glasses. My husband and I washed them all, only to find out later that the rental service expected to pick them up dirty because washing was part of their service.

2. Don't count on your garden for cut flowers. As the day of the event nears, the last thing you'll want to do is denude your garden.

3. You may need tents rain or shine if you

don't have shade trees. It's hard to sit down to a meal in the blazing sun. Pavilions — peaked tents with no sides — are particularly festive and can be decorated with pretty banners.

4. Keep decorations light, natural and organic; for example, ivy garlands rather than crepe paper streamers. You don't need expensive floral displays because the garden is already your main decoration. I keep little green herbal topiaries in 4-inch terra-cotta pots to stick on tables when I'm short of flowers. I've had them for a couple of years, and they just need a little pruning from time to time.

5. Alert your neighbors ahead of time. Ask them gently if they could refrain from using leaf blowers or chain saws during the ceremony. Similarly, warn them if you plan to have music, and opt for romantic harps rather than electric guitars. And, always observe a nighttime curfew for music.

6. Don't start any big garden projects just before a wedding. Do fix-up and tidying chores, especially ones that can affect safety. This is the time to stabilize that wobbly steppingstone or fix a broken step.

7. Don't water your lawn a day or two before the garden. Grass will hold up to heavy foot traffic better if the ground is dry and firm.

8. How to put this delicately? Portable toilets are not that expensive to rent. If you have a large crowd and lots of liquid refreshments, this may be a good idea. It beats a line at the guest bathroom or having guests go upstairs to see your unmade beds.

9. And the toughest tip of all to observe: Beware of last-minute hysteria that your gar-

den isn't good enough. Resist the urge to go out and spend a fortune on annuals because you suddenly imagine all sorts of holes.

AUGUST 16, 2001

HARMONY HAPPENS
Organic practices, combined with maturity, bring gardens into balance

I BECAME AN ORGANIC GARDENER QUITE BY accident. I would like to take great credit for environmental consideration, but the fact is I am just too lazy to spray, coat and otherwise apply chemicals to my garden.

Many of the gardeners I talk to regularly say the same thing. And the thing is, our gardens have never been so free of disease and damage. This will undoubtedly freak out the new gardener who is battling fungus and bite holes that look as if Godzilla himself had been dining al fresco on their foliage.

But I have a theory. Most of the gardeners I hang out with have fairly mature gardens, and I think, as a result of that maturity, they are balanced. I mean the gardens, not the gardeners, because most of us are a bit crazed. By balanced, I mean that these gardens have as many good bugs and birds as bad ones, and the good ones are doing a pretty good job of devouring the bad ones. Also, over time, we've probably discarded most of the plants that are most vulnerable to fungus and other diseases.

That's one way to tell old gardeners from new ones. We old hands are ruthless about dispatching troublesome plants. And, if you really want to know how ruthless we are, you should hear what we do with slugs. Snip, snip.

The reason I relate this is to give hope to those of you who are relatively new gardeners and have been dismayed at the kind of damage you see. Believe me, when I started my current garden some 16 years ago, I too was dismayed. A giant tulip tree dripped aphid juice, as did the street trees. I believe we drove the stickiest cars in town. Black spot and fungus were rampant, and the leaves of several plants, particularly hostas, had more holes in them than a lace doily.

> *If you really want to know how ruthless we are, you should hear what we do with slugs. Snip, snip.*

Back then, we did put out slug bait; we sprayed a little and had our tulip tree and street trees injected with systemic insecticide. Then, after years of systemic injections, we forgot one year to do it in the spring when the sap was rising. So we gritted our teeth and waited for the aphids to arrive. They never did. That was years ago, and they've never come back and we've never had to apply insecticide since.

We did notice some changes once we stopped the chemicals. Suddenly, we had a lot more ladybugs in the garden. In fact, one winter they stayed over and lived on our den ceiling. Fortunately, we didn't mind. I presume other good bugs also have moved in and stayed.

One of the biggest changes is the number of birds. When we started the garden, we put out feeders, but decided to stop because, well, duh, we have cats. But, in the past few years, we've seen a huge increase in the birds, even without feeders. And fortunately, without a specific target like a feeder, we haven't lost any birds to our feline friends.

This is one of those wonderful and rare things where the less you do to the garden, the better it is. So, although I didn't set out to be virtuously organic, I have turned out to be by default and can recommend it highly.

I think another thing has come into play in making gardens healthier and more insect free. Through the years, there's been a distinct trend toward the layered garden. Shrubs used to be pretty much confined to foundation plantings, and flower beds tended to be flat. When you wanted to attract birds, bees and butterflies to your garden, you were handed a list of nectar-filled plants that would do the job. Now shrubs and small ornamental trees are very much at home in flower borders.

I believe Seattle garden writer and designer Ann Lovejoy coined the term "naturalistic" gardens, referring to this layered effect. I have found that the layered garden, one with canopy and smaller understory trees, shrubs and hedges, plays an even bigger role than flowers in attracting insect-devouring birds.

Or, maybe the birds are back because my cat, The Perp (short for Perpetrator), is now old and quite fat.

AUGUST 21, 2003

MAKE ROOM FOR REFLECTION
It's time to take stock as summer wanes

I ALWAYS THINK OF AUGUST AS "TAKING STOCK" month. That is, of course, a euphemism for doing nothing.

A comfortable chair and shady porch make the perfect spot to contemplate summer's lessons.

The neighborhood dogs and I are lounging around doing quite a lot of thinking this month. We are thinking about what went right this summer and what went wrong, although some of us are thinking about how good it would feel to bite someone's leg.

Thinking about what went wrong always leads me directly to the pond, which now should be called Lake Lazarus. A tree branch came down on mine last winter and ripped a big gash.

Naturally, all the water drained out, the fish disappeared (raccoons are suspected) and the plant life died. Plus, a bunch of blue herons had to go into therapy because our fish weren't available for them to scarf up in spring.

Fortunately, pond liner is patchable and ponds come back to their natural state pretty rapidly as long as you stick enough plants in them.

What's gone right this year is, for the first time, the pond water, at least under the floating duckweed, has stayed clear all year, even on the hottest days.

The only thing we've done differently is tinker with the pump. It's the same pump, but instead of letting it burble up from the water like a gentle fountain, we ran tubing through a hollow fish statue, which now spits out the water in a forceful stream.

Apparently, the turbulence created by the stream is sufficient to keep things stirred up so that we haven't had an algae problem. There is probably no scientific basis to this beyond the fact that it seems to work.

If the large pond has been a series of disasters, a tiny new pond put in by our new garden helper, Doug Wilson, has been anything but. Last winter, a dogwood toppled over in a corner of the garden that is almost a perpetual bog. Instead of trying to fight the dampness, we went with it.

Doug peeled back the vegetation, stuck in a bit of liner rimmed with rocks where the tree had been, and set the vegetation back in place. We stuck in a gunnera plant for a waterside look, and within a day, the pond looked as if it had been there forever.

The other major lesson of the year has been that farmers really do know what they're talking about when they preach the virtues of crop rotation. This year, I planted roses in the old vegetable garden, and the vegetables where the roses had been. All the new roses are healthy, disease-free and blooming like crazy.

The vegetables look as though they're on steroids. The tomatoes have clambered up their wire cages, been reinforced with wooden stakes, knocked these over and are now marching toward the house, apparently intent on devouring it.

Naturally, not all has been successful on the rose front. The new roses are doing fine, but the roses we transplanted into borders from the old rose garden in late winter are decidedly anemic.

A couple bit the dust outright, and most of the rest are anything but robust. I'm going to give them another year before I say that transplanting roses isn't worth it. If I've learned anything, it's to be patient.

Patience has paid off with perennials. Several that are absolutely glorious now were wimps for two or three years. Not everything is a one-season wonder. That's especially true if you've planted from seed.

And, while I'm sitting on the back porch in this deeply thoughtful mode enhanced by a bowl of ice cream, I've decided that, come fall, I'm going to get tough.

First, I'm declaring war on floppy plants.

I will banish the swooners that refuse to stand up without being rigidly corseted. I will consign lilies to pots to put in the borders when they bloom and remove when they become gangly skeletons.

And, for perhaps the sixth or seventh year, I am going to consider taking out the Oriental poppies, which, although they look glorious in bloom, turn to brown mush and leave gaping holes.

I definitely am going to remove shrubs that bloom fleetingly and remain dark, light-sucking vortexes the rest of the year. In their place will go shrubs of variegation or colored foliage. I'm also going to move plants around to get better color combinations.

The first to be dug up will be the orange crocosmia under a rosy pink hydrangea. I have absolutely no memory of putting such a hideous combination together and think it must have been the work of garden gnomes.

A recent visitor to the garden took diplomacy to new heights when she looked at this combination and pronounced, "It's your Brazil look."

Anyway, all of this should be evidence that, while it appears we gardeners are sitting on the back porch reading and succumbing to the dog days of summer, many of us are actually in deep thought about projects for the fall. And, perhaps one or two of those projects might actually get done.

AUGUST 14, 1997

Part 4

FALL

Thinning Out, Timely Teachings and Thanksgiving

❦

For all its beauty, fall is not a time for reflection and repose for a gardener; chores pile upon chores.

BODY CHECK

The tussle between garden and gardener can get brutal

I AM NOT SURE WHEN IT HAPPENED, BUT SOMEone has lowered the ground. I know because I used to be able to get up in one fluid motion. Well, no, that's not quite true. I was never fluid and graceful. Let's just say, I used to be able to get up, period.

Lately, when I've been down on my knees weeding and try to get back up, it has become something of a herculean effort. The problem may be with my knees. Or possibly all the bendable joints.

There have been times when I've had to knee-walk, so to speak, over to something to hang onto just so I could hoist myself up. As I finally make it up, I can almost hear that music from *Chariots of Fire* celebrating my triumph. I try not to do this maneuver when anyone is around, because it is not a pretty sight.

Balance, too, is a challenge, particularly for those of us who are innately clumsy. There is always a dead flower to be snipped or a weed to be pulled just beyond reach. That means stepping into the flower beds and trying to position your feet so that they don't trample anything precious while you're reaching at an unnatural angle to get at the offending plant. This is about the time when the dog chases a cat through my legs and has led to the discovery that if you grab for something upright and soft, such as a canna plant, it will not support you.

Then, when I am finally working my way out of the shrubbery, there's always something with stickers to grab at me. But the scratches on my arms are not the worst of the garden's assaults on my poor body. There's the thing with the hands.

Sometimes when I look at women with long tapered nails painted in pearly colors, I wonder if we are even the same species. Not only do I have perpetually stubby nails, but I've noticed these days that there is a dirt stain engrained in the grooves of my right index finger. It seems to defy scrubbing, and I have a growing suspicion that it may be permanent.

The eyes aren't helpful, either. These days it takes bifocals just to weed or deadhead, lest I snip off a new bud rather than a dead flower. And I have been known to snip the living tendril on a vine rather than the dead one. All these physical tests wouldn't be so bad if gardening did the body more good. But, alas, gardening seems to be the one physical labor that does not lead to appreciable loss of weight. I suppose it would if I were double-digging, but having done that in my younger days, I now regard double-digging as one of life's idiocies.

As I consider the increasingly nasty struggle between my garden and my body, I can't help but remember one of Martha Stewart's first gardening books. There she was on the cover all peaches-and-cream looking, not a hair out of place and a crease in her jeans. But what really got to me is that she was wearing shiny white sneakers and gloves with not a dirt smear on them.

Me, I must be the anti-Martha. By the time I make it into the house after a foray in the garden, I look as if I've been on safari for

> *By the time I make it into the house after a foray in the garden, I look as if I've been on safari.*

days. I'm brushing leaves out of my hair, swiping spider webs off my face, and trying to reach the bug that is waltzing across my back. I've got grass stains on my baggy pants, dirt on my clogs, dripping hair because I picked up the sprinkler the wrong way, and pockets jammed full of weeds because it was easier to do that than find a basket.

Well, at least I have the satisfaction that, while the body may be going, at least I still have my mental faculties. Now, if I could only remember where I left my trowel.

SEPTEMBER 1, 2005

❧

CHOOSE LIFE ON THE DARK SIDE

Forget your garden's sunny spots and try your hand at subtle shades of difference

THIS WAS THE SUMMER I FELL IN LOVE WITH shade.

If you had asked me to describe my fantasy plot 10 years ago, I would definitely have said something with lots of sunshine. Today I'd still want some sun, but if I had to choose between the two, I'd opt for shade in a minute.

Unlike sunny patches, shade has infinite variations and subtleties. When people say shade, they can mean dappled light coming through trees. They can mean light shade under high trees. They can mean sun for part of the day and shade the rest. Or they can mean deep shade under a dense canopy.

By comparison, sun lovers are much more straightforward. If you have decent soil and moisture, they're going to make it. But there's really no such thing as a simple shade plant. There are plants for light shade, for deep shade and for every blurring line between.

Finding out which is which is the challenge. I haven't had this much fun since I started gardening. It's the thrill of the hunt.

A scruffy mutt, of all things, prompted this new interest in shade plants. Meriwether wandered into our lives 17 years ago and wandered out one morning this summer when he simply didn't wake up. We never knew where he came from, how old he was or what breed.

For all 17 years I remained amazed that I owned a dog that ugly. Of course, we adored him. And that's how we came to clear out an overgrown corner way in the back to make the Meriwether Memorial Garden, complete with a corny statue of St. Francis.

Since the area is under a large silver maple, the shade is fairly dense. We had to whack out a large laurel, which was the only thing growing there.

In a rare fit of conscientious research, I compiled lists of plants that do well in full shade according to seven different source books. I turned up 111 recommendations, including ground covers, perennial flowers and shrubs.

The surprise was that not a single plant appeared on all seven lists, and only the beautiful glossy ground cover wild ginger (*Asarum*) was mentioned six times. That should give you an idea of how imprecise the art of shade gardening is.

Hostas made it to five lists, and another ground cover, vinca, was on four. The only plants that appeared on even three lists included the common ground cover pachysandra, bleeding heart (*Dicentra*), Solomon's seal (*Polygonatum*), our woodland trillium, the shrub *Fatsia*, the large umbrella plant (*Peltiphyllum*) and mondo grass (*Ophiopogon*).

This could give you the impression that

Bright colors strut their stuff in garden dark spots.

you are limited to only 10 plants or so if you have full shade, and most of them ground covers. Yet I have a whole cast of characters doing well back in Meriwether's garden. They even include crocosmia, which spread to the area and is not on any of the lists for shade plants. Thanks to a bird, the shrub form of St. John's wort (*Hypericum*) also is growing back there.

When anything started looking brown or droopy in brighter areas, I moved it back to this corner. Thus, some tovara and astilbe that were about to turn toes up are now flourishing.

Sometimes the opposite happened — the May apple (*Podophyllum*) shriveled and disappeared. The monkshood (*Aconitum*) that is supposed to be a deep shade lover got scrawny and does better in dappled light. On the other hand, the bear's breeches (*Acanthus*) didn't flower like it does in lighter areas, but the leaves got bigger and shinier and it was magnificent as a foliage plant.

Among ground covers, the epimedium has been slow to spread, the mondo grass has done zip and the sweet woodruff is just about as invasive as it is in the sun. As for bloomers, hardy fuchsias and hardy geraniums, especially *Geranium phaeum*, do surprisingly well in fairly dense shade. That goes for phlox, Japanese anemone, several lobelia and euphorbia varieties, corydalis, ligularia, rodgersia and *Actaea* (used to be called *Cimicifuga*).

The moral of this story is that it pays to experiment. It's like cooking. You don't need to follow recipes slavishly. Sometimes experimentation produces stunning results. Of course, I feel like a hypocrite using a cooking analogy because I am among the world's worst cooks, but my favorite chocolate metaphors fail me here.

SEPTEMBER 24, 1995

❧

A LESSON IN SUBTRACTION
Taking out can be as vital as planting — but may be hard to do

M Y NEIGHBOR RECENTLY RIPPED OUT ALL her evening primrose (*Oenothera*). They were looking weedy, she pronounced as she dragged the offending plants off to the gallows.

Other friends who live on a hill overlooking Portland just guillotined a couple of large holly trees. Although they say they'll miss the red holly berries for winter bouquets, they have lots more light inside and can look down into the best part of the garden from their bedroom balcony. They also see more birds at the balcony feeders now.

As gardeners mature along with their plants, they often find that taking out things is almost as important as planting things. So why is it so hard to do? Why did it take me almost 10 years to rip out those Oriental poppies?

I guess it goes against our nature to dispatch a perfectly healthy plant. But sometimes we have to be tough. The poppies had dazzling tissue-paper orange petals, but alas, they bloomed early in the season when everything else was soft pink, violet and blue.

Now that I've taken the plunge, I'm feeling a bit ruthless. It gets easier once you've made your first eviction. It also helps me to think of this process as editing rather than destroying.

There are lots of reasons for a good clearance program. If you don't know where to start, here are some things to consider.

- Are there plants that flop over year after year because you hate staking? Those should be the first to go.
- If high maintenance isn't your thing, consider tossing plants that get black spot and mildew year after year, even if this means doing without certain roses.
- Are there views that are blocked? Are some of your rooms dark because foundation plants have grown up over windows?
- Are some of your favorite plants (lady's mantle comes to mind) losing their charm because they've seeded all over?
- Are some plants are out of proportion for their spaces?
- Are plants too crowded and appear to be engaged in a shoving match?
- Are things looking all mushy?

Let me explain what I mean by that scientific phrase, "looking all mushy." I'm about to dig up some *Filipendula*, not because their pale pink color offends me and not because they are high maintenance. In fact, they are well-behaved. The problem is that they grow tall and straight with feathery flowers between some plume poppy (*Macleaya*) and *Artemisia lactiflora*, both of which also grow tall and straight and have feathery flowers.

The three plants run together in a blur, leaving one end of the border looking mushy

> *Now that I've taken the plunge, I'm feeling a bit ruthless.*

and ill-defined. It needs a texture change to bring things into focus. I don't know what I'll put in there, but it will have to be big-leafed and mounding to give nice contrast to those other tall fuzzies.

Sometimes editing is needed because a plant doesn't fit in. I tried some goat's rue (*Galega*), which turned out to be a lovely purple meadow flower. But in a more manicured garden — not that mine is that manicured — it looks shaggy and weedy.

So if you have flowers that flop or borders that run to mush, get out your shovel and loppers. September is a swell time to edit the garden. If you take something out, and it leaves a gaping bare spot, there's still plenty of time to give a new plant a good start before cold weather arrives.

SEPTEMBER 2, 1999

❧

HEDGE YOUR BETS

English gardeners know how to weave their shrubs into charming rows as screens, frames and accents

WITH FALL — BARRING AN UNSEASONABLY hot Indian summer — comes a special window of opportunity. The days should be misty and overcast, but the nights still will be mild. Perfect planting weather.

It's the best time of year for planting shrubs and trees. Roots can get some solid growth before they go dormant, and you'll have a head start on spring. It's also the ideal time for planting hedges, which, after all, are simply a row of shrubs.

Hedges are an underused gardening feature. Other than separating one yard from the other, they're hardly ever used. That's intriguing because, despite a plethora of rock and brick walls, hedges are a part of nearly every English garden. Versatile hedges are used as dividers to create separate garden spaces, frames for special plantings such as rose and herb gardens, privacy screens (a favorite way to hide the compost pile) and fences.

Hedges are commonly pruned, and commonly pruned incorrectly. They should not have absolutely vertical sides; instead, the bottom should be slightly wider than the top. This allows light to reach all the leaves and keeps the hedge verdant and healthy. For larger hedges, gently rounded or undulating shapes are attractive.

On the other hand, no rule says hedges have to be pruned at all. Where space and proportion allow, let the hedge grow to its natural shape.

The English have made an art of hedges. Their specialty is the tapestry hedge, where different plants are woven together in one hedge. Such combinations are most successful where the texture and growth habit are similar but leaf colors vary — dark and light greens, bronze and wine reds and lemony yellows.

The quintessential hedge material, both dwarf and medium-sized, is boxwood (*Buxus*). It is splendid both pruned and unshorn and stays evergreen. Check out Korean and Japanese varieties as well as English. But boxwood also is pricey and slow-growing. For tall divider hedges, Northwesterners seem to be in a rut with arborvitae (*Thuja*) and laurel (*Laurus*). One snowstorm can bend arborvitae out of shape forever, and fast-growing laurel is labor-intensive if you're trying to keep it pruned.

So consider some of the following plants that make suitable hedges west of the Cascades:

A privacy hedge can add lushness and mystery to a garden.

- *Abelia grandiflora* — An evergreen with delicate pastel flowers in late summer; can grow to 8 feet; best kept to an informal shape.
- Barberry (*Berberis*) — Striking reddish foliage; both deciduous and evergreen varieties; ranges from 1 to 7 feet.
- Blueberry (*Vaccinium*) — beautiful deciduous hedges up to 6 feet, and fruit is an extra. 'Bluecrop', 'Blueray' and 'Rancocas' are all good for unshaped hedges. Others may be too floppy.
- Canada hemlock (*Tsuga canadensis*) — Superb for heroic-sized windscreen hedges.
- European hornbeam (*Carpinus betulus*) — Tall and perfect for a rich, dark green hedge; deciduous.
- Flowering quince (*Chaenomeles*) — 2-10 feet, brilliant early flowering, Asian feeling; leave natural shape; usually deciduous.
- Holly (*Ilex*) — English holly (*I. aquifolium*) makes a great barrier hedge. It gets big but is slow-growing and easy to prune.
- Lawson cypress (*Chamaecyparis lawsoniana*) — An Oregon native that grows fast and tall; good for screening.
- Roses — Look for types called shrub or hedge roses. For full, tall hedges, try *Rosa rugosa*. It will provide both spring flowers and autumn hips, but no winter leaves.

SEPTEMBER 3, 1993

STINKY OR SWEET

Plant's common names dig up some healthy laughs

THE OTHER DAY A COLLEAGUE AT WORK started talking about tending his stinky Bills. When I looked puzzled, he said that was what the Irish on one side of the line called the flower sweet William. It dates back, he said, to their animosity toward William of Orange.

Intrigued, I did a little research and found a source that corroborated the origin of the term stinky Bills, and said the original nickname of sweet William dates back to William the Conqueror. Then I made the mistake of reading another source that claimed the name sweet William comes from St. William of Aquitaine and that stinky Bill was the Scots' retort after William, Duke of Cumberland's 1745 victory over Scottish clans.

The sentiment, at least, is the same. This convoluted history of the sweet William (*Dianthus barbatus*) is a prime example of the vices and virtues of common names. On the one hand, common names are not precise, and this is exactly why we should learn our botanical Latin like good little gardeners.

But, on the other hand, common names are delightfully rich in history, legend and whimsy. For that reason alone, I do not hold with tossing them out.

There's something oddly moving about the fact that someone, possibly in another century, looked at our little native plant *Limnanthes douglasii* with its yellow center and white rim and dubbed it poached egg plant. Whoever it was got it exactly right.

No other name would do for love-in-a-mist (*Nigella damascena*), a pretty little flower encased in a foam of thready greenery. And doesn't love-lies-bleeding (*Amaranthus caudatus*) just break your heart? Maybe that's what happened to the mourning bride (*Scabiosa atropurpurea*).

In some cases, a common name just presents itself. Wallflower (*Cheiranthus cheiri*) really does grow all over English walls. Christmas rose (*Helleborus niger*) does bloom around Christmas. Morning glory (*Ipomoea*), four o'clock (*Mirabilis jalapa*) and evening primrose (*Oenothera biennis*) all seem to follow the day.

Could those florid pink and leafless *Amaryllis belladonnas* be anything but naked ladies? How could you not chuckle over the fact that someone came up with the name mother-in-law's tongue for the razor-leafed *Sansevieria trifasciata*. If you've seen the wispy tufts left after clematis petals drop, you'll also recognize a plant known as old man's beard.

Other plant names take some digging into. Youth-and-old-age (*Zinnia elegans*), for example, is named for its long-lasting flowers. But candytuft (*Iberis umbellata*), which looks a bit like flossy candy, is a name derived from Candia, an alternate name for Crete. And cherry pie plant (*Heliotropium arborescens*) doesn't have cherry-red flowers as you might expect, but its purple flowers are said to smell like cherry pie.

London pride (*Saxifraga umbrosa*) is another one of those plants with dueling legends. Some say it was so named because it

> *Common names are delightfully rich in history, legend and whimsy.*

was the first plant to come back in the rubble of London after World War II bombings. The less romantic claim the plant got its name for its ability to withstand the city's pollution.

Still other names are elusive. What clever story is behind meet-me-in-the-entry or kiss-her-in-the-buttery (*Viola tricolor*)? And what about mind-your-own-business (*Soleirolia*), humble plant (*Mimosa pudica*) and bats in the belfry (*Campanula* subspecies)? What's the story with sops-in-wine (*Dianthus* subspecies) or dame's rocket (*Hesperis matronalis*)?

Some of the most popular common plant names arose because someone thought a plant looked like something to wear. This brings to mind monkshood (*Aconitum*), Dutchman's breeches (*Dicentra cucullaria*), granny's nightcap (*Aquilegia*), wee folks' stockings (*Corydalis lutea*), lady's eardrops (*Fuchsia*) and blue lace flower (*Trachymene coerulea*).

Humans also seem to see animals in plants. Consider there's snapdragon (*Antirrhinum*), heron's bill (*Erodium*), toad lily (*Tricyrtis*), hound's tongue (*Cynoglossum*), dogtooth violet (*Erythronium dens-canis*), foxtail lily (*Eremurus*), turtlehead (*Chelone*), snake's head (*Fritillaria meleagris*) and cranesbill (perennial *Geranium*), just to name a few.

Speaking of animals, I'm happy to report there are no leopards or wolves in my garden thanks to leopard's bane (*Doronicum*) and wolf's bane (*Aconitum*). But I wish I could say that fleabane (*Erigeron*) was equally effective.

And speaking of common named plants, it seems like poetic justice that an Oregon native — darmera, also known as *Peltiphyllum peltatum* — is known as the umbrella plant.

SEPTEMBER 10, 1998

TIMELY TEACHINGS
Be smart with annuals

I ALWAYS HAVE HAD AN AMBIGUOUS RELATIONship with annuals. I've had to learn several lessons about them. The first was that there is more to annuals than the marigolds and petunias I grew up with. It turns out that not all annuals are sticky and in need of constant deadheading.

I indulged in the likes of sweet-smelling nicotiana, lacy cosmos and perky little zinnias. But at some point I stopped planting even these because it seemed so labor-intensive to plant the same flowers each year. I decided I was a perennials-only gardener.

That's when I learned a second lesson.

I missed the color and freshness that annuals can bring late in the summer. So the lesson this time was that planting annuals need not be labor-intensive to give effect. I didn't need to put out bedding plants like some Victorian throwback. Annuals in a few judiciously placed containers could perk up my late-season garden.

This summer I learned yet another lesson about annuals.

I learned to stop thinking of them as just flowers. There are some terrific foliage annuals. Sweet potato vine (*Ipomoea batatas*) is an example. There are varieties with chartreuse leaves, nearly black leaves and a pretty mottled leaf. They trail delightfully out of pots or send tendrils out along the edges of paths.

The silvery licorice plant (*Helichrysum petiolare*) also is a great annual to stick into pots, where it will billow out horizontally and gracefully in no time at all. Its foliage is a lovely foil to plants with reddish leaves and flowers in oranges, reds, blues and purples.

Then there is coleus (*Solenostemon scutellarioides*), with as many colors as Jacob's coat. There has been an explosion of new color variations and variegations, not to mention ruffled leaves.

Zonal geraniums (*Pelargonium* hybrids) are right behind coleus in the new-fashions department, as each year more varieties seem available. I bought a sweet little geranium with purple-and-green serrated leaves and stuck it in a pot. To my horror it sprouted flaming orange flowers. I went back and looked at the tag and saw that it was called 'Happy Orange'. I didn't mind too much, however, because as I plucked off the flow-

The "perennial" fountain grass Pennisetum setaceum *'Rubrum' acts like an annual for us, but is well worth growing for its arching, dark red leaves and frothy flowers.*

ers, I loved the old-fashioned geranium scent that was released.

One tends to think of nasturtiums (*Tropaeolum*) as flower plants, but they have lovely rounded leaves of green and yellow. They earn their keep with the way they billow out and fill in bare spots.

This summer, on a garden visit, I saw some of the new purple-leafed pineapple plant (*Eucomis comosa* 'Sparkling Burgundy') growing out of a golden ground cover. It was stunning. You might argue that eucomis is a perennial, but in my garden it seems to be an annual. I came right home and planted some. They didn't flower, but it didn't matter. The leaves alone are worth it.

And, of course, there are a number of annual grasses that are most dramatic in September. The fountain grasses (*Pennisetum setaceum*) are particularly gorgeous and sometimes even live over. There's also an increasing number of dark-leafed dahlias with foliage almost as pretty as the flowers.

So, my final lesson about annuals is not to be a perennial snob.

SEPTEMBER 16, 2004

"SPRING FORWARD, FALL" PLANT

For Northwest gardeners, the timing is good if the sudden urge arises to re-create your masterpiece

I MAGINE MY SURPRISE WHEN I PICKED UP THE September issue of *Practical Gardener* and found the following quote by one of the goddesses of horticulture.

There, blown up big under a picture of garden author and designer Rosemary Verey, was the following statement. "Gardening is about plants and good design, it's not about cramming a garden with odd bits and pieces."

Well, that shoots my whole gardening style. Bits and pieces jammed and crammed in perfectly describes my long border in the back.

It was the first of the garden to be developed nine years ago when we moved in. Over the years, some plants have died off (the lupine), others have spread (the asters) and some are mere wimpy shadows of their former selves (the delphiniums).

> *We all need this reminder to dispel a recurring Northwest fantasy that we actually have spring here in the Northwest.*

As holes have appeared, I've responded by simply, in Verey's immortal words, jamming something in to fill the hole. Meanwhile, the spreaders have taken over and gotten all out of proportion. All semblance of balance has been lost. Strange things have happened, such as the infamous orange-red crocosmia suddenly appearing next to the salmon pink phlox.

This whole incident, naturally, provokes one of those crises that gardeners are episodically prone to. You're going along just fine thinking your garden is starting to look pretty good. In fact, you're getting smug.

Then, something happens to knock the rose-colored glasses off, and you take a new look at your garden and want to rip the whole thing up. This is normal. You don't need to start making reservations at the Betty Ford Center for Depressed Gardeners.

Fortunately, this is the time to take action. In the Pacific Northwest, if you're going to redo anything in your garden, autumn is absolutely the very best opportunity. Unfor-tunately, your body clock may be out of sync. Mine certainly is. By this time of year, most of us are winding down, while in spring, we're positively tingling to get out there and dig.

That's why we all need this reminder to dispel a recurring Northwest fantasy that we actually have spring here in the Northwest. To be brutally honest, spring is simply a warmed-up extension of winter.

Spring rain, even when it's gentle, falls on thoroughly waterlogged ground, which makes digging pretty sloppy. Plus the clever people, such as our extension agents, who know about things like soil structure, tell us we can actually compact our clay soil even more by digging when it's wet.

Autumn rain, however, is hitting drier soil and provides just enough moisture to make even clay nice and crumbly for digging.

Another plus is that the soil is still warm at this time of year, which helps new plants and transplants get root systems established before the first hard frost. In spring, on the other hand, soggy soil can stay cold into June.

I recently read an excellent article on fall planting Kate Jerome in *Fine Gardening*. She described which kinds of plants do better in fall planting, and which should wait until spring. Evergreens, for example, need to be planted in early autumn or left until spring. That's because they don't go dormant like deciduous trees and will need to get better established to survive the winter.

Some plants, such as magnolias, which are slow to send out new roots, are the few exceptions that are best left to spring. As a rule, anything that's described as difficult to transplant or divide should wait until spring for that very reason.

There are, however, plants that actually prefer fall planting, even where springs are warm and sunny. Lilies and peonies do better with fall planting, as well as many ornamental trees such as Japanese maples.

The tricky thing is knowing how long it's safe to plant and transplant at this time of year since, obviously, there needs to be enough time for roots to get firmly anchored before temperatures dip and all growth shuts down.

Jerome's formula should work wherever you live. She advises you get things in the ground before all the leaves have fallen from the deciduous trees.

SEPTEMBER 17, 1995

❧

THINK SHORT AND STURDY
Tall, loose-petal flowers collapse in spring rains

W HEN CHOOSING SPRING-BLOOMING BULBS for fall planting, think small. It's easy to get carried away with glossy pictures and promises of multicolored tulips with double petals, ruffled edges and exotic pedigrees. They're a bit like the old Cadillacs resplendent with tailfins, chrome and flashing lights.

Unfortunately, their mileage may be just about the same. Tall, fancy, loose-petaled flowers simply collapse under the typical spring rains in Western Oregon and Washington. If you're absolutely in love, go ahead and get a few for some pots or a clump here and there. But if you're planning to plant great drifts of bulbs, invest in the little Volkswagens of the bulb family.

These are the bulbs often referred to as the "minor bulbs." They're short, sturdy and reliably carefree. They hold up under heavy rain and bloom their hearts out early in the season.

Consider planting these charming miniatures under deciduous trees. They lend themselves to a woodland look and, because they bloom early, they'll flower before the trees leaf out to block the light. They're also ideal for rock gardens.

None of the minor bulbs are more than 18 inches high, and most are under a foot. They look particularly splendid planted in drifts of all one color. Because they're small, don't be stingy. Be brave and think in terms of clusters of 50 to 100 bulbs.

The minor bulbs below are ranked in approximate order of bloom.

Snowdrops (*Galanthus*): Nodding stems under 8 inches high bear white blooms resembling tear-shaped pearls. They're among the earliest flowers to bloom.

Winter aconite (*Eranthis*): Only 4 inches tall and blooming early, winter aconites spread in bright yellow patches, resembling pools of sunshine.

Species crocus: They're tinier and bloom earlier than the more common Dutch crocuses. Nothing beats them for holding up to spring deluges.

Glory-of-the-snow (*Chionodoxa*): Tiny blue stars are surrounded by strappy leaves only 4 or 5 inches high.

Iris reticulata: Imagine perfect miniature blue iris only 6 inches high. They are the first iris to bloom.

Snowflake (*Leucojum*): Miniature white bells dangle amid strappy leaves about 9 inches high.

Miniature daffodils (*Narcissus bulbo-*

codium): Some of these tiny yellow daffodils are only 6 inches high.

Siberian squill (*Scilla siberica*): The bell-shaped flowers only 6 inches high are an exceptional sapphire blue.

Dogtooth violets (*Erythronium*): Just over a foot high, these charming flowers have purple, white or yellow star-shaped flowers on bending stems. The flowers resemble tiny lilies.

Checkered lily (*Fritillaria meleagris*): These are among the most exquisite and unusual flowers. The veining on the greenish-purple bell-shaped blossoms gives a distinctive checkered pattern. They are about a foot tall.

There's an important caveat to buying bulbs. Take the trouble to find out if they've been propagated by growers or dug in the wild. The wild forms of many common bulbs are now on the endangered list because they have been harvested indiscriminately, particularly in Turkey, Greece and Spain.

Beginning in 1992, all bulbs sold out of Holland (about 60 percent of the bulbs available in the United States) will be marked either "bulbs grown from cultivated stock" or "bulbs grown from wild source."

Until then, buy only from reputable dealers and, if ordering bulbs, specify that you want only "cultivated" or "propagated" bulbs. According to the Natural Resources Defense Council, the following wild forms of bulbs are particularly endangered: winter aconite (*Eranthis hyemalis*), snowdrops (*Galanthus elwesii*), snowflakes (*Leucojum aestivum* and *L. vernum*), and the following narcissus: *Narcissus triandrus, N. asturiensis, N. cyclamineus* and *N. bulbocodium*.

SEPTEMBER 20, 1991

PLAN A GRACEFUL AUTUMN

Resist the tendency to coax those summer buds a little more, and enjoy the bitter-sweet beauty of fall flowers and foliage

SOMETHING WAS CLEARLY WRONG. I WAS OUT in the garden this past week madly clipping dead roses, cosmos, dahlias and other late flowers trying to coax a few more weeks of bloom out of them. Somehow it didn't feel right.

Oh, sure, deadheading will prolong some flowers until a hard frost, but summer flowers just don't have the right feel now. The cosmos, for example, are still bravely pumping out blossoms, but the foliage is getting

Enjoy the last of the roses but don't deadhead them. You don't want to encourage new growth just before the first frost hits.

frankly crummy looking. Finally, it occurred to me what's wrong.

Prolonging the bright summer garden is a lot like an aging belle piling on the gaudy makeup in a desperate attempt to hold the years at bay. A lot is to be said for aging gracefully, whether it's people or gardens. Calculated, color-bold plantings are magnificent in the youth of the garden. Now a more natural look, akin to the season, is fitting.

Why have tired flowers when you can have fresh berries? Why prolong pretty but wimpy pink and yellow blossoms when you can have the drama of scarlet and wine and gold? Why try to tease one more month out of summer when you can enjoy the magnificence of autumn?

It's time to stop deadheading like a fiend. It's time to pull up the wilting cosmos and nicotiana and browning marigolds. Forget trying to coax a few more weeks out of the roses. The rains will rot them anyway. Instead, let them go to seed and enjoy the rose hips.

It will be a while before a hard enough frost will deliver really good color. But think of these next few weeks as a mini-season — the green season. Not just flowers are gone, but the yellow lawn is gone, too. Even those of us who aren't particularly lawn people suddenly find ourselves with a lush patch, thanks to some rain.

During this green period, enjoy the textures and shapes that you didn't see when you were blinded by flowers. Big-leafed plants such as hostas, bergenias and ligularia are getting tatty but still are magnificent. The ferns and grasses are a sight to behold. The smart gardener is one who has spent as much time building on foliage as on flowers. It will pay off now.

The idea is to look at the garden with new eyes and enjoy it for what it is now, not mourn for what we're losing. Not every day will be sunny; enjoy the freshness and humusy smell that comes after a rain. Sure, you think, easy for me to say. Everyone who has visited my garden is aware I'm a slob.

We garden slobs let vines ramble all over the place. We only get conservative when it comes to pruning. If we make plant lists at all, they are out the window at the first plant sale. "Neat" is not in our vocabulary; natural is. In short, autumn is our season.

Let me make a case for enjoying the later garden. Don't think of it as messy; think of it as relaxed. Don't think decay; think decadence. It is ever so much classier. Don't view the garden season as ending. Think of it as the beginning of a new season.

SEPTEMBER 23, 1994

POLITE SHRUBS
The good guys get repeat invitations to garden parties

THIS GRAY SUMMER TAUGHT ME A GOOD LESson. The shrubs I've been insinuating here and there among flowers paid their garden dues. When flowers were slow to open or, in some cases, didn't open at all this summer, the shrubbery structure held things together.

With gray fall around the corner, it's an ideal time to adopt even more shrubs. In fact, as I move more into my garden dotage, I become more and more enamored of shrubbery and less and less dependent on annuals and perennials.

I find the combination of shrubs and smaller plants charming. But not every shrub

Often looking more like a shrub than the small tree that it is, the white-edged leaves of Azara microphylla *'Variegata' add light to dark corners.*

is a great mixer with flowers. I've made my share of mistakes.

One year, I fell madly in love with the idea of winter color, so I planted a Siberian dogwood (*Cornus alba* 'Sibirica') for the show its scarlet twigs would make in winter. But by summer, the dogwood had grown to an immoderate dark mass that soaked up all the light like a black hole in space. Eventually, it moved to a friend's country garden.

Then there are shrubs with which I entertain a tempestuous up and down relationship. At times I adore lavatera. After all, it blooms so profusely and so long, it seems perfect. But after a while, lavatera starts to look like an aging showgirl who's still waggling her tassels well past her prime.

Other shrubs sound alluring, but the jury is still out. I planted a *Philadelphus* 'Belle Etoile' after seeing it in glorious and fragrant bloom in English gardens. After four years, I am waiting not so patiently for the first bloom. Then there have been the flirtations with hebe and ceanothus, which didn't survive the first cold winter.

Even hardy shrubs that are divine may not be suitable for a flower border. Most shrubs just get too big. Shape plays a part, too. Witch hazel (*Hamamelis*) is one of the loveliest of all shrubs, but its open vase shape cries out for space. Crowd it and you diminish its grace.

Luckily, there's no end of delightful shrubs to select from that are polite about sharing space with flowers. Here are seven of my favorites.

Hydrangea serrata 'Preziosa': Hydrangeas in general are the nearest thing to the perfect shrub, and this one in particular. It stays small, takes sun and blooms from late spring until September. The leaves are suffused with a pretty rosy tint that matches the rosy flowers.

Hydrangea quercifolia — Oakleaf hydrangea is one of the finest of all garden plants. It's difficult to say which is the greater asset, its clusters of creamy flowers or its beautifully sculpted foliage. I vote for the foliage, which has a burnished quality and turns a lovely burgundy in autumn.

Cotinus 'Grace' — I have four smoke bushes and am still looking for space to stick in this relatively new cultivar. The leaves are the color of a garnet ring I had when I was a little girl. This shrub can be cut way back each spring to maintain a discreet size and rounded shape.

Hypericum 'Hidcote' — I'm not especially fond of the ground cover, St. John's wort, but this shrubby cousin is another thing altogether. It has a lovely billowing shape and adorns itself profusely with buttery yellow flowers all summer long. The cultivar 'Elstead' is very popular with reddish tinged leaves, but I think 'Hidcote' has better flowers.

Spiraea japonica 'Golden Princess' — I suppose it's most unfashionable to include such a common shrub, but I do think this is one of the best mixers with perennials. The rosy flowers are really secondary. In spring, the foliage has a stunning copper color, then it turns to a greenish gold. 'Goldflame' and 'Gold Mound' are similar.

Sambucus racemosa 'Plumosa Aurea' — This is the common elder in its most glamorous dress, with finely cut golden leaves. Like the smoke bush, it needs to be pruned to keep it border size. It also needs light shade to keep the leaves from scorching.

Rosa glauca — Often you won't find this rose in the rose section of nurseries. It'll be consorting with the shrubs. You don't grow *Rosa glauca* for its flowers, which are pretty but small and fleeting. The smoky blue leaves with wine veins and stems are the attraction. Later in the season, *Rosa glauca* has fine hips, too, which is more than I can say for myself.

SEPTEMBER 16, 1999

❧

HOLD THAT MULCH!
Just watch your basil for a hint about bedtime for Northwest gardens

TSK, TSK, AS THEY SAY IN THE COMICS. I SEE it is time for my annual lecture. Mini-mountains of compost began appearing curbside around our city soon after Labor Day. Now they are reaching the proportions of a Lilliputian mountain range.

With autumn officially here, the instinct is to start putting the garden to bed, and of course, that's what most of the magazines advise. But pay no attention to the calendar or those East Coast-edited publications.

What should dictate how we treat our gardens is our special Northwest weather. And rushing to put the garden to bed too early can be detrimental in our mild-mannered climate.

If you plan to dig that compost into the soil to prepare planting beds for next spring's annuals and vegetables, you get two green thumbs-up. But if you plan to put it on top of the soil as a wintertime blanket, slow down.

Compost or any other material put on top of the soil is called a mulch. And rushing the fall (and spring) mulching is one of the most common garden mistakes we make around these parts.

Mulch does three things: It keeps weeds down. It conserves water by preventing rapid evaporation. And it acts as insulation, keeping the soil temperature warm if it's already warm or cool if it's already cool. And therein lies the problem.

If you mulch the soil too early in autumn, you help it retain summer warmth. The longer the soil stays warm, the longer you delay triggering dormancy in your plants.

Bears aren't the only creatures that need a winter's sleep. Going dormant is a protective process that helps most plants survive the winter.

But plants need to be helped into dormancy, and there's nothing like a few light frosts to do the trick. Where mulch is applied early, the soil's warmth will keep things growing and blooming, making plants extremely vulnerable to the inevitable hard frost later.

So when is a good time to mulch? We know how fickle our Northwest weather can be, so pay attention to what the weather fore-caster says. As a rule of thumb, green thumb, of course, the last week in November is usu-ally ideal.

In fact, to help you remember, plan to mulch the weekend after Thanksgiving. It's a great way to burn calories from the extra feasting.

In-ground plants aren't the only ones that benefit from three or four light frosts. The same is true of potted tender plants such as fuchsias and geraniums. Let nature take a hand in starting the shutting-down process before you rush them into protection.

Anyone who wants to know when the first light frost occurs should grow basil, which is the botanical equivalent of the canary in the coal mine. Basil is always the first to go, turn-ing black at the mere hint of a temperature dip.

Other clean-up jobs can wait, too. Debate seems to rage eternal about whether to prune roses in fall or late winter. I vote with the pruners who hold out for late winter. A Feb-ruary holiday, Presidents Day, is a great re-minder when to prune roses.

It won't hurt, though, to take tall roses down a bit to keep them from whipping around in the winter wind. And if you must hard-prune roses in autumn (it's hard to shake what Mom told you to do), hold off as long as you can. Early pruning will spur new growth and keep roses from settling down.

You also should resist the temptation to pick that proverbial last rose of summer af-ter mid- to late October. Letting roses form hips is another helpful way to get them to go to sleep.

And, speaking of cutting things down, there's a growing school of thought that wait-ing until late winter to cut down perennials

provides a slight advantage in helping mar-ginally hardy plants survive should we get one of those gosh-awful winters.

But that's easy for me to say because I'm kind of a natural slob and not at all offended by dried stalks sticking up at odd angles throughout the winter.

SEPTEMBER 25, 1997

DIG, MOVE, REPEAT
Welcome to the season of heavy lifting

I HOPE YOU HAD A REST IN THE HAMMOCK TO-ward the end of summer because it's time to get moving now. And by moving, I mean really moving, as in digging up and trans-planting plants.

The mild Northwest autumn is the per-fect time for making course corrections and getting things just right. There's nothing like a little rearranging of the plant furniture to give new pizazz to a garden that's gone bland.

If the idea of digging things up scares you, let me assure you that most plants are oblig-ingly portable. I am an inveterate mover, which is another way of saying I make my share of mistakes.

In all the years of lifting plants and plunk-ing them in new places, I've rarely lost a plant. And that covers some sizable specimens, in-cluding good-sized rhodies.

So why would you go to the trouble? There are lots of reasons for moving plants around, and here are a few signs to check out:

The solar eclipse. As gardens mature, trees and shrubs cast bigger shadows. Plants that once were in sunshine might find them-selves in unwanted shade for a good part of the day. If your plants resemble little towers of Pisa, leaning noticeably toward the sun, they're telling you they need to move.

Overexposure. Similarly, if you've done serious pruning or lost a tree or large shrub, you might find shade plants frying. Check for plants that had crispy edges or brown patches in summer. Even some plants listed as sun lovers can't take afternoon rays. Variegated and gold foliage plants have particularly sensitive skins and will be happier if moved to light shade.

> *I am an inveterate mover, which is another way of saying I make my share of mistakes.*

Size 10 feet, size 6 shoes. If you find yourself constantly whacking a shrub back, consider that it might not be a pruning problem but rather a placement problem. For some reason, a lot of houses have ended up with foundation shrubs that grow rapidly up windows and porches, making for dark, brooding homes.

Harsh pruning just makes the giants look graceless. Move the behemoths to spaces where they can stretch, and replace them with plants that don't need to be nuked to stay in proportion.

Godzilla meets Bambi. In spring when you planted them, they were in perfect proportion. Of course, if you were like me, you planted everything too close because you wanted instant gratification. Now you have little jewels of plants nearly engulfed by overly aggressive monsters. Cite irreconcilable differences and split them up.

The boring straits. Some sections of a garden can get just plain boring. If you have an area that's bland maybe everything's green or the same shape (iris, daylilies, ornamental grass) think about moving something out and replacing it with a contrasting shape or color.

Niche marketing. Sometimes you put a plant in, and it simply doesn't do anything. It doesn't grow, and it doesn't have the decency to die. This could be a sign that you dropped it in heavy clay without enough organic material to break up the soil and give the roots a chance to grow. But if you did everything right, it probably means — and who's to reason with plants — that the plant is just unhappy in that spot. So give it a move, and you might be surprised to find that the pouting plant suddenly shines in a new environment. Kind of like kids.

Out-and-out atrocities. Finally, there's the "what was I thinking" category. Sound familiar? When orange daylilies popped up next to a pink hydrangea in my yard, I knew that it was only a matter of time before the taste police would come after me. I don't know who perpetrated this evil pairing. These are the kinds of combos that must be split up before they catch on.

Tips for moving day. Most perennials, shrubs and small trees can be moved safely in autumn. Roses are an exception. Wait until they are dormant. Here are tips for transplanting now. Many rules for putting in new plants apply to transplanting existing ones.

- Dig a hole larger than the root system and add plenty of organic material for good drainage.
- Choose an overcast or misty day, so roots don't dry out.
- When digging up a plant, leave as much dirt as possible around the roots.

• If you have to trim some roots, reduce the top of the plant proportionately so the reduced root system has less plant to support.

• Transplant as soon as possible. If you've dug a plant and can't replant it right away, put it in the shade and cover roots with wet burlap or wet newspapers.

• Even if it's raining, water the transplant to ensure that the soil settles and that there are no air pockets. Don't let it dry out.

• Above all, watch your back. Don't try to lift something that puts undue strain on you. Lift with your knees. Drag heavy rootballs on canvas rather than trying to lift them. If you have to, interrupt your spouse's John Wayne movie and get help.

SEPTEMBER 28, 2000

GET A DATE
Coordinate chores with holidays

I WAS VISITING MY FRIEND CAROL KELLY THE other day, and I noticed that her autumn sedums (*Sedum spectabile*) were standing up straight as good soldiers. Much as I like the late-season color, I had been thinking about taking mine out because they sprawl out like a certain fat cat in our household. In fact, they look as if The Perp has slept on them, not that she would do such a thing. Hah!

I asked Carol what her secret was, and she said she'd gone to a workshop on how to keep your garden fresh. Noted plantsman Dan Hinkley, who conducted the workshop, recommended cutting back sedums, asters and chrysanthemums on the Fourth of July. "He told us that while everyone is out setting off fireworks, we should be whacking our flowers back," Carol said.

That, according to Hinkley, is the secret to having bushy, stand-up-straight flowers into autumn. This is good to know, since I thought the term "urban sprawl" had been invented for my asters.

It occurs to me that there are other rule-of-thumb dates that Northwest gardeners, at least those in the Willamette Valley, might find handy.

Halloween: This is the time to take the last of the tender plants into protection. This includes nonhardy fuchsias, geraniums and tropicals. Of course, if there's an unseasonably early hard frost, you'd want to get them in earlier. But generally this is the right time.

Thanksgiving weekend: The Friday after Thanksgiving is an excellent time to work off calories from the big dinner by mulching your garden. Resist the urge to do it much earlier because mulch acts as insulation, and, if it's put on too early, it will keep the ground

Sedum spectabile *'Autumn Joy'*.

too warm. A few light frosts and cold ground help send plants into dormancy.

Valentine's Day: Instead of a dozen red roses, give someone a bare-root rose. This is the perfect time to plant it.

Presidents Day: I sometimes think they give you this day off just to prune your roses. In many parts of the country, people prune their roses in fall. But mid-February pruning seems to work best in the maritime Northwest. It's late enough so that roses aren't likely to get nipped by a cold blast, but early enough to ensure rapid growth for early bloom.

St. Patrick's Day: This is the time to start feeding your lawn, and it should be an easy one to remember — taking care of your green on a green day.

April 15: Work off the tension from filing your income taxes by planting dahlia tubers. This is the time to start getting them in.

Mother's Day: In the Northwest, this is generally when the ground is warm enough to put tomatoes and warm-season vegetables directly into the ground. This is a hard one to wait for since tomatoes start to appear much earlier in nurseries, but they simply won't grow until the ground warms up. Days may have been warm, but nights usually remain cold until May, which keeps the ground cool.

These are only rule-of-thumb dates, since Northwest weather can be mighty unpredictable, but they are reasonably good guidelines for remembering to do what and when.

Meanwhile, I'm going to go out and tell my sedums, which were on the list to be dug up, that they have won a reprieve. And, I know what I'll be doing next Fourth of July.

SEPTEMBER 30, 2004

DON'T STOP YET

The party's not over for winter beauties

AUTUMN OFTEN IS TOUTED AS AN IDEAL TIME to plant; some say it is even superior to spring. Well, it is, and it isn't.

In many cases, a dry October is a better time to plant than a wet June. But there are exceptions.

I am reluctant to plant anything that is hardy only to USDA Zone 7 this time of year. It's true that a Zone 7 plant will survive winters in the Willamette Valley, but not necessarily in its first year. A new plant does not have the strong root growth that will help it weather whatever winter could throw at it.

As a rule, I generally consider a brand-new plant at least one zone more tender than it will be once established. Wait until spring to plant daphne, crape myrtles, hebes and other marginally hardy plants.

If you're wondering why I said Zone 7, when most maps in garden books show Portland as a Zone 8, it's because sad experience has taught me that some of my plants have not read the right books.

We are in Zone 8 when all the right conditions exist: normal winter, no elevation, southern exposure, shelter from wind and no depression forming a frost pocket. In short, most of us have a range of more than one zone in our garden.

Fortunately, there is a plethora of plants that will be better off with fall planting. The ground is more workable and warmer now than it will be if we have a cool, damp spring, which weather forecasters are saying we could have the next century.

If you get these hardy plants in now, they'll produce solid root growth and have a head start come spring. Trees and shrubs in

Boxwood makes a great backdrop.

particular seem happy with October planting. You might consider especially planting for winter interest.

Just remember, if you have a smaller garden, you'll want to consider how the plant will look the rest of the year. Many plants have charms for more than one season, and several ways exist to approach winter interest, from winter foliage to bare-branched beauty.

Here are my personal winter favorites in different categories.

Sculptural shapes: Contorted shapes might be fun, but for grace and beauty, I opt for the gentle curves of a well-pruned (which means opened-up) laceleaf Japanese maple. *Acer palmatum* 'Dissectum' is a splendid example. The maples are one of the reasons the Japanese garden is sublime even in winter.

Frosty flowers: The leading favorite for winter bloom seems to be the elegant witch hazel (*Hamamelis*). But my favorite is the more plebian winter jasmine (*Jasminum nudiflorum*). Its buttery flowers last from December through February. True, the plant is frankly boring the rest of the year, but it doesn't take up much room.

Cool conifers: A small conifer that's softly, not stiffly, conical is just the thing to perk up a winter scene, especially if the needles have a golden cast. *Thuja occidentalis* 'Rheingold' fills the bill.

Graceful swan songs: Many plants have attractive seed heads that should be left on over winter. I particularly love the way grasses dry. *Miscanthus sinensis* turns a beautiful amber color, and I wouldn't think of cutting it down until spring. 'Morning Light' is a choice cultivar.

Sparkling bark: The bare branches of coral bark maple (*Acer palmatum* 'Sango-kaku', also called *A*. 'Senkaki') positively glow on a winter day. In summer it will still dazzle with finely sculpted leaves that run the gamut from pinkish yellow in spring to apple green in summer and bronze-yellow in autumn.

Berried treasures: My personal favorite is beautyberry (*Callicarpa*) for its brilliant and opalescent purple berries that last much of the winter. *C. bodinieri* var. *giraldii* 'Profusion' is a cultivar that lives up to its name.

Broadleaf beauties: When it comes to evergreen in the winter, my choice isn't exotic. Common boxwood (*Buxus sempervirens*) is the perfect winter evergreen. Its defined shape, whether as a hedge or a topiary, gives a winter garden structure. As a bonus, its branches, which stay green for quite a while even when cut, are perfect for plumping out winter bouquets.

Many plants have charms for more than one season.

OCTOBER 7, 1999

THE LAWN YAWN

Not all grass is half baked

ANY DISCUSSION OF GRASS THIS YEAR CON-jures up visions of baked lawns.

But not all grasses were a disaster this summer of our discontent. The deeper-rooted ornamental grasses shimmered like hazy fountains in the borders and spilled over like silken tassels at the edges. Those few grasses that suffered from the drought had the good grace to dry to a lovely pale, wheaten color.

Ornamental grasses reached fad proportions on the East Coast, where summers are hot and humid — in short, flower-wilting weather. They are relatively new to Northwest gardens.

Here, where summers, even though hot aren't humid, gardeners haven't needed to find a replacement for flowers. Instead, ornamental grasses play a different role, complementing rather than co-opting the garden. You aren't likely to find an all-grass garden, but you are more and more likely to run into grasses used as sculptural accents among the perennials.

And this is their season. With their rippling edges and hazy colors, grasses were made for the soft, golden light of autumn. They shimmer in burnished versions of blue, gold, silver, scarlet, green and bronze. They rustle and dance in returning breezes. And they show to advantage against their late-blooming companions such as rudbeckias, autumn sedums and asters.

Landscape architects and garden designers often refer to grasses as great season extenders, because many send up their flowers in September and October. Several grasses even remain green throughout the winter.

Others have attractive dried foliage that need not be cut back until early spring.

The ornamental grasses available today are a far cry from the dusty old pampas grass your elderly aunt stuffed in jars around the house. Not long ago, the only grasses available in local nurseries were the ungainly pampas and the pretty but wildly uncivilized zebra grass that spreads like bamboo. No wonder grasses didn't have much of a following.

Now, though, an array of grasses is available to the gardener. All of the following, with the exception of the *Miscanthus*, sprout less than 3 feet and are suitable starter grasses for even small urban gardens.

Pennisetum: Several varieties send up rose- or cream-hued flowers that resemble fuzzy caterpillars. Bloom lasts from midsummer through much of autumn. It is questionably hardy, but well worth growing as an annual. Reasonably sized varieties include *P. setaceum*, *P. alopecuroides* and *P. villosum*.

Imperata cylindrica 'Rubra': Japanese blood grass is a gorgeous scarlet that glows like a flame when the light shines through it. Only a foot high, it's perfect for the front of the border or even in a pot. It takes some shade, but colors best in sun.

Carex buchananii: Leatherleaf sedge is a bronze year-'round beauty about 2 feet high. It's a sun lover but also tolerates shade. The unusual color is best set off by orange-and-yellow flowers or dark green foliage.

Milium effusum 'Aureum': Golden grass brightens shade with its bright, almost chartreuse color.

Festucas: These are the blue grasses. *F. ovina glauca* forms short, blue-gray tufts. Combine it with Japanese blood grass for dramatic effect.

Arrhenatherum elatius bulbosum: Bulbous oat grass is a pretty, foot-high green-and-white striped grass that does best in damp spots, although it will survive a dry summer.

Hakonechloa macra 'Aureola': This thicker-bladed grass grows in lush mounds of green-gold in sun or shade. It's got a reputation as a difficult grass to grow in most parts of the country but seems to like the Northwest climate.

Helictotrichon sempervirens: Blue oat grass grows to 2 feet and looks good year 'round. In spring, it sends out slender wands of flowers that go from blue to gold.

If there's room to try a tall grass, choose one of the handsome *Miscanthus sinesis* grasses, with their fountain shapes and graceful arcing stems of flowers. These usually start at 5 feet, but among the varieties, some soar as high as 12 feet. So be sure to ask about their habits.

Part of the beauty of grasses is that most are maintenance-free. Those that die in winter just need to be cut back in early spring to make way for new growth. Those that fizzle in summers that are too hot and dry likely will return with vigor, just like a lawn, once normal weather returns.

OCTOBER 2, 1992

❧

MURDER SHE WROTE
But kind heart spares formerly doomed plants

OH, MY. I SEEM TO HAVE RUFFLED FEATHers.

Recently I wrote a column about "editing" the garden, that is, removing plants that have overstayed their welcome. I mentioned specifically that I was heading toward the compost pile with some filipendula because it didn't offer sufficient contrast to neighboring plants.

Some readers took me to task for ruthlessly murdering plants rather than finding homes for them. I could feel the stings as all over Oregon people rubbed nettles on chubby voodoo dolls with red hair.

It seems visions of dragging perfectly healthy plants off to the compost pile evoked an image of poor Marie Antoinette being carted off to the guillotine. People could hear the poor things screaming, "Save me, save me."

Let me say, first of all, that I am vacuuming up the considerable cat hair in the house

> *I could feel the stings as all over Oregon people rubbed nettles on chubby voodoo dolls with red hair.*

and plan to spend the winter weaving a hair shirt. Second, I want you to know that I do understand how everyone feels.

I know there is some primordial taboo against doing away with a plant. That must be the only reason that I have faithfully watered a 30-year-old houseplant that passed the stage of resembling anything attractive about 20 years ago.

I can't seem to put it out of its misery because its sheer tenacity fascinates me. It's gotten so that I associate its well-being with my own. It makes no sense, but when that plant dies, I will get very, very nervous.

But when distaste for uprooting a healthy outdoor plant prevents you from having the garden you want, I stand by what I said before. You have to practice tough love and dig it out. Don't be held hostage by a spreading, seeding, crowding, creeping, clinging botanical monster.

But readers are right. One person's monster might be someone else's darling. Many are perfectly good plants that just don't fit in a particular setting or delightful plants that have a tendency to have too many babies.

So, with the exception of egregiously invasive demons (you know who you are), I promise to find good homes for my exes.

To that end, I called the Ronald McDonald House, which is looking for plants for its butterfly garden on the Legacy Emanuel Hospital & Health Center campus. This is a state-certified backyard wildlife habitat.

Readers who shivered at my cold-bloodedness will be happy to hear I'm sending the filipendula there, along with other plants that I'm digging up this fall. If you didn't know it before, the Ronald McDonald House is a place where families of seriously ill or injured children can be together.

The Feral Cat Coalition also wrote after the column appeared to note that it has an annual plant sale in June to raise money for neutering and spaying. The coalition has volunteers who will provide pots and dig up any unwanted plants. Because its sale isn't until next spring, I've told the coalition to call me then as I do my spring dividing and sorting.

I would be happy to share with readers information from other nonprofit groups that will take plants for a worthy cause. It is nice to know in our gardening mecca that we can have it both ways. We can edit our gardens without being killers.

Still, I have to admit, there will be certain plants that will continue to head toward the compost pile. I doubt whether anyone will be offended if that's where I toss some English ivy.

OCTOBER 14, 1999

❧

PERK UP YOUR WINTER GARDEN
In the garden's dead time, berries offer spots of color and attract birds

As SURE AS THE GARDEN GOES INTO ITS WINter slump, my heart turns to berries at this time of year. I even found myself admiring some pyracanthas along the road, despite the fact I have had near duels to the death with these thorny monsters.

Cotoneaster is another instance of how the season scrambles my brain cells. Normally, I'm not crazy about their stiffness, but wow, do they have berries and wow, do the birds like them. And frankly, those stiff, berry-laden branches look fantastic in winter bouquets.

Whether it is to attract birds or just have winter color, you have to have a berry shrub or two or more. But since many are quite large for urban plots, it pays to be judicious in selection.

As a group, the pyracanthas, cotoneasters and nandinas are some of the heaviest fruiters. Most also are evergreen, which makes them extremely useful for winter foliage around the front of the house.

You won't get a bad crop with any pyracantha, but *P.* 'Mohave', which has orange-red berries, is particularly showy. It eventually reaches 12 feet. Some of the best cotoneasters are *C. buxifolius*, *C. lacteus* and *C. microphyllus*, all hovering around 6 feet. *C. lacteus* is among the most prolific with its red berries.

Nandina domestica is one of the most

graceful shrubs, with its fountain shape, delicate leaves and heavy clusters of red berries. It is a fine size for small gardens, seldom more than 5 feet, and there is a dwarf form as well. This is a true multiseason plant, and one to grow even if it didn't have berries.

Some of the smaller shrubs don't have huge clusters of berries, but their size and the fact that they are evergreen makes them ideal for providing winter interest around an entryway.

Red-berried skimmia is modest at 2 feet to 5 feet. The diminutive (about 3 feet) *Viburnum davidii* is another low-growing evergreen. It bears gleaming blue berries. Both of these shrubs need cross pollination to produce berries, so be sure you have a male and a female.

Still in the evergreen category, *Elaeagnus multiflora*, a 6-footer, doesn't produce berries in great profusion, but the birds find the orange-red fruits exceptionally tasty. Some of the barberries also are evergreen, or ever-red, depending on the variety. *Berberis darwinii* (6-7 feet) has dark blue berries.

Arbutus unedo, the strawberry tree, is the hardy member of its family for our zone. You may not want the common variety, which can shoot up to 35 feet, but if you can find the cultivar 'Elfin King', you'll have a heavy-fruiting shrub under 5 feet.

Then there's holly (*Ilex*), which is both evergreen and fruiting. For the most part, I can't seem to work up much enthusiasm for holly because it is so ever-present.

But there is one holly that is a berry-lover's delight, and oddly enough, it's not evergreen. *Ilex verticillata*, also called winterberry, has an enormous crop of fat red berries on bare winter branches. Its fruits have been compared to polished rubies by more-romantic garden writers. When you see those expensive branches brimming with berries

in florist shops, this is the holly. Alas, it will eventually grow to 15 feet.

Like this particular holly, some of the best berry bearers aren't evergreen, although many have good fall leaf color. The best of the deciduous berry bushes is a plant I rave about every year, but every year it seems to get better.

The beautyberry, *Callicarpa*, has smashing, iridescent purple berries that arrive in late summer and last well into winter. *C. bodinieri* 'Profusion' is a choice cultivar that stays within a reasonable 6 or 7 feet. The white-berried beautyberry, *C. japonica* 'Leucocarpa', also is splendid.

If you favor the traditional red berry, you can't go wrong with the deciduous *Viburnum opulus*, which is the flashiest of the viburnums. *V. opulus* 'Aureum' has golden leaves. If you don't want a 20-footer, look for *V. opulus* 'Compactum', which is just 5 feet.

Aronia 'Brilliantissima', the chokeberry, is another superb red berry producer, as its varietal name suggests.

The mature size of some of these shrubs may sound scary, but remember most are slow growers, and you can always sell the house and have moved on by the time they've gotten out of hand.

OCTOBER 15, 1995

❧

RAPID TRANSIT
A new fire pit and "bus stop" rumble in to replace the ruined gazebo

THERE IS NOTHING QUITE SO MUCH FUN AS A new garden toy, and I have a couple of new ones. But first let me tell you how they came to be.

This garden gathering spot looks as if it's always been here.

I've mentioned that we lost our gazebo this summer to an errant branch. After we had dragged out all the debris, we found we had an almost perfect circular clearing.

So Doug the Wonder Boy laid a cobblestone circle with a fire pit in the center. I must hasten to explain, in case any city inspectors are reading, that the "fire pit" is one of those readymade copper bowls on a stand with a domed screen.

It was very easy to make, or at least Doug made it look easy. I'm not the one who had to wheelbarrow in several loads of cobblestones.

You can buy a package of cobblestones in a 7-foot circle or a 10-foot circle. The advantage to the package is that you will get stones that are cut at angles that facilitate laying out a tight circle. If you need to make a larger circle, you can buy the individual cobblestones because by the time you are 10 feet out, you don't need the slanted cobbles. The cobbles are available at several building suppliers.

Forming the circle went pretty fast, with Doug doing the work and me supplying hamburgers and fries.

First, Doug made sure the soil underneath was compacted and level, then he laid down landscape cloth to suppress weeds but allow drainage. Next he put a bed of sand, about 3 inches deep, on top.

Here's a little bit of practical advice. If you have cats, do not let the sand sit there uncovered for a day or two as we did. I don't think I need to describe the consequences of this foolish action. Put the cobbles on right away.

After the cobbles were laid, we spread

more sand on top and swept it in to fill all the cracks. You can make the cobbles a little looser and spread in finely crushed rock, and some people prefer this look. But I've had such bad experiences with weeds between cracks of stones that I wanted the cobbles to fit as tightly as possible.

When it was finished, we set our old Adirondack chairs around the fire pit, and it looks as if it's always been there.

Still, while I didn't miss my old gazebo, I did want a place to stop if I'm out in the garden and there's a sudden shower, or just a place to sit comfortably and drink a cup of tea on a drizzly but still mild day. I'd always loved the idea of those little shelters with a covered seat that you see in Asian gardens. They kind of look like attractive bus stops.

As luck would have it, Doug the Wonder Boy knows a carpenter, Majo Arens, who recently arrived from Germany. The three of us got together and pored over pictures in books and magazines and came up with an idea. Doug leaned toward something that looked more Asian, and I flirted with something brightly painted that would look very English.

Majo brought us down to earth, and we have something simple and rustic and very fitting for its space, a dry shade area under tall trees where nothing much grows. Majo built the little "bus stop" — that's what we've taken to calling it — in less than a week without plans. He did lovely finish work, rounding edges so we wouldn't scrape our legs.

I had an old stained-glass window that we set in the back so the afternoon light would shine through. It's simply an open shed with a U-shaped bench and a shingled roof.

The whole thing is cedar and smells glorious. Sitting in it sort of reminds me of summer camp. I had intended to paint it, but now that it's built, I think I'll just let it weather. Anyway, I love my new toy.

If you want to know, and I suspect you do, the whole thing cost $2,800, including labor and materials, but would be a lot less if you or your spouse did the labor yourselves. That was out of the question at our house because my spouse's idea of being handy is putting a stool in front of the counter so The Perp, who is aging, can get up to her food.

OCTOBER 13, 2005

MUCKING ABOUT
Amid the mud, try some shortcuts with bulbs

NEARLY EVERY SPRING, YOU'LL FIND ME fervently wishing my back yard was a mini-Holland. But this time each fall, the idea of mucking around in the mud and planting a thousand little onionlike objects has no appeal. Besides, my fingernails have finally started to grow back after a summer of scrabbling in the garden.

This leaves me with two options. I could either have a major guilt trip, or I could find creative ways to expend minimum effort for maximum impact (an effect I've learned from watching our cats).

Oh yes, there's still time to plant bulbs. The bulb deadline isn't so much a particular date as it is particular conditions. You're supposed to get your bulbs in before the ground is frozen or waterlogged, and those of us who live in Oregon can pretty much ignore the latter condition or else we'd never get bulbs planted, period.

The thing I hate most about putting in bulbs is using that cylinder thing with the handle on top that's supposed to make neat bulb holes in a jiffy. If you've ever tried twisting that thing in clay soil, you know what it feels like to pitch nine tough innings. And that's after only a dozen holes.

So my bulb planting site is the one place where I know the earth is nice and crumbly without any roots. That's in the veggie garden where we've just pulled up the tomatoes and other leftover healthy things. Bulbs and vegetables are perfect companions.

The bulbs will give you a cheery carpet of color and be done before it's warm enough to replant the tomatoes. When we're ready to put the salad stuff in, we lift our bulbs, taking care not to break the leaves off, and store them for the summer. The same sort of crop rotation would work with annuals.

Another lazy trick I've discovered is that it's easier to dig a couple of inches down and plant the minor bulbs — crocus, winter aconite (*Eranthis*), snowdrops (*Galanthus*), snowflakes (*Leucojum*) and miniature varieties of iris and daffodils

Maybe planting mushrooms would be easier.

— than it is to dig a bunch of 8-inch holes for the big fat tulips and daffodils.

The perfect place for these jewel-like plants is under deciduous shrubs and trees. Ordinarily, you don't get much color in the shade of woody plants, but the bulbs will bloom before the larger plants leaf out.

I'd love to have more bulbs in my flower beds, but it's a bother the way I keep turning up bulbs and accidentally chopping them to mincemeat when I put in new plants. Besides, it's hard to get attractive drifts of bulbs without disturbing roots of existing plants. So I pretty much limit myself to tall flowering bulbs that look good without being planted in drifts. Giant alliums and lilies are ideal. It's true that lilies don't flower in spring, but November is the best time to plant them.

A super-easy way to plant bulbs is to use the plastic pots that your perennials came in. Use ordinary potting soil sprinkled with some bone meal, and cram the bulbs right in to the desired depth. Group the pots side by side in an area where they'll get light and rain. Drizzle some compost around and between the pots and a little over the top for insulation.

When the bulbs are ready to flower, stick them among your perennials or slip the plastic pots inside pretty containers or baskets for a terrace. When they're bloomed out, store them in an out-of-the-way place, like behind a garage. To my surprise, I've gotten several years of bloom from bulbs planted in plastic pots.

In the ground, the best way to get high impact with little effort is to concentrate bulbs in clusters and place them strategically. I've planted some on each side of the entry to my new long arbor. Many gardeners ring a birdbath or ornamental tree with bulbs, or place them along an entry path. It doesn't take many bulbs for these special spots, and the effect gives you more razzle dazzle than thinly spreading around the same number of bulbs.

Finally, consider the effect that will please you the most.

If you're after the showy look of tall, fancy-petaled tulips in Dutch paintings, go for bulbs labeled late blooming. Tall bulbs and those with floppy or ruffled petals don't stand up to early spring's heavy rain and wind. If your heart leaps at the thought of very early flowers, select the ground-hugging species tulips and minor bulbs that withstand inclement weather.

PLANT A SPECTACULAR POT

You can get a high-voltage bulb display with just one pot. Here's how to get at least two months of bloom.

1. Select a weather-proof pot at least 14 inches across the top. Fill the bottom with two inches of gravel, and add about an inch of potting soil mixed with a dusting of bone meal on top of the gravel.
2. Set late-blooming tulip bulbs about a foot below the rim and gently tamp down enough soil to settle the bulbs firmly with pointy ends up.
3. For the next layer, place mid-spring-blooming narcissus positioned between the pointed tips of the tulips. Again sift in enough dirt to hold the second set of bulbs in place.
4. Next, sit early-spring blooming hyacinths on top and cover with two inches of soil.
5. On top of that, put a layer of very-early-blooming crocus and cover with an inch of soil. As one set of flowers dies down, the next group of bulbs will begin blooming and should hide the dying foliage of the bulbs that have already bloomed.

OCTOBER 22, 1998

IMPORTANT POINTS OF ENTRY

Good landscaping will help create an unbeatable path to your door

OOPS, YET ANOTHER NAG. YOU'VE BEEN hearing this is the season to plant bulbs. This is the season to divide perennials. This is the season to clean up. And now here comes one more. This is the season to do something about that entryway.

It's the part of your garden that's going to get the most attention in the coming winter months. Like the postman, the entry garden must perform through rain, sleet and snow.

I wish I had thought of this when I landscaped around my own front porch years ago. I planted attractive, low-growing shrubs on each side of the entry. They have flowers in spring, berries in autumn and gently rounded shapes.

Sounds perfect. The trouble is, one side is evergreen and the other is deciduous. In winter, my entry area looks as lopsided as a bride standing at the altar without a groom.

Not everyone has the problem of winter bareness. In our area, entries are just as likely to be socked in by dark, overgrown rhododendrons that loom like brooding Druids and are just about as inviting.

If that's your problem, the quickest fix is to open up your entry area by pruning your rhodies into graceful multistemmed trees and underplanting them with ground covers.

Where bareness is the problem and you have the room, go for the real thing. You can't do better than one of the 100 or so varieties of Japanese maple (*Acer palmatum*) that range from 4 feet to 30 feet. Stick with a multistemmed selection. Even without leaves, they have exquisite shape and handsome red or green branches.

Small and dwarf conifers are another way to go, giving you a range of needle colors — gold, green, blue-green and silver.

For golden winter color, look for the pine called *Pinus mugo* 'Winter Gold', the false cypress *Chamaecyparis obtusa* 'Fernspray Gold' or the even smaller 'Nana lutea'. English yew also has two outstanding golden varieties, *Taxus* 'Standishii' and *T. baccata* 'Aurea'. Among the smaller junipers, there's *Juniperus chinensis* 'Aurea'. The false cypresses have some beautiful blue needles. There are *Chamaecyparis pisifera* 'Boulevard' and 'Mikko'. Another blue is the dwarf spruce *Picea pungens* 'Fat Albert'.

There are fewer selections among broad-leaved evergreen shrubs, especially the smaller ones (3 feet to 6 feet). *Abelia grandiflora* 'Francis Mason' has golden leaves. So does the Japanese holly *Ilex crenata* 'Golden Gem'. This small-leaved holly resembles boxwood.

There is, of course, nothing wrong with green, especially if it's evergreen. You can't go wrong with boxwood, either the common variety *Buxus sempervirens* or Korean boxwood *Buxus microphylla koreana*. The boxwoods also can be pruned to sophisticated or whimsical shapes.

If your entry faces south and is sheltered from wind, take a chance with the lovely but somewhat cold-sensitive winter daphne, *Daphne odora*.

Skimmia is much overused in this area. Still, it is small, pretty and evergreen. The same can be said of heavenly bamboo, *Nan-*

> *In winter, my entry area looks as lopsided as a bride standing at the altar without a groom.*

dina domestica, except that it's underused. Never fear, it is neither a real bamboo nor invasive.

And speaking of evergreen, we should count our native Oregon grape, *Mahonia aquifolium*, among our winter blessings. After all, it hugs the right side of the entryway to the world's most famous garden, England's Sissinghurst. Those English know a good thing when they see it.

Fill in under trees and large shrubs with perennials and ground covers that retain winter interest. Grasses are a superb winter accent because although they go dormant, they dry beautifully. Good selections include *Miscanthus sinensis, Pennisetum alopecuroides, Calamagrostis acutiflora* and *Carex comans* 'Bronze Form'. New Zealand flax (*Phormium*) also stays evergreen, and hellebores, which can be used as a tall ground cover, are at their peak in winter.

OCTOBER 22, 1995

AN OVERLOOKED PRIZE
With its fall berries and winter foliage, the state flower is highly regarded — just ask the gardeners in Europe

A PROPHET IS NOT WITHOUT HONOR, SAVE in his own country, Matthew said in the New Testament. Botanists might substitute the word "plant" for "prophet" because that seems to be the case with the Oregon grape, Oregon's state flower.

It is highly regarded in Europe for its fall

berries and winter foliage. The English consider Oregon grape a prize garden ornamental and use its holly-like leaves for Christmas decorations. When it was introduced in England in the early 1800s by Scottish botanist David Douglas, individual plants sold for as much as 10 pounds each. One of Europe's most spectacular examples of Oregon grape is the hedge at the Château of Amboise in France's Loire Valley.

Here in the Northwest, this versatile plant gets relatively little attention. Yet it is the answer to one of the Northwest gardener's biggest problems: what to plant under tall trees.

Oregon grape will tolerate not only shade but also dry shade, which makes it an excellent underplanting for large trees. Despite the "state flower" designation, Oregon grape is actually a small shrub. It grows upright to a height of 3 to 6 feet with leaves that closely resemble those of the holly.

In late summer and fall, it bears beautiful deep blue berries, from which it derives its common name. The berries are edible, but bitter on their own. (They do, however, make excellent jellies.) Clusters of yellow flowers that are attractive, but not spectacular, appear in spring. This is a plant grown primarily for its foliage and berries.

A member of the barberry family, Oregon grape is sometimes known by the botanical name *Berberis aquifolium*, while other references call it *Mahonia aquifolium*. It is interesting that the governor's mansion is known as Mahonia Hall in honor of this state flower, while the state's own Blue Book uses the berberis designation rather than mahonia.

In addition to its use as an underplanting for trees, Oregon grape also makes an ideal informal hedge in a woodsy garden. It takes to almost any soil, as long as there is drainage, and will easily tolerate subfreezing temperatures.

Oregon grape, which grows naturally west of the Cascades from Northern California to British Columbia, has been the state flower since 1899. Meriwether Lewis and William Clark brought back seeds from their 1805-06 expedition, according to the Oregon State Federation of Garden Clubs, which researched the plant as part of a bicentennial project in 1974-76.

One of the United States' first nurserymen, Bernard M'Mahon (which may be the origin of "Mahonia") germinated the seeds for the horticultural trade. On a visit to the East Coast, David Douglas bought a sample of the plant and took it back to England, where it was a sensation. He later collected more specimens when he visited Fort Vancouver.

In addition to making jelly from the berries, early settlers used the roots of the plant for medicine and its foliage for holiday decorations. American Indians used the berries for food and the bark for dyes.

OCTOBER 27, 1989

BARKING UP THE RIGHT TREE
Trees and shrubs with beautiful bark give the winter garden its own special magic

FALLING LEAVES DON'T ALWAYS SIGNAL THE end of a plant's performance. For some trees and shrubs, the show is just beginning.

We rarely think of choosing a plant on the merits of its bark, but anyone interested in a year-round garden should. The tracery of branches against the winter landscape has a riveting beauty of its own. But add color, and the impact is nothing short of sensational.

A surprising number of plants boast gorgeously colored bark, and a few have winter flowers that bloom on bare bark. Because November is a great month to plant trees and shrubs, let's review some of the winter performers.

The two standouts among the shrubs that bear winter flowers on bare branches are the witch hazels (*Hamemelis*) and winter jasmine (*Jasminum nudiflorum*).

Witch hazels bear fragrant spidery, lemony-yellow flowers in January and February. They do double duty because of their attractive golden autumn foliage.

On the other hand, the small winter jasmine is really rather dull most of the year. All is forgiven in winter, when from December to March,

Witch hazels are true four-season shrubs.

its bare branches are smothered with buttery yellow flowers the size of popcorn. Of all the plants, it is most like a spot of sunshine on a bleak day.

Parrotia persica is a large shrub that resembles a witch hazel and gives us a double dose of winter color. Not only does it display a prettily mottled trunk of gray, brown and green, but it also bears crimson winter flowers on bare stems.

There's even a flowering tree that blossoms in November and may continue throughout mild winters, or repeat bloom in early spring. *Prunus subhirtella* 'Autumnalis', the autumn cherry, bears pale pink blossoms on bare twigs. It is a lovely small ornamental tree, growing only to 25 feet.

As for bark, the best and the brightest may well be the dogwood shrub, *Cornus alba* 'Sibirica', whose scarlet branches glow like hot embers. Lucky us, since it prefers damp soil. For a dramatic effect, pair the dogwood with the stems of the golden willow, *Salix alba* 'Vitellina', whose branches have been described as egg-yolk yellow. Another dogwood, *Cornus stolonifera* 'Flaviramea', also has brilliant golden stems.

Since new growth produces the most vivid color, hard-prune these shrubs every other year. That will also keep them to modest size. When planting shrubs or small trees for their winter effect, place them against green backgrounds or where winter sun can show off their color. For small shrubs, group plants for a glowing color effect.

Some of the Japanese maples — which don't seem to have any off season — also have good winter bark color. The showiest is the crimson-branched *Acer palmatum* 'Sango-Kaku'. This is one of the larger Japanese maples, growing up to 30 feet, although slowly.

Two shrubs of the willow family have especially noteworthy purple bark. The dewy willow, *Salix irrorata*, grows a modest 15 feet, and *Salix purpurea*, or purple osier, a mere

10 feet. Its branches also are popular among basket-weavers.

The birches are known for their white bark, and one of the creamiest whites is *Betula jacquemontii*. You'll need room, however, since it gets to 40 feet. The leaves also have outstanding autumn gold color.

One of the most dramatic bark effects belongs to those trees whose satiny bark seems to wrap around trunks in bands, peeling horizontally. It's an effect you frequently see in Japanese gardens. Two cherries are outstanding examples. *Prunus serrula*, known as the birch-bark cherry, also has good foliage color in the fall as well as polished mahogany bark. *Prunus maackii*, also called the goldbark or amur chokecherry, is slightly taller and has golden brown peeling bark.

Another bare-branched beauty is *Corylus avellana* 'Contorta', commonly called corkscrew hazel but really a filbert. Its branches are sought after for their curling and twisting shapes rather than for any remarkable color.

Branches from all of these plants make splendid winter arrangements in vases.

OCTOBER 30, 1992

❧

CHRYSANTHEMUMS NEED A FAIR SHAKE

The late bloomers, often maligned, offer a great variety of colors and forms

FOR MANY, THE LAST GARDEN BLOOMER OF the year is the chrysanthemum, which can bloom all the way through November. It's also the oldest known flower that has been cultivated for its ornamental appearance alone. References to chrysanthemums appear in Chinese literature as early as 500 B.C.

The name, from the Greek, means golden flower, and anyone who has seen the exquisite Chinese and Japanese paintings of a great globe of sun yellow can understand how the flower got its name. To the Chinese, the chrysanthemum is a symbol of nobility. To the Japanese, it is a symbol of the emperor. To everyone, it is a symbol of autumn.

Chrysanthemums belong to that odd group of flowers that elicit strong likes or dislikes. They are among those cult flowers — roses, orchids and dahlias are other examples — that growers devote themselves to, eschewing all other flowers. Others dismiss chrysanthemums on grounds they are exhibition flowers, not good garden mixers.

Well, yes and no. It's true, they are superb exhibition specimens, and you can see an example of that at a flurry of chrysanthemum shows this time of year. But one cannot relegate chrysanthemums to the exhibition hall alone.

Given that there are hundreds of varieties, you can bet there's a chrysanthemum — or two or three — that will be delicious in your late fall garden. In my book, the bronzy reds and cinnamon-oranges are a must for mixing with scarlet autumn foliage.

Just listen to how Seattle garden writer Ann Lovejoy describes the colors of a cultivar called 'Fine Feathers', and tell me you can live without it. She describes ruffled heads that open "molten bronze rinsed with auburn, and cool with time to the color of dry sherry or tawny port with highlights of peach gold." Then she invites us to imagine that picture brushed with the scarlet leaves of a Japanese maple.

That woman could write for a crayon

Chrysanthemums and flaming red maples — quintessential symbols of fall.

company. But, besides displaying that she knows a lot of names for autumnal colors, Lovejoy makes a convincing case that a chrysanthemum is more than a great corsage.

Purple, pink and rosy chrysanthemums have their garden roles, too. They are splendid mixed in with late-blooming perennials such as pink Japanese anemones, rosy sedums, purple-blue asters and frosty white boltonia.

So how did chrysanthemums come by such a bad garden reputation? Perhaps it is because of the way they are frequently packaged. Although an autumnal bloomer by nature, they often are forced into flower in spring simply because some clever marketers have discovered that flowering plants sell faster.

So what you get are stiff, tiny little blooming plants that stay stiff and tiny because all their energy is going into the flowers. You have to be tough and cut those flowers off as soon as possible.

If you're growing chrysanthemums for the garden, and the overall appearance of the plant is what's important, stop pinching back in early July. That will give the plant time to grow into the graceful, loose sprays of autumn.

But if you're growing for exhibition, you'll want to keep pinching off all but a few buds to channel the plant's energy into a few grand, champion blooms. Remove the buds that won't be allowed to bloom before they start to show color.

Speaking of stiff and forced, yes, you can transplant those potted gift chrysanthemums into your garden. Most have been treated with growth retardant to keep them pot-sized, but the next year the plant will take on its looser, natural and decidedly more graceful shape.

The downside of this easy adaptation is that mums are multipliers. If you see a lot of baby chrysanthemums in spring, dig up the old clump and discard it and keep a few of the babies. They'll eventually have better and bigger bloom than the older plant. If you've got an older plant that wimped out this year, it needs dividing right now.

Some favorite cultivars of fall-blooming chrysanthemums are the dwarf *C.* 'Mei-kyo', rosy flowers with yellow centers; *C. nipponicum*, green-centered white flower; 'Emperor of China', old rose with red tinged foliage; 'Apollo', dark red; 'Venus', pink; 'Clara Curtis', pink; 'Duchess of Edinburgh', coppery-red with yellow centers; 'Apricot', orange with yellow centers; 'Peterkin', orange; 'Bronze Fairie', bronze; 'Salmon Fairie', salmon; 'Anastasia', pale pink; 'Emerald isle', greenish-white; 'Silver Lace', white; and 'Waikiki', orange.

If there is variety in color, there is even more in form. The great golden globe of Oriental screen paintings is but one face of a multifaceted plant. Chrysanthemums range from the giant "mums" that make up corsages at football games to the little nosegay flower called feverfew. The latter is as pesky as it is pretty because it seeds all over, which is fine for a romantic cottage garden but not so swell elsewhere.

The various forms of chrysanthemums have descriptive names such as spoons, buttons, cushions, daisies, spiders, quills and pompons. Incidentally, for those of you who collect trivia, most of the garden books have it wrong. They spell the flower type as "pompom."

Actually, a pompom is a large gun or small cannon, and a pom-pom girl, according to Webster's, is a lady of the streets, to put it discreetly. The correct word for those tasseled colors cheerleaders wave and the chrysanthemum form is pompon.

I thought you'd like to know before you go bragging about your pompoms at the next meeting of the genteel ladies of your garden club.

OCTOBER 27, 1996

BARE-BONES OPPORTUNITIES
Giving your plot a solid structure creates charm in the cold months

FOR MOST OF THE COUNTRY, WINTER IS SIMply something to be gotten through. Gardeners kind of put themselves in a holding pattern, like planes circling O'Hare Airport, waiting for spring to signal that they can come on in.

But the temperate Northwest climate gives us the luxury of a fourth season. The upside is that, unlike places such as Minnesota, we won't go for five months without seeing bare ground.

The downside is that, if we don't do something about it this month, that's all we'll see — bare ground.

The secret to a great winter garden is all in the bones. Like people, the gardens that look best as they age are those that have good underlying structure.

In winter, there's little foliage to mask imperfections. There's no riot of color to distract, no perfect rose to focus on. With the garden laid bare, we see the whole. This is where good design pays off.

It either works or it doesn't. If it doesn't, November is the ideal month to do something about it. As the garden undresses, you can suddenly see why shape and proportion are so important. This is the time to address that fuzzy feeling that something's not working quite right and make those famous midcourse corrections.

Subtle changes can reap big dividends. Simply widening a too-skinny border or path can bring it into better proportion with the rest of the garden. Subtly remolding the shape of the lawn or a flower bed can make the curve more pleasing to the eye. Moving an ornament or fabulous pot to just the right location can transform an otherwise "lost" area.

Details, too, are more important in the winter garden. Crisp edges to lawns, trimmed hedges and artfully pruned trees and shrubs keep things from looking all mushy, even on the drippiest of days.

This is the season when fine stonework pays off. Wet stones and bricks glisten like a polished floor. Little details that you wouldn't have noticed in summer, such as a border of river rock, come into exquisite focus.

Structures, from fences to buildings, stand

A stunning pot can bring drama to a bare spot.

out with greater clarity. This is time to make sure they are in good repair because no vines hide their imperfections. This also is the season when an investment in a good-looking, not just functional, fence pays off.

A few judicious additions to plantings can make a big difference, too. The assortment may be limited compared to other seasons, but the selection is choice.

Unlike the warmer months, the emphasis isn't on an abundance of plants. Play to winter's spare beauty by using plants as sculptural effects. Choose for shape and for the rare, sweet-scented flower.

The indispensable shrub for the winter garden is witch hazel (*Hamamelis*). Not only does it have a graceful vase shape, but it bears fragrant, spidery, golden flowers in January and February. As a bonus, the witch hazel also has attractive autumn foliage.

Viburnum bodnantense is another staple of the winter garden. It bears small intensely sweet-scented white flowers in the dead of winter. Like the witch hazel, it has an attractive shape throughout the year.

The small winter jasmine, (*Jasminum nudiflorum*) on the other hand, is really rather dull most of the year. But from December to March, buttery yellow flowers the size of popcorn smother its bare branches. It is like a spot of sunshine on a bleak day and perfect for putting by the back door, where it will cheer you when you're carrying in the groceries.

Sasanqua camellias also are popular for their winter flowers. They need a bit of shelter and do best, because of their vining nature, when they are leaning against a wall or hedge. They provide better value than the spring-blooming camellias that have larger, looser flowers that manage to time their blooms for downpours and turn brown instantly.

Evergreens, such as boxwoods and conifers, won't flower but they give the garden backbone, and not necessarily all of it is green. Evergreens come in a wide variety of leaf colors, including golds, silvers and blue-grays, as well as different shades of green.

For a finishing polish, introduce carpets of evergreen ground covers, including the flowering hellebores and heaths. Then, of course, there are the real jewels of the winter garden, those early-blooming bulbs.

Speaking of that, I sincerely hope you're not like me. Here it is November already, and there's a big bag of about a zillion bulbs still sitting on my kitchen table.

OCTOBER 29, 1995

❧

WHAT'S IN FASHION?
When it comes to your garden, the best style is your own

SPRING MAY BE THE SEASON OF RENEWAL, BUT there are certain advantages to reworking or renewing a garden in autumn.

Things that didn't quite work are fresh in your mind. The ground is easier to dig. As you cut back dying foliage, you can see the bones of the garden.

You might not feel so ill at ease moving plants around at this time of year. In spring, it's painful to disturb fresh little plants just beginning to bud or leaf out.

So gaze about your realm and consider what, if anything, you'd like to change.

The first thing many people do when they rework a garden is try to figure out what style they want. I personally think too much is made of style. Let me put it a different way: A garden will benefit from being stylish. But it doesn't need to be a particular style.

Stylish means the garden has a logical and pleasing structure with harmonious planting and accessories. That doesn't mean it has to fit into a category, such as cottage, formal, Victorian, Asian or natural. Although I think those styles are terrific, I think some of the best gardens are intensely individual and a bit quirky.

The term "stylish" isn't as easily defined as "style." The elements of a stylish garden are not much different from those that make clothes stylish: good lines, good-quality materials, pleasing proportions and attention to details.

> *I personally think too much is made of style.*

You often hear that a stylish garden starts with good "bones." Think of bones as the garden's floor plan. You move plants around in a garden, just as you might move furniture in a home. But both need to have a floor plan that works. A solid underlying structure will provide definition to the garden regardless of the season and however you flesh it out.

A stylish garden pays attention to proportion. The elements that make up the floor plan — paths, terraces, decks, planting beds, lawns — must have a pleasing balance. It's easier to describe proportion by its absence: a dinky terrace overwhelmed by a large, sweeping lawn; a flower bed that's too narrow for its length; a skimpy path.

A stylish garden has good lines. Without crisp lines, a suit will be baggy and shape-

Style can mean different things to different people — this is the "casual living" style.

less. The same is true in a garden. Straight lines must be perfectly straight. Circles and ovals must be neat, not squishy or flat along one side. Curves are robust and sweeping rather than crimped or ragged.

A stylish garden pays attention to details. Edges are finished neatly. Focal points guide the eye. Hedges, arbors and other boundaries keep transitions from one part of the garden to another natural rather than abrupt or blurred.

Finally, and for me this is the toughie, a stylish garden has discipline. It is well-maintained. It has consistency and pleasing repetition of plant and hardscape materials rather than an assortment of many materials and elements. It is definitely not hodgepodge.

OCTOBER 21, 1999

BRING GARDENING YEAR INTO FOCUS

A notebook and camera can keep track of some eye-opening things such as when color slumps occur

REMEMBER STANDING UP IN FRONT OF YOUR fifth-grade glass and reading your essay, "What I Did on My Summer Vacation?"

Well, it's time to do the equivalent for the garden. It's time to review how things went, and make a few notes and resolutions for next year.

The first resolution for next year should be to keep a notebook to jot down what's in bloom each week. Taking a picture to go with the written entry is even better.

Memory has a way of blurring reality. A notebook gives a sharp picture of what the gardening year really is like. That way, when you're buying plants next year, you'll have a better idea of where to make your horticultural investments.

Reviewing the past gardening season will raise some interesting points. For example, there are two color slumps in most gardens in the Willamette Valley. If you can remember when they are, you can steer those little red wagons straight to the plants that fill in during those stretches.

May, believe it or not, is one such stretch. Poets rave about the beauties of the month. There are May flowers, Maypoles and May queens. With all that propaganda, gardeners get fooled into thinking it's a great flower month.

But these poets who sing the praises of May probably live in places where spring arrives in April at the earliest. Here, we've got bulbs popping up as early as February. By the first week in May, the tulips and daffodils already have strutted their stuff.

It's a few weeks off before the June flower explosion. So jot down the exceptions — the May bloomers we may want to secure to fill in this color slump. First to come to mind are the peonies, lovely as roses and blooming a month earlier.

Others on the list might include the wall-

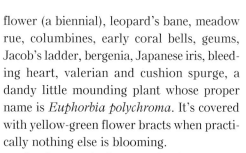

flower (a biennial), leopard's bane, meadow rue, columbines, early coral bells, geums, Jacob's ladder, bergenia, Japanese iris, bleeding heart, valerian and cushion spurge, a dandy little mounding plant whose proper name is *Euphorbia polychroma*. It's covered with yellow-green flower bracts when practically nothing else is blooming.

Gardeners who kept notebooks and continue to scan back over the year will find another color slump in July. The first wave of roses has come and gone, and the plants are storing up energy for a second rush of bloom (that is, if they're even repeat bloomers).

The stately plants — delphiniums, foxgloves, lupine and the like — have marched through the border and are in retreat. So there's July, sandwiched between the glories of June and the brilliant garden of August when the dahlias, coneflowers, rudbeckias, sunflowers and other flashy plants take over.

That's the beauty of a notebook. Would you have remembered that July wasn't so hot? So you'll need to put in an order for astilbes, coreopsis, hardy geraniums, verbascum and veronica. Add to that list lots of daylilies (July is their prime month) and early blooming lilies.

A review of the notebook is handy for other things, such as noting what plants look great even out of bloom. Then you're sure to buy more of the lovely *Iris pallida* 'Variegata', whose green- and white-striped leaves make such superb accents that they're worth getting even if they didn't bloom.

Conversely, notes can tell you that some plants get shabby quickly after bloom-

Astrantia *adds complex and delicate beauty to a border throughout summer.*

ing and should be stuffed in places where something else will hide them. Oriental poppies head the list here. When they're in bloom, they lure us in every time. But if they're at the front of the border, they'll just be eyesores in a few weeks.

Weekly notes also give some good information about bloom periods. It may turn out that some things don't last long enough to merit a place in a small garden.

Camellias may be one such overrated, short-blooming plant. The flowers are exquisite, but they manage to open precisely during the year's biggest downpour and turn brown almost immediately.

Camellia sasanqua is an exception to this regrettable performance. It blooms in true winter (December-January), and its smaller, single blossoms hold up well.

The beauty of a notebook with a postseason review is that it will make us aware of things we saw but didn't really notice. We're so used to reading that May is a great month, that flowers bloom continuously from June on, that camellias are perfect flowers, that we don't always pay attention to evidence to the contrary.

OCTOBER 27, 1991

> *I turn 60 years old next week. I am not at all shaken by the fact.*

FOLLOW THE LEADER
Like Gertrude Jekyll, I'm getting better all the time

TODAY I'M GOING TO PAY HOMAGE TO ONE of my heroes, Gertrude Jekyll. She was one of the most influential gardeners of the past century, and there's a reason I want to talk about this particular lady at this particular time.

I turn 60 years old next week. I am not at all shaken by the fact, and the person I have to thank for this is Gertrude. I like to think she'd let me call her that, but never Gertie. She definitely was not a Gertie.

The thing is, Gertrude did not become a famous garden designer until well into her 50s, and she didn't reach her stride until she was 60. She went on to design gardens until nearly 90. She wrote her most influential book, *Colour Schemes for the Flower Garden*, when she was 65.

So, I have Gertrude to thank for the realization that I am about to enter my prime. She is evidence that 60 does not mean being over the hill, which is good because I do not remember ever being on top of the hill. Besides, I've already had my midlife crisis. It occurred when I was 12 years old and looked in the mirror and saw freckles, braces and winged glasses and realized I was not then — nor was I ever going to be — a beauty, and maybe I had better think about a career. It was a defining moment.

Gertrude's defining moment arrived in 1891, when she was 48. She suffered from acute and progressive myopia, and her doctor advised her to give up painting and embroidery work. This would have been difficult for anyone, but Gertrude had studied art. Painting was her life's work and embroidery a favorite pastime.

Rather than give in to frustration, she found another way to express herself artistically. She became a garden designer, and one of the most influential to boot. In fact, she is considered the mother of the English flower border.

In her day, it was the fashion to have sweeping lawns and large shrubs surrounding manor houses, but few flowers. Gertrude loved the cottage gardens in the countryside. But throwing seeds out willy-nilly, while charming in a small space, wouldn't work in grand spaces.

So she devised the idea of borders to contain and display flowers in large properties. She wasn't the first person to plant a border, but she did the most to popularize the idea. More to the point, she popularized the idea of "painting" with flowers. Using her artist's eye, she carefully planned drifts of color and textures to harmonize throughout the year.

Early in her career she met a young architect, Edwin Lutyens, and eventually they became a design team. He designed the homes and garden hardscapes and she designed the plantings for the Duchess of Bedford and others of England's landed gentry. Both were influenced by the Arts and Crafts movement, and the house Lutyens designed for Gertrude at Munstead Wood is a classic example of that movement.

After Gertrude's death in 1932, her own garden was not kept up and eventually disappeared. But when I visited Munstead Wood a few years ago, the house was in excellent condition and the new owners had found the blueprints for her borders and were having them restored. I remember this visit particularly well because the new gardener was very hunky, so we ladies hung on his every word.

Don't get me wrong. At nearly 60, I am very discriminating. I am saving myself for Harrison Ford. Unless my husband comes up with a really great birthday gift.

NOVEMBER 1, 2001

GET PLANTS READY FOR WINTER REST
Protect tender ones now, but leave hardier plants until after a few frosts

I HAVE BEEN PINCHING THE PERP TO SEE IF she has grown a thicker fur coat and checking out other signs that might indicate a longer and colder-than-normal winter.

We gardeners can be forgiven if we're on the nervous side. After all, last winter Mother Nature threw just about everything she had at us — wind, ice, snow and floods. As a result, this year I, for one, am paying a lot more attention to putting the garden to bed for its winter nap.

November is certainly the month to do the tucking-in chores, but timing is everything. There are some chores to do now and others that should wait until the very end of the month. Applying mulch is a case in point.

Mulch is simply any material — from newspapers to compost — that acts as an insulating blanket. Organic materials have an advantage in that they break down and can be turned into the soil in spring to help break up our hard clay.

Whatever you use, you need to mulch tender plants early and hardy plants late. The reason is frost. It kills tender plants, but it aids hardy plants by helping them go dormant.

Very tender plants, such as nonhardy fuchsias and geraniums, should be put under protection immediately. If you don't have a greenhouse, tuck them in a sheltered area, such as a garage, cold frame or basement window well, preferably on the south side of the house. Mulch all around the pots right up to the plant's toes.

Marginally tender plants can be left where they are but will benefit from loose mulch mounded up around their toes. Typical marginal plants include daphne, hebe, ceanothus, New Zealand flax, canna, dierama, some euphorbias, gunnera and Chilean potato vine (*Solanum crispum*). Also, any newly planted plants that have not had time to establish good root systems should be treated as marginally tender.

Put your garden to bed before it ends up on ice.

It's also a good idea to keep a pile of newspapers, old carpet scraps or burlap sacks around to cover these semi-tender plants on nights when extreme cold is predicted. But hold off on mulching the really hardy plants until after Thanksgiving. Weathering a few frosts will actually help them survive. A few cold nights will trigger their dormancy and put them safely to sleep.

What kills hardy plants in the winter is temperature fluctuations rather than the degree of cold. We'll get a few warm days in winter and things will start to wake up. Then it'll get cold again, and the plants are suddenly vulnerable because they've begun to come out of dormancy.

Wind and snow can wreak as much havoc as temperature. Many of us lost trees, particularly evergreens, in last year's windstorms. This is the time to check tall evergreens and make sure they are open enough so that wind passes through. If growth is too thick, it will form a sail and take the full brunt of the wind. Remove broken and dead branches from any trees. Also, remove the ivy that girdles a tree. I didn't believe that was important until an arborist told me that ice coating the ivy leaves can add 300 pounds or more to the weight of a tree, making it more likely to topple in an intense windstorm.

Shrubs and hedges are more vulnerable to snow than to wind. Boughs break or bend irreparably from the sheer weight. Boxwood, yew and arborvitae can be bent permanently out of shape. It's a good idea to run some wire or twine along hedges that have been problems in the past.

Any girdling device will give them some support until you can get out and brush off the snow.

Getting roses through the winter always is a special concern in our rose-crazy world. Old-fashioned roses and roses grown on their own rootstock generally do not need special protection. But hybrid teas may need protection, especially in higher elevations or windy areas.

Don't prune roses in the fall. Wait until late February. The exception is tall roses that may be susceptible to wind rocking (roots heaving up out of the soil). Trim some off the top to prevent the wind from catching the rose.

Pour some compost or other type of mulch around the bottom of the rose so that it mounds up to about a foot or at least high enough to cover the knob that indicates the graft union. Don't use peat moss because it will retain too much water, and don't use manure because this is not the time of year to fertilize.

Strip leaves from roses to make sure any disease won't winter over. Don't put any foliage on the compost pile if it has signs of black spot or other problems.

Tree roses, with their naked stems, are more vulnerable to cold. It helps to wrap the stems with burlap or newspapers.

As to whether these protective measures will be necessary or not, here's a late-breaking sign from nature. The Perp already has taken early to her winter habitat. She is firmly curled up under the electric blanket.

NOVEMBER 3, 1996

❧

SET ASIDE A LITTLE SPACE
And sit back for the fireworks

I HAVE SPENT THE PAST TWO MONTHS WANdering around the garden, trying to figure out where I could stick a burning bush or yet another viburnum. I covet them for their autumn foliage.

In a moment of weakness, I fell in love with and purchased something called a *Disanthus cercidifolius* for its scarlet leaves. It will, I've learned, get the size and shape of a witch hazel, and I have not a clue where to put it.

The problem is that I want an autumn garden, a true garden of the season, not just an extended bloom of leftover summer flowers. But even in a yard as large as mine, about three-fourths of an acre, you shouldn't go overboard on shrubs that offer nothing but a month of leaf color.

What do you do with them the rest of the time when they're 6 feet tall, just as wide and nothing but dark-green lumps?

Before autumn slips away entirely, I'm making note of select perennials that can give

an autumnal show even in the tiniest gardens that have room for nary a shrub. They fall into three categories: late bloomers with good autumn flower color, past-their-prime bloomers that offer good leaf color and over-the-hill bloomers that dry prettily.

LATE BLOOMERS IN AUTUMNAL SHADES

Flowers the colors of wine, gold, peach, coral, brick and russet can complement or replicate fall leaf color. Asters, sedums and chrysanthemums are the obvious choices, but there are more. Before we get into that, however, I have a confession about chrysanthemums.

I thought I could never love such a flower, thinking it too much of a potted plant. That was before I discovered a fabulous chrysanthemum at my local nursery called *Chrysanthemum* x *morifolium* 'Dark Grenadine'. Imagine the finest glowing-red Japanese maple, and you have the flower color.

Big, fat dahlias in sunset colors also are indispensable autumn flowers. I prefer the spidery shapes because their rag-tag edges seem to go with the look of the season.

Knautia (also sold as *Scabiosa macedonica*) is a simple little plant with unremarkable flowers, but it sends them up in claret-colored profusion from midsummer into early November. It's a good plant for weaving among others because its slender stems allow it to lace through with little interference.

The toad lily (*Tricyrtis*), on the other hand, is remarkable. It will present you with a cloud of spotted purple flowers like miniature lilies from late summer into November.

Another plant in the blooms-forever category that looks splendid in the late garden is the hardy fuchsia, its arching stems dripping with garnet flowers.

Japanese forest grass in its tawny autumn splendor.

Most Japanese anemones, also late and long bloomers, are white or pale pink and don't look particularly autumnal. But if you can find a warm peachy pink, such as 'September Charm', it will blend nicely with the russets of the season. Try it behind *Sedum* 'Autumn Joy' for a striking combination.

PERENNIALS WITH GOOD LEAF COLOR

A few perennials past their bloom have autumn foliage the equal of many shrubs. Hostas and peonies turn gold, and bergenia takes on a scarlet tinge.

Red-leafed coral bells (*Heuchera*), spurges (*Euphorbia*) and New Zealand flax (*Phormium*) don't change color, but they equal some of the finest fall trees and shrubs.

Some ferns color nicely, particularly the cinnamon fern (*Osmunda cinnamomea*).

Using the term "perennials" loosely to take in ornamental grasses, you can extend your choices of fall leaf color for small spaces.

A few to try include Japanese blood grass (*Imperata cylindrica*), flame grass (*Miscan-*

thus sinensis 'Purpurascens'), golden Hakone grass (*Hakonechloa macra* 'Aureola'), northern sea oats (*Chasmanthium latifolium*) and fountain grass (*Pennisetum alopecuroides*).

For standout leaf color, it's hard to get past the canna. It comes as a surprise that such a tropical-looking plant is terrific for the fall garden. But there is nothing like a peach-colored dahlia backed by a great fan of wine-red canna leaves in the autumn sun.

Cannas are marginally hardy, so it's best to cut them back this month after a couple of frosts and put them in a sheltered spot.

FLOWERS THAT DRY WELL

Let the plumes of astilbe, goatsbeard, plume poppy (*Macleaya*) and Joe-Pye weed dry right on the stalk, and you will be rewarded with a rich russet glow in the autumn light.

When the petals fall off rudbeckia, leave their chocolate centers standing. *Eryngium* and *Echinops* (globe thistle) also dry well on stalks, and finding other standouts is just a matter of experimenting.

NOVEMBER 6, 1997

HATS OFF TO THE IMP
An unknown prankster leaves an embarrassing but usable gift

IT IS INTERESTING HOW MUCH GARDENING CAN insinuate itself into one's life. When I learned this fall that my cancer had returned, the first thing I asked my oncologist was, "Should I return the bulbs I ordered?" "Oh no," she said with a smile.

That's good enough for me. I expect to be around another spring, but I figure I ought to say something in case anyone spots me with no hair. Who needs hair, anyway? I plan to buy outrageous hats and stick silly flowers on them.

So I am already planning for next season. I planted two trees last summer, and I am anxious to see what kind of growth they put on. I am also eager to see if my garden sprouts any more fake flowers.

Did I tell you about that? No, well, here's what happened:

One day in late summer, I came home from work and opened the gate to my garden. I noticed a pretty, vivid purple flower just to the right of the entry. I assumed Doug the Wonder Boy had planted it. It looked like a lavender, and as the days went on, I marveled at how it kept its flowers.

Then, one Sunday morning, a group of ladies came to tour my garden. They surrounded the still-vivid plant and asked what it was, and I said I wasn't sure. Then someone bent over, touched it and gasped, "It's fake."

Oh golly, it was. Imagine my embarrassment. Obviously an imp had come into my garden and planted it.

Something similar happened in the spring. I got up to go to work and was still a little bleary when I opened the back door to let The Perp out. She demands I open the door despite having a pet door two feet away.

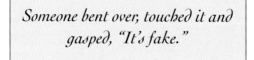

Someone bent over, touched it and gasped, "It's fake."

I couldn't believe it. There were rabbits all over my back lawn. It reminded me of mornings in England, when you'd see them in the fields. Where had they come from? Perhaps from the golf course adjacent to my neighborhood.

I'm not real swift in the morning, and the weather was misty, so it took a moment to register. They weren't real. Someone had gathered up all my fake bunnies and placed them on the back lawn. I think I know who the someone was.

Certainly Doug cackled when I mentioned it, and he has been known to practice a little "gardener's humor." We have pottery birds feeding in the vegetable garden and a stone rat peering out of a hole in the boxwoods. There's a pottery dog looking up at a wire cat in the crotch of tree, and various faux critters tend to move around mysteriously.

Still, he swears that he's not the one who put the fake lavender in the garden. So I haven't a clue. I suppose the plant will remain a mystery, much as we never discovered how goldfish appeared in our pond a few years back.

I don't mind a little practical jokery in the garden so long as it's friendly.

But while someone's adding things, let me put in an order. I'd like a few rose bushes that don't get black spot and some of those stately delphiniums that refuse to grow for me. Also, how about some colorful penstemons, which never come back in my clay soil.

While we're at it, the imp should also plan to put in a *Melianthus* shrub and a banana plant next spring, since those are the two plants I manage to murder every winter.

As for the fake lavender, I am leaving it

there in case it magically seeds. I can wear the flowers in one of my new hats.

NOVEMBER 3, 2005

THE HUES OF AUTUMN
Fourteen small trees, including dogwoods and maples, can provide the home gardener with brilliant fall colors

QUICK, LOOK NOW, OR THAT MAGNIFICENT autumn color will be gone with the next deluge. While the Northwest may not get the eye-popping colorama of New England, Oregon and Washington do put on a respectable show. That's thanks to a variety of deciduous plants that don't require the traditional hard frost to turn on the neon.

Fortunately, some of that color comes in small packages that even ordinary city lots can accommodate. If you've thought about adding autumn drama to your garden, now is the last chance to check out the candidates. Enough leaves should be left on nursery specimens to give you an idea of which ones produce the most vibrant hues.

Here are 14 small trees that do well in this region with guaranteed great fall color. This selection is limited to trees that are normally under 30 feet, so they will work well in gardens of any size. All are beautiful specimens even before leaves turn, and nearly all have the happy combination of a flowering season as well.

Like many smaller trees, these tend to be shrubby and can either be left as is for a delicate multistemmed look or trained by early pruning to a single trunk.

It's a toss-up on which is the most beautiful Northwest garden accent — the dogwood or one of the smaller maples. Don't debate; get both. Two small dogwoods head the list for spectacular late color. Leaves of the flowering dogwood, *Cornus florida*, turn plum red, while those of the Japanese dogwood, *Cornus kousa*, change to scarlet. Both have pinkish-white blossoms in late spring and red fruit in fall.

Of the maples, three stand out. Vine maple, *Acer circinatum*, will have red-orange fall foliage in the sun and gold in the shade. Autumn leaves of the Amur maple, *Acer ginnala*, are scarlet. Then there are the great favorites, the Japanese maples, *Acer palmatum*. This family includes cutleaf and laceleaf varieties and summer leaf colors of both red and green. In fall they'll shame the sunset.

With careful selection of trees and shrubs, your garden can charm you with fall colors ranging from glowing yellow to deep russet to eggplant.

So much for the best known colorists. The serviceberry, *Amelanchier*, is an up and comer. It has showy white drooping clusters of scented flowers in spring, late summer berries for the birds, and red, orange and yellow leaves in fall.

Washington thorn, *Crataegus phaenopyrum*, a member of the hawthorn family, is another delicate specimen with arching branches. Its white June flowers are modest, but its orange-red leaves in autumn are anything but. It also has red fruits that birds find delectable.

Creamy white flower cups weigh down the branches of the Franklin tree, *Franklinia alatamaha*, in late summer. In autumn, the tree blazes orangey red. The sourwood (sometimes called sorrel tree), *Oxydendrum arboreum*, is another late-summer bloomer with drooping clusters of white flowers. Its late dress is vivid scarlet.

Bare branches of the Persian parrotia tree, *Parrotia persica*, are covered with rosy blossoms resembling witch hazel in March. In autumn, it runs the gamut from gold to rose to scarlet. It also has attractive winter bark.

Two cherry trees of the *Prunus serrulata* variety stand out in autumn, as well as spring. Look for the cultivars 'Shirotae' (also known as 'Mt. Fuji') and 'Shogetsu'. They are delights for their red-bronze autumn foliage as well as for their spring blossoms.

The pear, *Pyrus calleryana*, is another outstanding spring bloomer with good late color. The cultivar 'Chanticleer' has orange-red foliage and 'Autumn Blaze' is red-purple.

Stewartia monadelpha lacks a common name but nothing else. White summer blossoms and bright red autumn leaves are a charming combination. Japanese snowdrop, *Styrax japonicus*, rounds out the bevy of small

beauties. It flies red and gold colors at the end of its season, and bears white summer blossoms.

NOVEMBER 9, 1990

FLOWERS MAKE A LAST STAND
Let the garden go out in a blaze of glory

IF PASSING AWAY IS INEVITABLE, IT SHOULD BE done as gloriously and stylishly as possible. The crimson and golden blaze of autumn is certainly the right way for plants to go, as opposed to the sickly browning that ushered out lawns this summer.

Some of the best things about this season, in fact, are the plants that linger, like Camille, milking their demise for every inch of drama. If "malingerer" has a nasty connotation, maybe we need to invent the word "bellelingerer." That would describe summer flowers that stay on into autumn, brilliant even in their decline.

These aren't flowers that are supposed to bloom now — such as chrysanthemums and asters. No, we're talking about flowers that are well past their prime but that loiter in glorious decadence.

Take rudbeckia, for example. It is a blaze of golden glory from August to September. But when the petals fall, it leaves us with the mahogany buttons that form the centers and give the plant its nickname, black-eyed Susan. For weeks, these make a very pretty stand, until eventually they lose their crispness and turn soggy with the rains.

The purple and white coneflowers (*Echinacea*) are even more glorious when denuded of petals. Their centers glow with a lumines-

The autumn garden fairly shouts its seasonal swan song.

cent quality. Japanese anemones are other flowers that keep their "eye" long after petals are gone.

Then there are the flowers themselves that dry elegantly right on their stalks. Nothing beats the astilbes for this act, although the plume poppy is a tempting second best. Both flower plumes bloom in mid-summer, then dry to a gorgeous burnt umber, a color of Crayola box fame.

There's a kind of poignant beauty in autumn's decay.

The dried flowers of the large stonecrops, such as *Sedum spectabile*, may be most effective when past their prime. When they first bloom, their delicate colors are overshadowed by other vividly colored flowers. Later on, without such competition, their subtle rosy-bronze colors literally shine. In this, they are similar to the hydrangea, whose flowers manage to fade in the most exquisite style.

> *All of this is an argument against getting too carried away with fall cleanup.*

A number of other flowers dry attractively right on their stems. The best have stiff stems that resist getting mushy until the last minute. The self-sewing annual *Verbena bonariensis*, has such stiff stems that it makes pleasant stands of purple hue well into late fall.

The globe thistle (*Echinops*) frankly looks more attractive after its purple ball-like flowers have bloomed and dried than it does before it blooms. Let's face it, its leaves are definitely weedy looking.

Even one perennial has terrific autumn foliage color. The big, broad leaves of hostas turn a brilliant yellow and make a fine splash for weeks, before they finally shrivel and disappear. One of the best displays is the *H. sieboldiana*, whose huge, blue-green quilted leaves turn into great yellow fans.

The russets and golds of flowers and leaves are doubly enhanced if you've got a good foil of silver-hued plants: the artemisias, santolinas, lamb's-ears, lavenders and the like. Many of these manage to stay evergreen, or perhaps eversilver.

All of this is an argument against getting too carried away with fall cleanup. Leaving some seed heads and stalks standing will add structural beauty throughout the winter and won't hurt your plants. Combine them with the berried plants — the hazy mounds of heathers, the hips of roses, and the rare winter flowers such as hellebores — and it's possible to have a year-round garden in our mild climate.

NOVEMBER 13, 1992

WINTER LULLABY

Don't let it turn into a springtime dirge for marginal plants

PUTTING THE GARDEN TO BED THESE DAYS has gotten more complicated. That's because we gardeners are becoming increasingly adventuresome, extending the diversity of our plants and flirting shamelessly with those that are marginally winter-hardy.

Case in point: cannas and daturas (trumpet flowers, also sold as *Brugmansia*) were big sellers this year. So were giant-leafed gunnera, a popular pondside plant, and papyrus, a favorite plant for in the pond.

In the Willamette Valley, you can loosely divide these marginally hardy or barely hardy plants into two categories. Category one includes plants that generally survive except for the occasional fierce winter (daphne, hybrid tea roses). Category two includes plants that generally don't survive except for the occasional mild winter (cannas, dahlias left in the ground).

The following list by no means covers all marginally hardy plants, but it does note plants that are increasingly common in Willamette Valley gardens. Some may be entirely safe on the coast, and almost none will winter over east of the mountains.

Perennials in category one, those that stand a fair chance of surviving but aren't fail-safe, include phygelius, penstemon, francoa, dierama (angel's fishing rod, wand flower), *Acanthus mollis*, alstromeria, *Euphorbia characias* and phlomis.

Some woody-stemmed perennials (or subshrubs) also fall into category one — lavender, santolina and caryopteris.

Shrubs in category one include daphne, potato vine (*Solanum*), crape myrtle (*Lager-*

stroemia), lavatera, rockrose (*Cistus*), abelia and hebe.

Those perennials in category two (really annuals most years) include many popular salvias (*S. patens, S. involucrata, S. officinalis,* for example), gazania, canna, phormium, gunnera, agapanthus, meconopsis (the blue poppies) and the famous chocolate cosmos (*C. atrosanguineus*) that all the books insist is perennial. I haven't found it so.

Category two shrubs include ceanothus, datura, abutilon, pittosporum, choisya (Mexican orange), olearia and osmanthus.

Fortunately, there are steps we can take to greatly increase the odds of category one plants surviving even a fairly rugged winter. But it will take a combination of protection and a mild winter for category two plants to live over if they stay in the ground.

They really should be dug up and taken in, but that's a lot of work, and, what the heck, El Niño may just mean we get that mild winter.

A key rule to winter protection is not too early and not too tight.

Category one plants should not be protected until two or three light frosts. Early frosts help the plant go dormant. Protection is put on to keep them cold and, therefore, dormant. On the other hand, category two plants should be protected before frost, because frost can destroy their cells.

Mulch spread over the roots of plants is the easiest and best protection. Its thickness depends on the material. Compost, grass clippings and other fine mulches should be 2 to 3 inches thick; shredded leaves and bark chips about 4 inches; and straw, the loosest mulch, should be piled about 8 to 10 inches high.

Straw is particularly good because it allows air circulation. Tie it loosely around your most tender shrubs. Evergreen branches piled about three deep also are excellent protection for perennial beds.

Avoid mulches of peat or whole leaves. These pack down and cut off air circulation, which can lead to rot. For the same reason, don't pack mulch against trunks of trees and shrubs. On perennials that die to the ground, put the mulch right over the top.

For tender roses, pour dirt or compost down the center of the bush and mound it up around the crown to about 8 inches. Don't prune roses until late winter.

Cut off the foliage on pond plants, such as water lilies, and sink them to the deepest section of the pond to keep them from freezing. This won't work for papyrus. It needs to be brought indoors and kept in a bit of water.

Leave the tops on the more tender perennials. This can add some slight additional protection for the plant's crown. For large-leafed plants, such as gunnera, fold the leaves over the crown, then apply a mound of mulch over the crown and roots.

Set aside a pile of old blankets, shower curtains, drop cloths, sheets or burlap sacks to drape over marginal shrubs when the temperature drops into the 20s. If there's a dry, desiccating wind, go for the protection even at higher temperatures. Wind can do more damage than cold.

And lay off the fertilizer. Tender plants also have a better chance where they get good drainage.

Alas, this may mean that my entire garden is doomed.

NOVEMBER 13, 1997

GARDEN FORGIVE US, FOR WE HAVE SINNED

From rocky horrors to Edward Scissorhands' designs, we have gone astray

TODAY, DEAR READERS, WE ARE GOING TO review our sins and promise never to commit them again. Of course, sin, like beauty, is in the eye of the beholder.

Who can say that a gnome isn't a suitable garden ornament, or that a cement goddess shouldn't adorn your fountain?

No one, of course. But that's not going to stop me. After all, the words opinionated and gardener have a magnetic attraction. So, herewith, a list of leading blunders, many of which I have committed.

Mixed media: Terra cotta pots here, Grecian urns there. Brick pathway here, stone walk there. You get the picture: It doesn't quite hang together.

The lineup: Okay, Mrs. Smith, can you pick the marigold that snatched your purse out of this lineup? Go ahead and put your shoes, but not your flowers, in straight rows.

Gumdrop pruning: Topiary is one thing, but otherwise plants weren't meant to grow in tight little balls.

Denial: You know that rose that gets black spot year after year, and that azalea that gets mildew annually? Toss them out. Mercy killing is okay in the plant world.

The tree monster: Invest in a little research before planting a tree that drops sticky blossoms and sticky leaves over your deck or pool.

The Calvin Klein look: Sorry, but underwear shouldn't show. Things like the black pond liner and the awkward space between deck and ground need cover-ups.

A huge old tree can be a blessing or a curse; make it work for you.

Polka-dot paradise: The one-of-everything look belongs in botanical gardens. Think fewer flowers, but in bigger drifts.

Unhappy marriages: Versailles-type fountains don't match well with ranch houses. Weathered-wood fences aren't compatible with stucco. House style and color should guide garden choices.

Future shock: It's hard to move behemoths. Before you plant, pay attention to how big that shrub or tree will be in five years.

Rocky horror show: In nature, rocks don't sit on top of the ground like bowling balls. If you have a rock garden, cluster rocks naturally and dig them in to give them a settled look.

Fighting Mother Nature: A lush foliage garden beats scrawny, light-starved flowers. People who live in woodsy settings should count their blessings, not fight them.

Fear of cosmetic surgery: Old growth is fine for forests. But urban gardens need thinning over time.

Chain-saw massacres: This is the corollary to fear of cosmetic surgery. A lot of plants simply don't need pruning. If they're healthy, let them grow naturally.

Scratching the surface: A couple of inches of rich dark compost on top of soil makes everything look nice — for about a month. Clay soil needs a lot more than a couple of inches of organic material, and it needs to be worked in.

Sun worshiping: Shade isn't an enemy.

As much as sun is ideal for growing many flowers, a garden without some shade is harsh and jarring.

Niagara Falls: Those huge, tumbling waterfalls look great at shows, but they can overwhelm a normal urban lot.

Walking the straight and narrow: That's a good philosophy for life but a poor one for designing garden paths.

No surprises: Assuming you don't live in a condominium, you shouldn't be able to open your back door and see everything all at once. Gardens need a little mystery.

The Great Plains look: A playing field can be too level. Vines and other verticals seem to be the forgotten plants.

Hit list: The following items should be banned forthwith from all gardens: chunky bark, chain-link fencing, planters made out of old tires, arborvitae, molded waterfalls and plastic flamingos (unless you hang their Latin name around their necks).

NOVEMBER 19, 1995

❧

GARDENING'S GIFTS
A shared passion causes friendships to sprout up and grow

GOOD MORNING AND HAPPY THANKSGIVING. When I was a kid, Thanksgiving was all about food and getting to see my cousins. When I became an adult, I realized all those movies about dysfunctional family gatherings were not, after all, fantasies.

My mother used to insist we have every Thanksgiving at her house. She was not a good cook, and her idea of mashed potatoes was out of a package. The salad was a wedge of iceberg lettuce, never tossed. Mr. Turkey was always overcooked. A bowl of peanuts served as appetizers. The vegetables were canned or frozen.

But the setting was magnificent. She put great store on good china, silver and crystal. Unfortunately, she also insisted on doing the whole thing herself. In her eyes, potluck was gauche. She would not let anyone help, and we all had to stay out of the kitchen. She'd sit down at the table, look wan and announce she was too tired to eat. You can imagine how that made the rest of us feel.

Then, as I got older I came to think of Thanksgiving in a different light. It was not about eating or dysfunctional family gatherings. It was exactly what it said. It was a day to give thanks. So that's what I'm going to do.

First, I'm thankful for husband Ted the Great Footrubber, wonderful friends and work colleagues.

I'm thankful for warm, fuzzy animals.

I'm also thankful for the end of election ads, the world's greatest oncology team that has kept me going for nearly eight years, a supportive place to work and editors who never nag and say, "But you don't put anything educational in your essays."

And then there's gardening to be thankful for.

One of the great joys of gardening, I've found, has nothing to do with plants, design or "a feeling of oneness with the Earth" — a phrase that gardeners often grab onto to describe why they love to garden.

I enjoy all these things, but most of all I am thankful for the people one meets through gardening. I have formed bonds that would not have occurred if we weren't fellow gardeners.

I love the conversations about gardening almost as much as the act of gardening. I love going with companions to nurseries, which almost always leads to buying more than I intended.

I love going to craft shows at this time of year to search out garden ornaments, mostly now as gifts, since I'm pretty much over the top in my garden. Well, not pretty much. I AM over the top.

I love seeing other people's gardens, especially small starter gardens that speak of so much hope and remind me how much fun my early gardening days were when I was discovering plants, toying with ideas and reveling in the delight of some modest successes.

I am thankful for all this, and also one more very important thing. I am thankful to readers who have sent me sweet messages, educational information and, who, in their gentle hearts, have never derided me for my flamingo fancies. The latter is more than I can say about my friends, who mostly think I'm nuts.

Now if you'll excuse me, I have to go out and check something strange that's going on in my garden. The flamingos all seem to have red pop-up devices sticking out of their feathers.

NOVEMBER 25, 2010

And so the garden rests . . .

A curving garden path beckons with promise.

INDEX

Dear Reader: Please also see the Listing of Columns by Date, which follows this general Index.

LISTING OF COLUMNS BY DATE